Willful Liberalism

Also by Richard E. Flathman

The Philosophy and Politics of Freedom
Political Obligation
The Practice of Authority
The Practice of Rights
The Public Interest
Toward a Liberalism

Willful Liberalism

Voluntarism and Individuality in
Political Theory and Practice

Richard E. Flathman

Cornell University Press

Ithaca and London

To the Memory of
George Armstrong Kelly

Contents

*Thou shalt have no other
gods before thee*

Acknowledgments

A slightly different version of Chapter 1 of this work was previously published, under the same title, in *History of European Ideas* 10, no. 5 (1989), 547–68, and is reprinted with the permission of Pergamon Press. A draft of the essay was presented to the Seminar of the Program in Moral and Political Philosophy at The Johns Hopkins University. Discussion in the seminar, and especially the comments of Sidney Maskit, prompted substantial and valuable changes. I have not been able to respond adequately to all of Sid Maskit's objections to my appropriation of Hobbes, but I will get even with him for that.

Chapter 2 was presented to a conference concerning James Fishkin's efforts to reconstruct liberalism held at the Law School of Emory University and later to the political theory group at Princeton University. I am grateful to Jim Fishkin, Tim Terrell, and Amy Gutmann for these opportunities and to the participants on both occasions for helpful critical comments. Ed Lindblom saved me from a blunder concerning William James, and Jerry Schneewind gave the paper a characteristically acute reading that enabled substantial improvements.

Chapter 3 was the basis for a discussion in the Law and Philosophy Seminar at Yale University. My thanks to Steven Smith for arranging this occasion and to Ian Shapiro for congenial hospitality and challenging discussion. With typical generosity, Bob Salisbury went well out of his way to read the paper. I am afraid that he found it mostly puzzling, but I much appreciate his willingness to wrestle with it.

Acknowledgments

Segments of Part Two were presented at the University of Texas at Austin, at Harvard, Columbia, the Murphy Institute of Tulane University, and at the annual meetings of the American Political Science Association in 1990. These bracing and otherwise highly agreeable occasions leave me particularly in the debt of Jim Fishkin, Anne Norton, Thomas Tseung, Jeffrey Tulis, Stephen Macedo, David Johnston, John Gray, Richard Teichgraber, Lee Auspitz, Tim Fuller, and George Kateb. I am also grateful to Jim Wiley for a reading of Part Two which helped me to a better understanding of Nietzsche's notion of strength.

I have not been able to decide whether to be pleased or disturbed by the fact that John Charvet, who read all of Part Two and some of Part One, finds my version of strong voluntarism fully compatible with his own neoidealist and communitarian moral and political theory. The conversation continues.

David Sachs responded so violently to the one chapter that he read that I didn't dare show him any of the rest. But he has helped me so much over the years, and I so much enjoy his company, that I won't be able to hold this failing against him much longer.

Bonnie Honig has seen and heard more of this manuscript than she could reasonably be expected to bear. In addition to thanking her for invaluable comments and suggestions, I hope that her reading of it has helped her to understand why it has been such a pleasure for me to be involved in her importantly analogous work over the past years. I express the same hope concerning the entire superb group of Hopkins political theory students with whom I have had the privilege to work for now more than a decade. Certainly I would not have found my way to these thoughts without their help.

And then there is Bill Connolly. Bill has read and commented in detail on all the materials here published. Yet more to my pleasure and profit, he has listened to, frequently contested, in all likelihood prompted much of what is said in these pages. As everyone who knows Bill will realize, there is therefore a lot of really baaaad stuff in this book and Bill is RESPONSIBLE for most of it.

R. E. F.

Baltimore, Maryland

Willful Liberalism

Introduction

The connected and cumulating essays gathered here continue the reflections proffered in my recently published works, most obviously in the immediate predecessor of the present book, *Toward a Liberalism* (Ithaca: Cornell University Press, 1989). The essay format common to all of the first and much of the second of the two volumes signals the exploratory, open-ended spirit in which I have tried to approach the issues considered, a spirit that I think is consonant with, and indeed engendered by, some of the most estimable features of the liberal tradition. At the same time, and undeniably in some tension with this appreciation, in the present work I have embraced positions more definite and substantial than those I defended in the predecessor collection. In advancing a "willful liberalism" I stand against tendencies in as well as around liberalism about which I previously expressed skepticism, and affirm and promote alternative tendencies to or for which I earlier acknowledged an attraction. For this and intimately related reasons that will quickly appear, I must be prepared for the possibility that some will regard this book—in my view mistakenly—as moving away from, not further toward, a liberalism, as illiberal and therefore antiliberal.

Dissatisfied (as all self-conscious liberals are?) with the available formulations of liberal theory, in seeking to refashion it to my liking I increasingly look to sources outside and thought by many to be at odds with liberal doctrine and practice. My appropriations, elsewhere and more extensively here, of elements in the thinking of Ludwig Wittgenstein and Michael Oakeshott are examples of this strategy. But these are modest and I should think largely unobjectionable departures from the liberal canon. Wittgenstein's philosophical works are almost entirely devoid of political and moral, certainly of ideological, argumentation. If there is reason to think that some of his personal views were illiberal, this is neither here nor there to my attempt to bring procedures and outcomes of his philosophical investigations to bear on topics in political philosophy. Oakeshott is a much more explicitly moral and political thinker than Wittgenstein and is frequently and in some measure rightly regarded as a critic of liberalism. It is increasingly recognized, however, and I hope it will become yet clearer from the discussions here, that his thinking—above all his powerful emphasis on individuality and plurality—constitutes a rich resource for securing and otherwise strengthening elements vital to, albeit too often recessive in liberalism.

The reaction I anticipate will be prompted in some quarters by the considerable and for the most part favorable attention I have given to the thinking of Thomas Hobbes. Of course numerous Left, Right, and Communitarian critics of liberalism (e.g., C. B. MacPherson, Leo Strauss, and Alasdair MacIntyre) have argued that Hobbes is a protoliberal, indeed that his thinking established the main elements of liberal thinking and practice. Perhaps in part for this very reason, and in any case because of Hobbes's political and legal absolutism, most self-declared liberals have wanted to distance themselves from his thinking. This stance seems to me to be mistaken several times over and in ways that betoken regrettable developments in liberal theory and practice. The readings of Hobbes's thought that we have from critics of liberalism, or rather those parts of their readings of him that are central to their claim that he is the founder of liberalism (albeit, pace Macpherson, Hobbes was not a "*possessive* individualist" and liberalism is not capitalism) seem to me to have important merits. As Oakeshott (who is deeply influenced by Hobbes and to whose reading of Hobbes as the theorist of "Will and Artifice" my own interpretation of the latter is heavily indebted) has insisted, Hobbes thought a quite robust individuality and a rich diversity of thought and action not only inevitable but highly desirable. Rejecting as at once philosophically untenable, practically unsustainable, and humanly debilitating the classical and leading Christian conceptions of the good, the virtuous, and the mode of political society necessary and sufficient to goodness and virtue, his Leviathan was predicated on and meant above all to serve individuality and the plethora of "felicities" that are individuality's yield and its "good." If various amendments and adjustments to his thinking are desirable, in my judgment these ought to be in the direction of strengthening his own—circumstantially remarkable— commitment to individuality, certainly not in the directions proposed by those of his critics mentioned above. If liberal theorists and publicists, whether because they are cowed by the animadversions of Hobbes's recent antiliberal critics or for any other reasons, abandon or diminish this commitment, they betray what is most estimable in liberalism.

In ways that I try to make evident in Chapter 1, Hobbes was primarily a theorist of self-assertion and self-making, of self-reliance and self-responsibility. His conceptions of divine and of human government, while absolutist in the sense that there are no de facto or de jure limitations on the former and few de jure limitations on the authority of the latter, stress the self-restraint that has in fact been practiced by God and that ought to be maintained by all human authorities. Perhaps more important, his conceptions of the languages and other instrumentalities through which God for the most part made and human authorities must make themselves and their wishes known to their subjects, presume heavily and in the latter case necessarily on the capacities of their subjects to construe and apply whatever directives are transmitted to them. Nor does Hobbes particularly regret these limitations on authority, the extensive domains of liberty in fact left by God to humankind and necessarily left to their subjects by human rulers. True, he believed that the estate of humankind is for these reasons more troubled and anxious than that of the "ants and the bees" to which God has provided a good that is indisputably common. And the least attractive features of Hobbes's thought derive from his desire partially to relieve the human estate of its difficulties by instituting a simulacrum of the order that obtains among subhuman creatures and from his notion of evils that, if not exactly common in the foregoing sense, are in his view indisputably evils for all human beings and hence warrant arrangements that create and sustain the order that he proposed. But Hobbes rejected the reality, possibility, and desirability of an ordering common good and sought no more political and legal order than is necessary to the activities of individual human beings pursuing a great diversity of goods.

Introduction

Interspersed in the essays that follow are attempts to identify and to underline respects in which both the most and the least appealing of these elements of Hobbes's thinking remain integral to liberal theory and practice. Contemporary liberals are at once attracted to and fearful of the diversity and unpredictability that Hobbes theorized; they are both in quest of and wary concerning institutions that promise the order he promoted. In important measure this is as it should be as well as the way it is and will remain. The tensions, indeed the conflicts and partial incompatibilities, between and among these desiderata are not to be regretted and in any case are almost certainly ineliminable.

On my own reading of their current characteristics, however (the reading that prompts and energizes the dissatisfaction that I have already recorded), liberal theory and practice have gravitated rather too strongly toward the less-engaging tendencies in Hobbes's thinking. It is true that most contemporary liberal thinkers and practitioners reject Hobbes's absolutism, most particularly by insisting on an array of individual rights that they believe are incompatible with that feature of his thinking.[1] But in arguing for a wider and more secure set of rights and for an expanded and deepened social justice, for greater cooperation and social unity, enhanced welfare and the like, they place their emphasis on commonalities not differences among individuals, on the conceptions and understandings, beliefs and values that have already achieved wide acceptance, the hopes and fears, desires and interests that are most generally recognized. Above all they stress the human capacities for rationality, reasonableness, and mutual understanding that they take to be the most secure basis for such unity as we have thus far achieved and for the augmented and intensified unity they seek. Their aspirations in these regards soar well beyond any that Hobbes himself would have entertained or even countenanced, and their estimations of the efficacy of government and politics as means of pursuing them far exceed his own. At the same time, the argumentative and rhetorical resources on which they rely are importantly similar to those which Hobbes marshaled in pursuing his own much more restricted objectives.

[1]This tendency is and has always been more pronounced in liberal circles in, say, the United States and France than in Great Britain. In Chapter 1 I argue that at a deep theoretical and conceptual level absolutism is a necessary feature of the state as we know it. On this view the British tendency is the more clearheaded of the two.

4

These developments seem to me to diminish both the security and the vigor of liberalism's commitment to individuality and other sources of diversity. In part because aspects of Hobbes's thinking can be read as licensing these developments, but more importantly because thinkers before and after Hobbes in what I will be calling the voluntarist tradition strongly complement the most potently individuality-promoting features of Hobbes's thought, in later chapters, and especially in Part Two, I explore and attempt to appropriate formulations of voluntarism significantly less qualified than his.

Chapter 2 moves in this direction by engaging the thinking of William James, which powerfully affirmed and promoted individuality. A radical pluralist in his metaphysics, his philosophy of religion, and his somewhat rudimentary social theory, a qualified volitionist in the theory of belief that was his epistemology, and an enthusiastic voluntarist in his axiology and metaethics, James's professional philosophical enemies were the idealists and the "block universe" to which their holism committed them. But the radical pluralism that he advanced against Hegel, Bradley, and Royce was above all for the purposes of a vitalistic "philosophy of life" that was addressed (as were other *lebensphilosophien* of the mid-to-late nineteenth century, such as those of Emerson and Nietzsche) to a substantially wider audience. Deeply distressed by the uniformity, monotony and conformity that he believed were stifling the human spirit, he promoted an individuality so radical that it threatened solipsism and even denial of the desirability of mutual intelligibility.

As with other of the strong voluntarists considered later in the volume (in particular Friedrich Nietzsche) against whom similar charges have been leveled (e.g., the charge of an unremitting and destructive nihilism), these radical tendencies in James's thinking present us with a complex but above all a deeply engaging array of challenges and provocations. James intended nothing so manifestly self-defeating as an unqualified solipsism or a privatism that would seal us off, hermetically as it were, from one another. The impression that he does so is due in considerable part to his animus against homogeneity and his corresponding zeal to promote the greatest diversity that the unalterable commonalities and the arguably essential communalities of human life (which James recognized but for the most part passed quickly over) would permit, an animus and a zeal more potent than his concern for philosophical nicety. But it is also and in more important ways due to complexities intrinsic to the project that he, along with the other voluntarists and with this work, had undertaken.

The differences and singularities that James sought to promote can be identified only by comparison with and against the backdrop of some number of recognized identities and commonalities. The initiatives and innovations that he admired presuppose constancies and continuities. Competitions and conflicts require some measure of cooperation. The mutual opacities and unintelligibilities that he was prepared not only to abide but to celebrate have as their condition respects in which we are transparent to one another, respects in which shared understandings obtain among us. Will and willfulness contrast with and hence implicate reason, reasonableness, and like notions. In making his case for the element in these and related modalities that he favored, he diminished and sometimes impugned the other, thereby appearing to fall into an incoherence of which the proverbial existential analogue is sawing at the branch on which one is sitting.

These considerations inform my decision to enframe the discussion of James—and, if much of the time implicitly, of the other voluntarists—by explorations in Wittgenstein's philosophy of meaning. As I now read him, Wittgenstein sees difficulties akin to those I have just attributed to voluntarism as endemic to language and hence to all thought and action.[2] His investigations, which crisscross in every direction over a wide field of thought, aim less to

---

[2]Along with many of those (anglophones) who responded to Wittgenstein's "later" thought during the 1960s and 1970s, I first read him as theorizing the enablement of meaning. Keying on his dissolution of the notion of a (logically) private language and his emphasis on the ordinary and the settled, on the conventions and agreements, criteria and rules that not only regulate but constitute practices, language-games, and forms of life, I took from him reassurance against the numerous anxieties, both philosophical and practical, generated by any very close attention to empiricism and positivism, behaviorism and emotivism. This was not and is not an altogether inappropriate reading. The elements just mentioned are prominent in his work, and, whatever his intentions, they are capable of providing a certain comfort.

As I argue below, however, and as in any case has been made evident by other commentators (especially, for me, Stanley Cavell), this reading overlooks and suppresses a great deal. As I now read him, and I have no doubt that the change is partly due to my now being in the market for kinds of comfort other than those I earlier sought, Wittgenstein is as much the theorist of unmeaning and the limitations and disablement of meaning as of their opposites. Or rather, by virtue of being a great theorist of the one he is a theorist of both.

promote or defeat this or that thesis or proposition than to identify
the conceptual and other resources out of which various and often
strange and conflicting theses and propositions are formed and to
sketch the complex and shifting relationships among them. Although not himself usefully characterized as a voluntarist, he locates
the conceptual, logical, or ontological "spaces" in which favored
voluntarist notions such as singularity and innovation, unintelligibility and mystery, will and willfulness are deployed, spaces that can
be seen and said to be "open" to use precisely because he shows them
to be variously bounded. These of his analyses, strongly reminiscent
of passages in Nietzsche that I consider in Part Two, help to fend off
philosophical dismissals of voluntarism as incoherent and rejections
of its leading concepts as figmental or obscurantist. More generally,
and whether or not we should attribute any very definite advocacy
to Wittgenstein himself, they seem to me to encourage receptivity to,
or a certain equanimity concerning, positions and proposals that
many find deeply disturbing.

In Chapter 3 I again summon Wittgenstein and Oakeshott, this
time in somewhat hesitant—on my part—support of a more substantive thesis concerning the relationship between individuality
and other forms of plurality, a thesis that I call complementarism.

Let us take plurality to mean an abundant diversity of sub- or
extrastate groups and associations, and let us call pluralism the
doctrine that there is and/or should be such a multiplicity. On this
usage, most liberal thinkers have embraced pluralism, and it is
widely thought that liberal societies are characterized by—and encourage or should encourage—plurality in the above sense.

As I have thus far stated them, however, these commitments and
understandings leave open the question of the relationship between
individuality and plurality. A major school of pluralist thought is
insistently anti-individualist. Some of its members argue that, in
F. H. Bradley's well-known phrase, the "mere individual is a delu-
sion of theory," others that individuals and individuality are all too
prevalent, a manifestation of the breakdown of social life (which for
them is first and foremost group and associational life) partly produced by the vicious doctrine called individualism. Reacting against
views of this sort, individuality-oriented thinkers such as William
James and in some respects Nietzsche became suspicious of groups
themselves and particularly of theories and doctrines that privilege
groups philosophically, surround them with special legal and politi-

cal protections, and promote their dominance in social and political life. For James and Nietzsche, groups and associations, valuable as they sometimes may be, are almost always sources of insidious and individuality-diminishing influence. And all too often they are concentrations of power used to suppress individuality.

The possibility that I explore under the rubric of complementarism is that the oppositions just outlined are false, that robust and widely distributed individualities are productive of group and associational life, and that the latter support and stimulate individualities. In a discussion that returns in a somewhat different context to the question of locating spaces for voluntarist and other individuality-affirming notions, I argue that complementarism is correct in its (often implicit) claim that individuality and plurality are conceptually interwoven and are in that sense mutually dependent. I also adduce various general reasons for thinking that as a practical matter they advantage one another. These considerations support the quite strong traditional association between liberalism and pluralism and hence also my claim that an emphasis on individuality is rooted in the liberal tradition.

There are, however, good reasons to be wary of complementarism. Its most grandiose versions, for example Hegel's, threaten to lose both individuals and groups in a Reason or a Geist the allegedly unifying qualities of which are responsible for the complementary relationships among the elements they encompass and subsume. Closer to the ground, the interest-group liberalism prevalent in the United States is careless of the individuality side of the individual-group relationship. Heavily discounting the Jamesian and Nietzschean apprehensions mentioned above, those among its proponents who have concern for individualities too readily assume that they will be taken care of by, will of themselves come along with, group and associational life. Most important here, complementarists tend to be indifferent and sometimes actively hostile to individualities of the kinds that voluntarists such as James, Nietzsche, and Oakeshott value most highly, those that may owe little more to group life than the Wittgensteinian spaces in which they are enacted by the persons whose individualities they are (and that may well detract from group life). Because the complementarisms that predominate in liberal theory and practice have these tendencies and deficiencies, if the views of Wittgenstein and Oakeshott are suitably appropriated and coordinated, they provide an invaluable corrective to and enhancement of a major characteristic of liberalism.

The argument of Part Two is that the most insistent forms of voluntarism can make such a contribution across a front much wider than that discussed in Chapter 3.

In a variety of respects that I sketch in the first section of Part Two, liberalism presupposes individuals whose conduct is for the most part voluntary. "Voluntary" in this regard means both that the actions taken are not coerced or compelled by other agents or agencies and that they occur because of the choices and decisions of the individuals whose conduct it is, because of desires and interests, beliefs, values and reasons that are in some sense the individual's own. In at least these ways, liberalism is committed to a form of voluntarism.

By comparison with Hobbes, Oakeshott, and James, and more especially with the thinkers explored in Part Two (e.g., William of Ockham and Nietzsche), however, liberal thinkers have embraced no more than heavily qualified versions of voluntarism, versions that do not provide a satisfactory account of the kinds of voluntary conduct that all liberalism presupposes and that are antagonistic toward the yet more vigorous forms of individuality theorized and promoted by the strong voluntarists. Moreover, or rather worse, as I read recent liberal responses to its Left and Right ideological critics, commitment to so much as a weak form of voluntarism seems to be on the wane in liberal theory and practice.[3]

Understood as an account or characterization of human doings and forgoings, the emphasis of strong voluntarism is always first and foremost on the wonder-ful quality or character of human conduct, on the ways in which our thinking and acting, in large part because they resist and finally defeat our own best efforts to explain

---

[3]At several points I suggest that the movement of liberalism toward democratic welfarism and hence more collectivist or communalist conceptions of politics and political action partly explains the decline of the voluntarist elements traditional to it. On this reading, commitment to the weak form of voluntarism mentioned above is now being sustained by the antiwelfarist and sometimes antidemocratic libertarians or free market theorists usually and for the most part correctly placed on liberalism's ideological Right. For reasons partly having to do with the relationship between theory and practice, to which I return later in this Introduction, this analysis doesn't settle any of the questions concerning public policy that are debated between liberals and libertarians. The analysis does have a bearing on ideological or public philosophy positions that may inform but do not settle policy debates, but it does not resolve those questions in favor of libertarianism. Libertarianism as it is now most prominently before us is not a version of strong voluntarism, and the willful liberalism for which I argue partly overlaps with, but in fundamental respects is in opposition to, libertarianism.

and understand them, ought to inspire wonderment in us. Understood as an ideal for human life, its emphasis is always first and foremost on the often-wonderful character of human conduct (notwithstanding its frequent vulgarity, ugliness, immorality, and the like), on the ways in which the inexplicable diversity of our thinking and acting should be celebrated by us.

In some of its earliest articulate formulations in the Western tradition, the ultimately mysterious quality of human action was accounted for by appeal to the Truth, which we can do little more than acknowledge, that we were created by and in the image of God, that is, by and in the image of the most mysterious of all beings. Endowed by God's grace with an analogue to God's own mysterious essence, Her will, our actions are like Hers in the respect that they are willful beginnings. We can explain or even understand our doings primarily in the weak sense that we can name their originating source, that is, primarily by saying that they are impelled by our wills. And those theological voluntarists who thought the diversity, unpredictability, and importantly inexplicable character of human conduct wonderful as well as a source of wonderment[4] did so for the reason that it precedes from this "power" that not only comes to us from God but is like unto that very power by virtue of which God is God. Later voluntarists such as Arthur Schopenhauer, Nietzsche, and Jean-Paul Sartre were "secular" thinkers in the limited sense that they scorned Christianity and its various theologies. As we will repeatedly see, however, in attempting to convey their powerful sense of the mystery and the sometimes majesty of human conduct they too turned to the notion of the will and they too invoked and projected will-suffused images of the divine and the otherwise super- and extrahuman.[5]

[4]Notoriously, Augustinian voluntarists think much of human conduct, especially instances of it that have the characteristics just mentioned, sinful and shameful. These thinkers, and yet more dramatically the theorists of "general," "group," "national," "real," and "true" will, remind us that invocation of will and willfulness is by no means a sure path to a more individuality-oriented liberalism.

[5]I use the distinction between theological and secular thinkers primarily in the sense indicated above, that is, to signal the fact that the thinkers I call "secular" understood themselves to be rejecting, not participating in, theological controversies. But the distinctions between theological and secular, religious and secular, certainly between spiritual and secular, are far from clean. As I have begun to indicate in the discussion above, in these respects my emphasis is on the similarities and continuities between and among the several strong voluntarists to whom I respond.

Some of the anxieties and antagonisms that these notions will of certainty provoke are diminished when we examine the details of strong voluntarist thinking. Human action as strong voluntarists conceive and valorize it is only finally or ultimately, not entirely or unqualifiedly, mysterious and unpredictable. (For Ockham and John Duns Scotus this is also true of the actions of God.) Will and willfulness as voluntarists conceive and especially as they promote them, are preeminently sources of self-command and self-control rather than means of commanding or controlling others. Will and willfulness, the at once animating and controlling sources of individuality and diversity, are essential to spirited, challenging, and hence engaging human lives. For theological voluntarists such as Ockham, however, neither will nor willfulness (which he and the other voluntarists subject to meticulous, closely textured analysis) would be possible apart from numerous further gifts and revelations from God, and the secular voluntarists are equally insistent on an array of cultural, social, and even political institutions and arrangements that provide settings within and against which action takes place. The strong voluntarists detail and even exult in the limitations on rationality and reasonableness, mutual understanding and cooperation in human affairs, but they also contend for respects in which all of these are necessary to the individualities and pluralities they exalt.

Misgivings and fears may also be somewhat allayed if we consider voluntarist conceptions of the relation between theory and practice, their thinking about the practical implications and implementation of their views. In the best sense of radical, that is, questioning beliefs and values very deep in a culture and tradition, strong voluntarists such as Duns Scotus and Ockham, Schopenhauer and Nietzsche, James and Oakeshott are clearly among the most radical of our thinkers. They are decidedly not in that company of utopians and ideologues who think it possible, desirable, and urgent to institute, by authority and power if necessary, rapid and sweeping changes in existing institutions, arrangements, and practices.[6]

---

[6]Jean-Paul Sartre is clearly an exception to these remarks; Hobbes and Hannah Arendt are partial exceptions to them. Even if we respect the important distinctions among the numerous and rapidly changing phases of Sartre's career as a thinker and political actor, he rarely manifests the skepticism, sometimes doctrinal, always temperamental, that informs voluntarist thinking at its best. I argue in Chapter 1

Introduction

The profoundly individuating character of the strong voluntarist ideal is by far the most important reason for what some will regard as this "conservative" tendency of the leading thinkers of this persuasion (a tendency better regarded as quite powerfully antiauthority and to this extent antipolitical).[7] Although clearly of the view that ideals and aspirations play a vital role in the human lives they most admire—and the higher, the more complex (one might almost say the less achievable) the ideals the better—nothing is more repugnant to these thinkers than the notion of a single substantive and life-encompassing ideal that is appropriate for all of humankind or all of the members of this or that society, culture, or civilization. Better, the notion *most* repugnant to the strong voluntarists is the fantasy of a life-encompassing ideal that is for everyone harnessed to the conviction that its requirements can and should be imposed on everyone by political, religious, or other kinds of authority and power. Transvaluations and transformations are indeed to be sought, but this is and must be the work of individuals.

---

that Hobbes was a deeply skeptical thinker and that the most admirable elements in his thinking are due importantly to his doubts about the reach of our knowing, understanding, and reasoning. But it is clear that he overcame or suspended his hesitations concerning both the truth and the utility of what he regarded as the fundaments of his civil philosophy. Arendt's skepticism in the domains of metaphysics and epistemology, historiography and social theory is clear from her earliest essays forward (see esp. her "What Is Existenz Philosophy?" *Partisan Review*, 8 [Winter 1946], 34–56), but she too conquered or concealed her doubts concerning the most distinctive claims of her political theory. It is in large part for these reasons that I give only passing attention to Sartre, distance myself from aspects of Hobbes's thinking, and am for the most part critical of—despite being much indebted to—Arendt.

This is perhaps an appropriate place to respond further to the suggestion of several readers of drafts of this work that in it I largely abandon the diffident stance or temperamental skepticism that is prominent in *Toward a Liberalism*. It is true, as I said above, that this work is more resolute than the previous one in affirming a certain point of view or assemblage of related ideas and ideals. These affirmations, however, are themselves informed by doubts concerning the more self-confidently rationalist, generalizing, and evangelical doctrines with which they contrast; and the ideas and ideals they affirm are marked as much by diversity or rather indeterminacy of content and application as by unity or specificity of form.

[7] "Conservative" is the disdainful term that radicals in the second and now more familiar of the above senses will disdainfully apply to it, thereby failing to recognize the genuinely radical character of strong voluntarism and once again uncritically reinforcing the homogenizing and impositional proclivities that are among the oldest, most deeply ingrained, and most objectionable characteristics of the culture and tradition they have inherited.

At the same time, and echoing main themes of Hobbes's thinking in ways I have already discussed, the strong voluntarists are convinced that individuals can do this work only in the setting of "language-games and forms of life," cultures and traditions, institutions and practices. James and Nietzsche see these first and foremost as sources of control and imposition that must be acted against; Oakeshott, Ockham and in important respects Arendt think of them in a more Hobbesian fashion as frames to act within and from; but all of the strong voluntarists presuppose and want to maintain substantial continuity in the variety of arrangements that are necessary to (albeit never sufficient for) individuality and plurality. And while the nineteenth- and twentieth-century voluntarists are without exception deeply wary of the modern state and the kinds of politics it engenders, the estimation I am attributing to them extends to this institution and these practices.

For these reasons, and because all of its major versions are internally complex and dissonant, strong voluntarism leaves open most of the issues of public policy. It is a public philosophy that informs, provokes, and orients thinking and acting, not an ideology, program, or technical manual that regulates, directs, or governs them. Our selves and our lives, our affairs and activities will be different to the extent that we entertain and embrace it, but the particular ways in which they will change, the shapes and characters they will acquire and assume, are left indeterminate—that is, are left for each of us to determine for ourselves.

These complicating but perhaps in some respects reassuring features of strong voluntarism bulk large in the pages that follow.[8] For

---

[8]Some will think that they bulk far too large, that in attempting to appropriate strong voluntarism to liberalism I domesticate and even denature thinkers such as Nietzsche. There is no short answer to this undeniably forceful objection. A long but inconclusive response to it is in the pages that follow.

I will take the occasion of first mentioning this objection to comment briefly on a perspective in which this work might be viewed, one that was somewhere in the back of my mind as I wrote the essays but is mentioned only briefly and casually in them.

Some of those who think I have made Nietzsche too tame will identify him as a precursor and quite possibly a major progenitor of anti-modernism and more especially of postmodernism. From this perspective, in which liberalism is likely to be viewed as a (perhaps *the*) modernist moral and political ideology, the project of appropriating Nietzsche to liberalism (toward which he is often openly antagonistic) is hopelessly misconceived if not wholly obnoxious.

The Nietzschean thinking that I construct here (and for that matter the Jamesian,

this very reason it is vital not to let them obscure or deflect attention from what is distinctive—and in my view distinctively valuable—in the ideas and images I will be considering. I repeatedly claim that strong voluntarism secures and enhances conceptions and valorizations that have been, are, and ought to remain central to liberalism. Its connected but greater contribution resides in the challenges it issues and the alternative possibilities it imagines and forwards, in its emphasis on will as well as and for many purposes rather than reason; opacities and other mutual inaccessibilities as complements to transparencies and shared beliefs and understandings; self-making and self-command wherever possible; mutual, collective, and above all governmental and political disciplines only as necessary or manifestly contributive to the former; *virtus* in preference to virtues; diversities and uncertainties rather than commonalities and assured regularities.

These are disturbing and no doubt risky ideas and ideals. Those who are satisfied with liberal theory and practice as they are will think it foolish, perhaps reckless, to entertain them. But it is not and can never be the case that all is well with liberal thinking or in liberal societies. The fundamental and abiding commitment of liberalism is to the most disturbing moral and political idea of all, the idea that each and every human being should be free to think and act as she sees fit. This idea is no more than barely intelligible, and the ideal of implementing it fully is manifestly impossible to achieve. For this and the connected reason that individuality and freedom compete or conflict with other revered liberal ideas and ideals, liberals them-

---

the Wittgensteinian, and even the Hobbesian thinking) includes many of the generous assortment of elements that are now encountered under the rubric of postmodernism. It will, I hope, be evident that I find these to be among the most engaging and salutary elements in his (and their) thinking. But "modernity" and "modernism," and of course liberalism, are hardly univocal notions, far from simple or monolithic phenomena. As is suggested by the rubrics *postmodern* and *postmodernist* themselves (concepts that like bedfellow notions termed *neo*, *anti*, and *after*, seem to me to manifest an inability or an unwillingness to break from—to be done with, as Nietzsche might say—the ideas and other phenomena they critique) modernity, modernism, and liberalism must include, if not precisely the elements that postmodernists forward, characteristics that could give rise to them. My project here is to think within liberalism, accentuating and where necessary adding (as liberal thinkers have always done) ideas that have been recessive in, subordinated by, or absent from it. I leave it to others to judge whether this effort, which is neither to be expected nor particularly to be hoped to yield a tightly integrated construction, might also be labeled in other ways.

selves are endlessly adjusting and revising liberal theory and practice in ways that, whether so intended or not, qualify its commitment to individuality and individual freedom. Often propelled by events that are beyond human understanding or control, and invariably pressed further by that great number of political thinkers and actors, easily a preponderance, who fear and hate individuality and freedom, these efforts have their effects, take their toll. For these reasons, and because individualities and the freedoms on which they thrive must constantly be reconceived and reenacted, by its own most important standard liberalism can never be satisfactory and liberals can never be satisfied with it.

Liberals and liberalism are forever in need of ideas and images that protect and invigorate, disturb, disrupt, and refashion their thinking and its arrangements and practices. The reflections that follow are out of this understanding and in this spirit.

PART ONE

INDIVIDUALITY AND PLURALITY, SOCIALITY AND POLITICALITY

Chapter 1

Absolutism, Individuality, and
Politics: Hobbes and a Little Beyond

Taking absolutism to mean rule qualifiable by nothing
other than the will or judgment of the ruler, the home of the most
literal formulations of the idea is in monotheistic theologies that
treat God as the omnipotent ruler of the universe. Theologies that
tend toward this view are likely to be regarded as incompatible with
human individuality and politics.

This reaction may confuse absolutism and totalitarianism in the
literal sense of a governance that in fact encompasses all doing and
forgoing in the "jurisdiction" of the God in question. It may ignore
or self-contradictorily exclude the possibility that God will choose
to restrict Her rule to certain aspects of human affairs, "ruling"
others only in a weak sense that permits of individualities and
politics in them. It might well be thought that individualities and
politics that, in this sense, are by God's leave, are thereby diminished or unworthy. Atheists and perhaps agnostics are eligible to
have (and might indeed be attracted by) this thought, but believers
in an omnipotent God who embrace or even entertain it thereby
blaspheme.

Here is one means by which an omnipotent God might permit
individualities and politics: She might endow Her human creations
with the firm belief that She exists and rules over them, but also limit
their access to the particulars of Her will concerning them. Firmly
believing that She exists and is omnipotent, but knowing that they
know only those parts of Her will for them that She unequivocally
reveals to them, they must perforce find or make their own way
outside the limits of that revelation. (Because they must navigate

within whatever limits She causally imposes on them, which, however, they can know only imperfectly, the very thought that there is an omnipotent deity may contribute to the anxious and unsettled character of their affairs.) Although absolute in the above sense, this characteristic of Her rule over them not only permits but obliges them to rule themselves in some parts of their thought and action. If in addition it has pleased God to create or to permit differences as well as commonalities among Her human subjects, individualities might develop among those subjects and numbers of them might devise a form of governance and a politics through which to accommodate their differences.

I argue that an articulation of this conception of divine absolutism and its relation to the human estate can be found in Hobbes's thought and that, on this reading, he can be said to project from and elaborate on the conception in theorizing the relationships among absolute government, individuality, and politics in intrahuman affairs.[1] As indicated in the Introduction, I further argue that this reflection, unpromising as the very terms in which it is cast might make it appear, yields much of continuing value for liberal theory and practice.

As with all accounts of Hobbes's multifaceted and in important respects mobile theorizing, this interpretation does well with some dimensions of his thinking, less so with others. I have tried to acknowledge a few of the difficulties with my reading, but I have not scrupled to subordinate exegetical and historical considerations to my primary objective, namely elaborating a distinctive and forceful attempt to locate and forward possibilities for individuality under circumstances apparently uncongenial to it. I do not endorse the particulars of Hobbes's absolutism, but I do accept one aspect of his argument that the only coherent political-theoretical (or anti political-theoretical) alternative to it is anarchism. I also argue that Hobbes has—or that his texts help us to formulate—a quite robust and instructive theory of individuality, one that is consonant with, though not entailed or otherwise required by, his arguments for

[1]Despite this interpretation, I hope to keep bracketed the much-disputed question whether in his personal beliefs Hobbes was an atheist. If we think he was an atheist, we can construe his discussions of theology and religion as Theophrastian moments in a secular political reflection or—especially in the case of his conception of divine absolutism—simply as taking advantage of readily available and otherwise convenient metaphors to articulate his reflection.

absolutism and for minimal political involvement for most citizens. Although clearly not a sufficient or adequate basis for a willful liberalism, Hobbes's thinking can help to move our own reflections toward such a conception.

I

If the will of an omnipotent God were completely known by humankind, human relations would be in principle unproblematic and problematic in fact only to the extent that some human beings, by God's leave as we would have to say, pridefully set themselves against God's commands. Human beings, who have this knowledge only in small part, but who also have a tendency to sinful pride, can handle the consequent practical problems by creating governments and investing them with absolute authority. Insofar as God's will is known, governments enforce it against prideful (and perhaps otherwise inappropriately willful) persons; and they supplement God's will with such further commands as prove to be necessary or appropriate. A government's authority to do these things, moreover, might be enhanced by the support and hence power that would be generated by general recognition of the divine grounding of some of its laws as well as the more general notions of law and command, enforcement and obedience.

Hobbes recognized that pride leads persons to set themselves against divine and other forms of authority, and some of the least attractive elements in his thinking result from his desire to tame pride sufficiently to sustain political order. For him, however, the epistemic conditions of rebellion against God's commands, and hence also the conditions presupposed by my foregoing remarks about human society and government, are satisfied in no more than special and narrowly restricted classes of cases. Having at best limited knowledge of God's will for them, for the most part humankind can neither obey nor disobey (albeit their actions can accord with or violate) that will, can neither order their affairs by reference to it nor rebel against such an ordering. Of course human beings often convince themselves and others that they know God's will and purport to rule or to rebel in God's name. While Hobbes's political argument places reliance upon the motivational effects of belief-based fear of God, in his view these epistemic conceits are primary causes of the disorders of his age. (Thinkers considered below, by contrast, regard such convictions as chief sources of oppressive control, of guilt and shame, and of ressentiment.)

There being no perceptual access to God, on Hobbes's epistemology human beings "cannot have any idea of him in their mind, answerable to his nature. For as a man that is born blind, hearing men talk of warming themselves by the fire, and being brought to warm himself by the same, may easily conceive, and assure himself, there is somewhat there, which men call *fire*, and is the cause of the heat he feels; but cannot imagine what it is like; nor have an idea of it in his mind, such as they have that see it; so also by the visible things in this world, and their admirable order, a man may conceive there is a cause of them, which men call God; and yet not have an idea, or image of him in his mind" (*Leviathan*, chap. 11, p. 85; also *Elements of Law*, chap. 11, p. 230).[2]

Within these limits, and among many other differentiations that he makes, Hobbes's extended and reiterated discussions of religion and religious belief include distinctions among (1) "natural religion" and its causes or "seeds," (2) what we can call natural but considered or reasoned religious belief, and (3) "true religion."

(1) Unique among the creatures of the earth in being endowed with both care about their futures and a desire to know the causes that affect them, religion arises among human beings out of fear (or anxiety) about the former fed by reducible but ineliminable ignorance concerning the latter. "This perpetual fear, always accompanying mankind in the ignorance of causes, as it were in the dark, must needs have for object something. And therefore when there is nothing to be seen, there is nothing to accuse, either of their good, or evil fortune, but some *power*, some agent *invisible*: in which sense perhaps it was, that some of the old poets said, that the gods were at first created by human fear" (*Leviathan*, chap. 12, p. 88).[3] Nec-

---

[2]In the absence of standard editions of Hobbes's main texts, and in particular because of the proliferation of widely used editions of *Leviathan*, I refer to chapters as well as to the pages of the particular editions I have used. Page references are to the following editions: *Leviathan*, ed. Michael Oakeshott (London: Collier Books, 1962); *Elements of Law* and *De Corpore* in *Body, Man, and Citizen: Selections from Thomas Hobbes*, ed, Richard S. Peters (New York: Collier Books, 1962); *De Homine* and *De Cive or The Citizen* in *Man and Citizen*, ed. Bernard Gert (Humanities Press, 1972); *A Dialogue between a Philosopher and a Student of the Common Laws of England*, ed. Joseph Cropsey (Chicago: University of Chicago Press, 1971).

[3]Although this passage refers specifically to ignorance of those lengthy causal chains that lead to the thought of God, fear is "always" (but not only) engendered by

essarily underdetermined by the deliverances of the senses, and among much of humankind very little disciplined by reason, out of this potent combination of causes (powerfully augmented by the deceits and dissemblings of the ambitious) "it hath come to pass, that . . . men have created in the world innumerable sorts of gods" (chap. 11, p. 86).

(2) Reasoned or considered religious belief is natural in that it springs from these same seeds and suffers these same epistemic limitations. It is distinguished by the fact that those who profess it recognize and respect its conditions and qualifications. "Curiosity, or love of the knowledge of causes, draws a man from the consideration of the effect, to seek the cause; and again, the cause of that cause; till of necessity he must come to this thought at last, that there is some cause, whereof there is no former cause, but is eternal; which is it men call God" (p. 85). Some human beings arrive at this conclusion "by their own meditation," that is by reasoning from the signification of names previously assigned or stipulated rather than by flights of undisciplined fancy, by gullible acceptance of the opinions of others, or, as in (3), by direct and unequivocal revelation from God Herself. Those who have proceeded in this more considered fashion "confess he is incomprehensible, and above their understanding, [rather] than to define his nature by *spirit incorporeal*, and then confess their definition to be unintelligible; or if they give him such a title, it is not *dogmatically*, with intention to make the divine nature understood; but *piously*, to honor him with attributes, or significations, as remote as they can from the grossness of bodies visible" (chap. 12, p. 89).[4]

(3) "True religion" results exclusively "where God himself, by supernatural revelation, plant[s]" it in a people of Her choosing. And where God has done this "he also made to himself a peculiar kingdom: and gave laws, not only of behavior towards himself, but also towards one another; and thereby in the kingdom of God,

---

the ignorance of causes. For example, fear may be aroused in me if I do not understand what causes you to act in ways that have consequences for me.

[4]In the same fashion, men of even modest capacities for ratiocination can reason their way to and choose to be guided (or not) by the "laws" ("theorems") of nature and can "piously" credit God with having created the universe in a manner such that those "laws" are operative in it. Pace Howard Warrander (*The Political Philosophy of Hobbes: His Theory of Obligation*, [Oxford: Clarendon Press, 1957], passim), they cannot claim to *know* that God promulgated those laws and hence cannot regard them as laws or commands in the proper or jural sense.

the . . . laws civil, are a part of religion; and therefore the distinction of temporal, and spiritual domination, hath there no place" (p. 94).

In the case of (1), human beings pretend to themselves or others that they know God's will (or the wills of their several gods) for them and that their conduct is or should be governed by it. The epistemic claim being unwarranted and in all likelihood fraudulent, in fact they are and can only be choosing their own actions, are and can only be ruling themselves. Case (2) is the same as (1), minus the hypocrisy of the latter. Thus in all cases of natural religion, God's decision largely to withhold knowledge of Her will from human-kind means that Her "rule," although absolute, is in actuality largely irrelevant to human conduct.[5] Again in actuality, God allows both uniformity and individuality, either robust and encompassing or meager and circumscribed politics, these being matters left to the determination of human beings.

In the case of true religion and thus God's kingdom Israel, God chose to further reveal Her will for humankind to a selection of human beings, those revelations constituting commands promulgated as *laws* to and imposing an *obligation* of obedience on the *conduct* of all those persons who are members of the "kingdom."

True religion being the case in which divine absolutism is most closely akin to the human variety, its rarity should not deflect us from considering it more closely. As the word *obligation* indicates, even in God's peculiar kingdom the subjects were *permitted* by God to disobey.[6] More important for present purposes, in Hobbes's view

---

[5]Hobbes's theology approached voluntarism in the sense of the Ockhamistic (see infra, Part Two, esp. Section II.A) emphasis on the will rather than the reason of God and, as we see later in this chapter and at other junctures below, his metaethics were also voluntarist or agent-relative in holding that the meanings of "good," "evil," and kindred terms are given by the will of each person who uses them. In his theory of belief, however, he was an antivolitionist. Thus, "laws are made and given in reference to such actions as follow our will; not in order to our opinions and belief, which being out of our power, follow not the will" (*The Citizen*, chap. 4, p. 163). Religious belief is as it were produced in human beings by God's existence and omnipotence, but neither this belief nor its cause is sufficient to bring about action. To repeat, the discussion above is not meant to deny that human beings may be motivated to act by fear of God. But if they think that their fear yields a particular action, they deceive themselves, perhaps in the hope of mitigating somewhat their fear, or—in the "Nietzschean" theme that is often very powerful in Hobbes—of establishing or consolidating their control over other persons.

[6]We might say that Hobbes attributes to God acceptance of the point that, conceptually, "law" in the strict jural sense entails the possibility of both obedience and disobedience. The importance of the point, however, extends well beyond conceptual considerations.

not even the "kingdom of God" was a theocracy in the strictest sense of rule directly by God. Although "Moses . . . governed the Israelites, that were not his, but God's people, not in his own name, with *hoc dicit Moses*; but in God's name, with *hoc dicit Dominus,*" this means not that Moses (as distinct from Jesus) was God incarnate or in thin disguise but only that Moses "personated" God (chap. 16, p. 127). Even in what he regards as the clearest cases of revelation, that is God's deliverances to the canonical prophets, Hobbes insists that God spake not "*in*" "but to them, by voice, vision, or dream; and the *burthen of the lord* was not possession, but command" (chap. 8, p. 66).

Of course Hobbes's chief purpose here is to discredit all forms of the arrogant and destructive claim to be possessed of God and hence to be entitled, in one's own person, to the obedience owed to God. Moses was not *an* authority to whom obedience was due owing to his personal qualities or characteristics; he was *in* authority by virtue of holding an office with which he had been invested by God following a covenant made by God's people.

This view, however, has the effect of diminishing further the role of God in human affairs. Except where it suffices merely to repeat what God has said to them (not easily or efficaciously done in the cases of visions and dreams!), it falls to the prophets-cum-officeholders divinely appointed not only to enforce God's commands in cases (if any) unequivocally covered by them, but to interpret and apply those commands to the much larger class of cases about which God's revelations are equivocal or to which She has not yet chosen to speak.

The relationship between God and the prophets with respect to the laws of "true religion" models one vital aspect of the relationship between human rulers and their human subjects. In God's kingdom, God promulgates the laws of true religion but the prophets must interpret and apply those laws (and the subjects, who, let us emphasize, are at one remove from God in this respect, must interpret and apply the interpretations of the prophets); in commonwealths, sovereigns promulgate laws but their subjects must interpret and apply them in their own actions. Together with the fact that both God and human rulers rule primarily by law and hence create the possibility of disobedience, these features of the ruler-ruled relationship, regardless of how absolute the authority of the ruler may be, make space for individuality and for politics (of course they assure neither).

25

Being omnipotent, God could speak again and further, thereby reducing or even eliminating the need for interpretation on the part of prophets and subjects.[7] Indeed God did speak further through Jesus Christ and Christ's apostles. But in doing so She eliminated the distinction between God's peculiar kingdom and all others, extended Her entire revelation to all of humankind, and, on Hobbes's view, left to sovereigns who are neither divine themselves nor "personators" of the divinity the task of interpreting and applying both those "laws" that God has made accessible to all rational creatures and those specially revealed (positive) laws that are applicable to kingdoms other than God's "peculiar" one. Moreover, while remaining silent Herself, God continues to permit (in the sense of not causally preventing) any number of falsely self-designated prophets to present and attempt to implement their own interpretations of both the natural and the revealed or positive divine laws. Along with the confounding effects of divinely unilluminated translations into other languages and of transmissions from generation to generation, the consequence of these of God's decisions has been to surround both the natural and the revealed laws with disagreement and conflict. In this light God's will or God's rule are seen to enter into human affairs primarily through the medium of diverse and self-serving appropriations of God's name by private individuals and groups. Although absolute, God's rule is far from total.

II

Later I will try to show that Hobbes's texts give us reason to think that he welcomed these among God's decisions, although it would be too much to say that he wished to banish God from the conduct of human affairs. Even if he was an atheist in some sense of that less-than-univocal term, he was convinced that most human beings will

[7]Note that human sovereigns who "personate" their subjects can, and in Hobbes's view should, interpret the laws they promulgate. The "mortal God" that is the sovereign is the *present* "God," the God who has no choice but to be *here* among us and hence positioned continuously to interpret herself. Hobbes sometimes writes as if sovereigns can thereby eliminate all uncertainty concerning the meaning of the laws they promulgate, leaving their subjects in no doubt as to what those laws require of them and hence with no choices other than to obey or disobey (of course in most cases they can disobey in a variety of ways). But there is a large question of whether or not human rulers, being merely absolute, not omnipotent, can accomplish this much.

26

be impelled by fear to some form of religious belief; and he very likely was convinced that this human propensity could be harnessed to the purpose of achieving peace and felicity. He labored mightily at the latter task, disputing religious doctrines that worked against this result and contending endlessly that true religion requires all but unqualified submission to an absolute government.

It would also be a mistake to think that Hobbes had nothing but regret concerning the limits on our knowledge of God or the uncertainties consequent on them. True, he insistently promoted absolute government to ameliorate difficulties in the human condition. True, it is the task of this "mortal God" to achieve among its subjects a *greater* uniformity and predictability than the immortal God has seen fit to institute in human affairs. But first, Hobbes's considerable skepticism concerning the extent to which human beings can know God and God's laws extended to his estimation of the extent to which human beings can know one another and can understand and act on one another's wishes and directives. Notwithstanding the (usually self-serving) fantasies of ancient philosophers and their scholastic acolytes (and of the collectivists and communitarians who are their descendants in our own time?), there is no *possibility* of so much as approximating in human affairs the commonality and integration that God has effected among ants and bees. And second, Hobbes regretted—or his texts give us reason to regret—these latter limitations no more than he did God's self-restraint in imposing Her will on humankind.

In pursuing this thought, I proceed on the partly erroneous assumption that Hobbes extended his skepticism-generating nominalism concerning God to all matters of fact and evaluation.[8]

---

[8]As I attempt to make convincing in the remainder of the chapter, this assumption is given plausibility by Hobbes's account of reasoning (and hence of science and scientifically warranted knowledge) as the adding and subtracting of "names" together with his repeated insistence that the categories of thought that names provide are the products of stipulation or "artifice" and are not determined by the nonlinguistic "properties" of the things and classes of things that they name. Hobbes did not accept this nominalist view without qualification. Despite his acerbic criticisms of Aristotle and the scholastic realists who were influenced by him, in *De Corpore* and elsewhere Hobbes followed them to the extent of recognizing pre- and otherwise non-linguistic thinking and in arguing that the categories or classes into which it organizes (some of) the data provided by the senses can and should be disciplined by the (perceived) characteristics of the things and classes of things they identify and collect.

He also insists, however, that these possibilities and capacities, which compose what he calls "Natural Reason" and which humankind partly shares with some

Our senses mechanically and (we are for the most part obliged to assume) reliably transmit the individual (radically particularized) "motions" *that* impinge on them. But (on the view I propose to develop) the data of sense do not present themselves to us in adequately intelligible form. Neither God nor nature has provided us with categories adequate to identify, combine, or otherwise to determine *what* those motions or properties are and are not. Indulging an anachronism, we might say that sense data become somethings rather than anythings (albeit Hobbes does not entertain the more radical possibility that they are nothings)[9] only if *I make* them into such by stipulating a name for them.[10]

Ratiocination, the "adding and subtracting" of names already assigned (*Leviathan*, chap. 5, p. 41), presupposes and cannot control the initial processes of assigning names and hence cannot determine how "things" are or should be identified and classified, distin-

---

subhuman animals, have done little to enhance the human estate. Those human beings who have not supplemented "natural" by "philosophical" reason or "ratiocination" remain in no better than a subsistence condition as regards their material or bodily needs and are in a state of war with one another. Misuses of the uniquely human capacity for language, ratiocination, and hence science (including overestimations of them, such as attempting to bring them to bear on theological questions and to derive a *summum bonum* from them) have gravely compounded the difficulties of humankind, but their proper use is the only way to relieve the latter. See esp. *De Corpore*, chap. 1, pp. 23–31.

Thus in ignoring the "realist" components in his thinking in order to accentuate his views about absolutism and individuality, my reading is incomplete but not unfaithful to his "civil philosophy." (I am indebted to Sidney Maskit for discussion of these points.)

[9]Cf. Ludwig Wittgenstein, *Philosophical Investigations* trans. G. E. M. Anscombe (New York: Macmillan 1953), I, 6. Wittgenstein was a conventionalist not a nominalist. For him, the conceptual system by virtue of which anythings and nothings become somethings consists not of a collection of stipulations but of a complex web of interwoven beliefs, rules, judgments, and the like that are shared among those who use a language. See infra, Chapters 2 and 3 for further discussion of Wittgenstein's views.

[10]For a particularly delightful presentation of these of Hobbes's views, see his story of how the man who pretended "to have been miraculously cured of blindness, wherewith he was born . . . discovered himself, and was punished for a counterfeit" by answering the question "What color is this?" "For though by his sight newly received he might distinguish between green, and red, and all other colors, as well as any man . . . , yet he could not possibly know at first sight which of them was called green, or red, or by any other name" (*Elements of Law*, I, chap. 6, p. 203). Here Hobbes treats the color concepts in question as shared among the counterfeit and those who exposed him.

guished and combined (albeit once some names have been assigned, reason can and should play a role in making further or altered stipulations). Licensing in at least this respect the charge of radical atomism so often leveled against him, Hobbes holds that even after they have been named, things as such remain entirely particular, connected or disconnected with one another only in the sense of having presented themselves to us, contingently and accidentally so far as we can know, in spatio-temporal contiguity or discontiguity with another. With a reliability and permanence that vary somewhat from person to person and more so from one circumstance to another, memory records these sequences in individuals, history does the same among peoples, and prudence draws on these essential but necessarily uncertain resources in estimating and acting into the future. It is only *after* names have been assigned that reason and the sciences of which reasoning is the method can draw inferences and conclusions that can be necessary and hence fully reliable. These inferences and conclusions, moreover, hold only so long as the reasoning respects the names that are the materials with which it works.

The individual, pre- or non-rational, and otherwise largely un-constrained act of naming or stipulating, then, plays a crucial role in all serviceable knowing, believing, and—as we see in more detail below—acting. In one of the senses now conveyed by the word *willful*, we might characterize Hobbesian naming as a process of willing. But because for Hobbes the will is merely "the last appetite in deliberation," and because some naming must have taken place before deliberation can occur,[11] it is better to classify naming in the wider category of "artifice," that is, as the chief instance of the process by which individual human beings make somethings out of things that God and nature have (so far as humankind is concerned) left in the condition of being anythings. Here the more skeptical side of Hobbes's nominalism asserts itself. Because reasoning cannot begin until artificing has occurred, and because the data transmitted by the senses do not fully determine the names that artifice stipu-lates, the first results of artifice cannot be understood without refer-ence to an agency that some will regard as of a less promising or

[11]Or at least deliberation that is rational or influenced by reason in the more estimable sense on which I am concentrating. Because Hobbes does attribute delib-eration to animals (*Leviathan*, chap. 6, p. 53), we cannot say that naming is necessary to all deliberation in the widest sense in which he uses the term.

encouraging character, that is, "The interior beginnings of Voluntary Motions, commonly called the Passions; and the Speeches by which they are expressed" (chap. 6, p. 47). "These small beginnings of ['animal' as distinct from 'vital'] motion, within the body of man, before they appear in walking, speaking, striking, and other visible actions, are commonly called ENDEAVOUR. . . . This endeavour, when it is toward something which causes it, is called APPETITE, or DESIRE; . . . And when the endeavour is fromward something, it is generally called AVERSION" (ibid.).

Generically, the passions "are the same in all men." This providential fact is a necessary condition of whatever mutual understanding and cooperation human beings can achieve and sustain. The "*objects* of the passions," by contrast, "which are the things *desired, feared, hoped, &c*," result from "the constitution individual, and particular education, [and] do so vary, and . . . are so easy to be kept from our knowledge, that the characters of man's heart, blotted and confounded as they are with dissembling, lying, counterfeiting, and erroneous doctrines, are legible only to him that searcheth hearts" (*Leviathan*, "Author's Introduction," p. 20). Those who have attempted the latter activity, Hobbes adds, have been "for the most part deceived" (ibid.).

Nor does the importance of the passions diminish after the conditions necessary to reasoning have been established. It is essential to Hobbes's larger theory that belief and action can be affected by education, persuasion, reason, command, threats, and so forth. Dependent on the generic commonalities among the passions and the faculties of sense and of reason, these effects are produced primarily when one person induces others to think within the set of names she has stipulated. Whether or not he is entitled to do so, Hobbes often writes as if this process is unproblematic. Postponing the difficulties lurking here, it remains the case that "the thoughts are to the desires, as scouts, and spies, to range abroad, and find the way to the things desired; all steadiness of the mind's motion, and all quickness of the same, proceeding from" the desires. For "as to have no desire, is to be dead: so to have weak passions is dullness; and to have passions indifferently for every thing, GIDDINESS, and *distraction*" (*Leviathan*, chap. 8, pp. 62–63). Thus while reasoning can play a part in artificing that takes place after a stock of names has been accumulated, we must think of artifice and hence of all the knowledge and belief that result from it as both first and foremost products of the workings of the individual's passions and hence of difficult and limited mutual accessibility.

This profoundly skeptical (but therefore also mutually insulating?) conclusion is strongly reinforced in the case of action. All human actions are taken in order to obtain objectives that the agent desires or to avoid states of affairs to which the agent is averse. One or more of the agent's passions having already played their role in identifying the object of the action, desire and aversion enter again in designating that object as good, evil, and the like. "But whatsoever is the object of any man's appetite or desire, that is it which he for his part calleth *good*: and the object of his hate and aversion, *evil*; and of his contempt, *vile* and *inconsiderable*. For these words of good, evil, and contemptible, are ever used with relation to the person that useth them: there being nothing simply and absolutely so; nor any common rule of good and evil, to be taken from the nature of the objects themselves" (chap. 6, pp. 48–49).

There is a good deal of redundancy in this famous passage. On the most robust formulations of Hobbes's nominalism, of nothing whatsoever can it be said that the nature of the object itself makes it simply or absolutely one something rather than any other. Again, one person may choose to adopt names initially stipulated by another, but all naming is and on Hobbes's theory can only be "with relation to the person" here and now using the name. Moreover, while Hobbes allows that a person will regard the same object sometimes as good, sometimes as evil, thereby accepting a version of the distinction between descriptive and evaluative naming, in the case of the names most important to action (for example, power and riches, glory and honor, death, injury, and dishonor), desire and aversion will be the passions responsible for the name of the object itself and hence no such distinction will be possible.[12] The manifestly advertent character of these redundancies highlights rather than diminishes their importance in Hobbes's moral and political argument. Hobbes might have left it to attentive and prudent

---

[12]It is therefore doubtful that Hobbes's epistemology and metaethic entitle him to his view that (even in the absence of a sovereign's stipulation) some things—civil peace, felicity—ought always be called good and others—civil war, death—ought always to be called evil. There is no doubt that he held this view (although he recognized that some persons whom he admired—in part for this reason—rejected it), but the larger arguments of his texts do not encourage us to follow him in doing so.

readers to notice the fractionating and conflictogenic tendencies of his theory, foregrounding instead the possibilities for cooperation that the theory makes available. Indeed this is precisely the tactic that one would expect from a theorist allegedly preoccupied by the problem of order and keen to reduce human diversity to uniform and manageable proportions. As his critics have gleefully proclaimed, his insistence on the deeply voluntarist, "agent-relative," and hence individuating character of his philosophical views makes difficulties for his argument that human beings can and should submit to the discipline of an absolute government.

Difficulties there may well be, but we are not yet in a position to determine for whom or for what. We have to consider the possibility that the prominence of the views just discussed (in the works of this most candid of thinkers) both reiterate Hobbes's (deeply skeptical) philosophical convictions and reveal his delight in the human individuality that those convictions at once project and protect. Is it possible that the "order" that Hobbes's views are said to jeopardize is one that Hobbes thought neither possible nor desirable?

III

As we have seen, for Hobbes actions follow the will and are susceptible to the influence of laws and a great variety of other considerations that enter into the deliberations of which will is the last appetite. Deliberation is impossible without the energy and direction of passion, but if it is not disciplined by prudence and reason, the agent degenerates into giddiness or even madness. But neither discipline nor for that matter sanity is good (desirable) in itself or in its own right; they are desirable, rather, because they assist the agent in avoiding the summum malum which is premature death, and in sustaining '*felicity*,'' that is, "*continual success* in obtaining those things which a man from time to time desireth" (p. 55).[13]

---

[13]Notions such as normality, sanity, and madness, then, are for Hobbes delineated by reference to the regularity of success and failure in satisfying desires that are given by the passions. It follows both that desires as such can be neither sane nor insane and also that someone judged mad by other criteria—say, clinical criteria—but who has good success in satisfying her desires would have to be judged sane by Hobbes. So far as I am aware, Hobbes departed from these views only in holding that those who desire to commit suicide thereby show that they are non compos

Returning to the notion of felicity in chapter 11 of *Leviathan*, Hobbes gathers and underlines the powerfully individuating elements of his theory of action. "We are to consider, that the felicity of this life, consisteth not in the repose of a mind satisfied. For there is no such *finis ultimus*, utmost aim, nor *summum bonum*, greatest good, as is spoken of in the books of the old moral philosophers. Nor can a man any more live, whose desires are at an end, than he, whose senses and imaginations are at a stand. Felicity is a continual progress of the desire, from one object to another; the attaining of the former, being still but the way of the latter. The cause whereof is, that the object of man's desire, is not to enjoy once only, and for one instant of time; but to assure for ever, the way of his future desire. And therefore the voluntary actions, and inclinations of all men, tend, not only to the procuring, but also to the assuring of a contented life; and differ only in the way: which ariseth partly from the diversity of passions, in divers men; and partly from the difference of the knowledge, or opinion each one has of the causes, which produce the effect desired" (chap. 11, p. 80).

The ends of action, then, are individuated several times over and in several respects irreducibly. For the most important purposes, the universe that I inhabit is what it is by virtue of the names that I assign to its components. I can adopt names that you have assigned, but it is only after and for so long as I adopt them that they identify elements in my universe. In every case, my choice of identifying names is partly a consequence of my passions, and my passions play a distinctively important role in my choice of the evaluating names (such as "good" and "evil") that I assign to the objects of my actions. My object in life is my own felicity. Insofar as you and I adopt the same names and endeavor to achieve or avoid the same objects, your felicity and mine can coincide; but because my felicity consists exclusively in the satisfaction of my desires and yours in the satisfaction of yours, your felicity cannot be mine and mine cannot be yours.[14] Your actions can contribute to or detract from my

---

mentis (*Dialogue between a Philosopher and a Student*, "Of Crimes Capital," p. 116).

[14]Insofar as I am able to discern the objects of your desires, my desire can be that you satisfy a desire of yours. It is only in this kind of case, instances of which Hobbes thinks are rare, that the satisfaction of one or more of your desires constitutes rather than merely coincides with the satisfaction of one or more of mine. Cf. infra, Part Two, where I discuss Nietzsche's importantly similar views concerning self- and other-regardingness, egoism and altruism.

felicity and vice versa, but calculations to this effect hold only so long as the passions and stipulations that inform them remain unchanged.

All of this is as it is; that is, it is a description of human beings and their circumstances that Hobbes holds to be warranted by experience and science. It is also as it *should or ought* to be in the only sense (apart from divine commands) in which Hobbes allows that we use those words, namely, that this set of characteristics and circumstances enables the felicity of individual human beings as they see it. Even if Hobbes wished that the human estate were otherwise in these respects (a speculation for which I have found no textual evidence), he thinks, therefore, that attempts to alter substantially the characteristics of human beings and their circumstances that his analysis singles out will continue to be both futile and harmful. Like the misguided efforts of his predecessors in moral and political philosophy, and like the yet more egregious attempts of the false prophets and sects of his own day, such endeavors will diminish felicity as they otherwise leave human beings pretty much as they are. It is thus no worse than an exaggeration to say that Hobbes (like other thinkers of a predominantly skeptical tendency) thinks that his own most important contribution is to have identified the limitations on and hence the possibilities open to human thought and action, thereby protecting them (to the extent that philosophy can do so) against misconceived and destructive enthusiasms.[15]

As Hobbes is at pains to emphasize, the lives of creatures with these characteristics are not likely to be easy. Even if insulated against pretensions and misunderstandings, the characteristics and conditions that establish felicity as the appropriate human objective and that enable its pursuit are far from sufficient to achieving and sustaining it. Although contemptuous of—as well as affrighted by—the utopian mentality that seeks the perfection of the human condition, Hobbes thought that he had devised affirmative means of diminishing somewhat its "inconveniences." Chief among these devisings is "that great LEVIATHAN" and its absolute authority.

---

[15]In this perspective, the parts of Hobbes's work that present his firmest convictions are chapters 1–12 and 31–47 of *Leviathan*, the analogous chapters of *Elements of Law* and *The Citizen*, and of course *Behemoth*; correspondingly, the more problematic parts are the "Author's Introduction," chapters 13–30, and "A Review, and Conclusion" of *Leviathan* and their analogues (if any) in the other moral and political works.

IV

Hobbes presents his arguments concerning Leviathan as inferences (in part the results of experience and prudential deliberation,
in part of deduction) from the analysis thus far discussed, supplemented by generalizations about the circumstances of human life
and the tendencies of human conduct. It is clear from this mode of
presentation that in his view this supreme example of human artifice
can do no more than ameliorate difficulties and that in attempting
to do this much it must respect the limits set by the characteristics of
human beings and their condition.

In considering his argument it will be useful to return to the
comparison between God's peculiar kingdom and Leviathan. As we
have seen, Israel provides an example of divine rule that is omnipotent and absolute but in practice quite narrowly confined. Knowing
that God is omnipotent, and being moved by piety to attribute the
most favorable characteristics to Her, should we not assume that it
is out of benevolence that God has chosen this combination of
ruling us and leaving us to our own devices? And should we not
imitate God's example as far as possible in conducting our own
affairs?

If we pursued these thoughts, we might say that (1) we should
accord to our rulers the closest thing to divine rule at our disposal,
namely absolute authority over us, but that (2) with our encouragement our rulers should follow God's example and exercise that
authority sparingly.

Hobbes accepts (1) in close to unqualified form. He does not
explicitly mention the consideration I just introduced as a reason for
doing so, but if we emphasize the role that covenanting played in the
creation of Israel and plays in creating Leviathan, we might argue
that the example of God and God's chosen people has influenced his
thinking. However this may be, the case of Israel helps us to notice a
distinction Hobbes makes between two moments in absolutism and
the different arguments he gives for each of them.

Deriving as it does from Her omnipotence, God's rule over humankind in general is necessarily unqualified except by Her own
will. But when the people of Israel covenanted to make God their
political sovereign, and when other peoples covenant with one
another to create governments, they necessarily claim (however
hybristically) entire right or authority to do so. How they exercise
that authority, for example, whether they make that government

absolute or qualify its authority in certain ways, is a question that they must regard as within their authority to decide. If they decide to make the government absolute on the ground that their ruler will be God and that God's majesty forbids qualification of Her authority, it is they who make (by God's leave) their decision on that ground. If they decide to limit, divide, or otherwise qualify the authority of government in certain ways (for example, because they believe that God has commanded them to do so, because to fail to do so would violate laws or rights of nature, to act imprudently, or for any other reasons), it is they who act on those reasons and who therefore claim (at least implicitly) the right to do so. Because it is the authority to make the decisions, not the reasons given for them, that validates those decisions, rejecting the reasons cannot invalidate the decisions. As Hobbes puts it: "This device therefore of them that will make civil laws first, and then a civil body afterwards (as if policy made a body politic, and not a body politic made policy), is of no effect" (*Elements of Law*, II, chap. 1, p. 318).

In this of its moments, authority is necessarily absolute. The alternative to absolutism is not limited authority; it is anarchism if not radical antinomianism. However it is exercised or implemented, absolute authority is the basis of all systems of rule. In Hobbes's view this is a truth of reason, an indisputable deduction (as we might put it) from the meanings of the words *authority, rule,* and *government.* (And while, largely contrary to Hobbes, these considerations are anything but good reasons against placing various limits and controls on the authority of governments, they are excellent reasons for wariness concerning politically organized societies and their claims to authority.)

Hobbes is aware that acceptance of these conceptual points will not of itself convince anyone to covenant with others to constitute a government or to honor that covenant if they find the resulting government harmful to them. Thus he gives reasons for making such covenants, for implementing them by instituting governments that are invested with the authority of those whose covenants create them, and for honoring the covenants by submitting to the governments thereby created.

One such reason that Hobbes frequently presents is that God has commanded us to make such covenants and to honor them in the manner just described. Thus far it is only in the case of the Israelites that God has demarcated the people among whom such a covenant should be made. For this reason, the rest of humankind are left with discretion in these regards. In all other respects, Israel exemplifies God's revealed will concerning government.

But here we begin to see the limitations of the reasoning I am now pursuing. Strictly, Hobbes cannot treat God's rule of Israel and human rule within God's general revelation as parallel. One reason is that he knows that the argument I just summarized will convince only those who accept his reading of deeply contested passages in scripture. Another and deeper one is that on his own epistemology we cannot *know* this much about God's will. Whether or not for these reasons, Hobbes also argues that such covenanting is essential to the felicity of each of us.

Hobbes also accepts the second of the conclusions that I said might be drawn from the example of God's rule of the Israelites and indeed from the yet-greater self-limitation that God has maintained vis-à-vis all other peoples. He accepts that those human rulers properly invested by their subjects with (all but) absolute authority should nevertheless exercise that authority only to the extent necessary (of which they must be the judges) to maintain the peace and defense essential to the felicity of their individual subjects.

In this case it is yet more obvious that Hobbes cannot use the example of God's self-restraint as the reason for his conclusion. Either to generalize from the example of God's relation to Israel or to claim to know God's intentions for the rest of humankind would be to indulge a "vain conceit" prohibited by his epistemology and theology and castigated on various other grounds throughout his works. If, however, there is no such parallel between divine and human rule, there are instructive analogies between them. The most important of these analogies are between the limits of our knowledge of God and of our knowledge and understanding of one another.

Although insistent that we can know no more than that God is, cannot know what God or God's will is, Hobbes thinks we can have partial and for some purposes serviceable knowledge of one another's desires and thoughts. Setting aside doubts whether his theory actually warrants this possibility, it is plain that on his theory our knowledge of one another can be no more than partial and can never be secure into the future. And just as his conception of our limitations in respect to God plays a vital role in his theology, so his theory of jurally absolute but practically limited government can be read as an elaboration on his conviction that in at least this respect each of us is like a God to all the others of us.

"Of the voluntary acts of every man, the object is some good to himself" (*Leviathan*, chap. 14, p. 105). For this reason alone, it is possible for the natural persons whom we make our sovereigns to pursue our ends if and only if our ends coincide with theirs. What is more, not being gods or even personators of gods, sovereigns can know our ends, and hence can know whether our ends coincide with theirs, only to the limited extent that a human being can know another's passions, deliberations, and stipulations. In this sense, and for all of their formal authority to act, the sovereign's abilities to do so are as severely limited as those of any person.

Why then should we create sovereigns and submit to their rule?

Perhaps we should answer, as in consistency Hobbes himself must answer in part, that we should do so on the wager that the sovereign's ends and our own will in fact coincide often enough that the advantages will outweigh the disadvantages.

But this is only part of Hobbes's answer. Although insisting that the authority invested in the sovereign should be (all but) absolute, Hobbes does recognize that ruling is a distinctive office and activity; he distinguishes good and bad ruling; and he counsels sovereigns to rule well rather than badly. Ruling well, however, does not require the impossibility of pursuing the ends of someone other than the ruler or the near impossibility of acting only if the ends of the ruler and those of the ruler's subjects coincide. Rather, it requires that rulers be especially attentive to a distinction that prudence and reason urge on all human beings, that is, between the ends of our actions and the conditions under which we are most likely to be successful in pursuing whatever ends we have. Although necessarily pursuing their own ends, and urged to consider that because of their position their ends will more often than is usual coincide with the ends of their subjects, sovereigns are especially well placed and have a responsibility to attend to the conditions necessary to the successful pursuit of such kinds of ends as experience and reason have shown to be most common among humankind. (Hobbes argues further that the sovereign's own ends will very likely be encompassed within these classes.)

It is a signal advantage of this view that on it the inherently uncertain business of "searching hearts" is irrelevant to ruling. To repeat, "let one man read another by his actions never so perfectly, it serves him only with his acquaintances, which are but few," while "he that is to govern a whole nation, must read in himself, not this or that particular man; but mankind." To discharge their offices well, then, rulers must discern "the similitudes of *passions*, which are the same in all men, *desire, fear, hope, &c.*; not the similitude of the *objects* of the passions."

Relieved of, or rather largely excluded by incapacity from, the duty to know and advance the particular ends of their individual subjects, the sovereign is nevertheless confronted with the arguably greater difficulty of "reading mankind" and pursuing what has traditionally been called the common good. Recognizing that from Plato forward the daunting character of these tasks had been taken as reason for pessimism concerning government and everything that has been thought (however absurdly) to depend on it, Hobbes continues the lines of thought I am tracing in ways that permit him to "recover some hope" that "the disorders of state" can be "taken away" (chap. 31, p. 270).

Concerned with the conditions of felicity, not felicity itself (nor even the conditions of the integration of self or self and community, moral perfection, perfect freedom, and like fantasies), the deep and transcendental truths that Plato and his successors thought good rulers must know are in fact irrelevant to governance. The "only science necessary for sovereigns and their principal ministers" is the "science of natural justice" (ibid.). Moreover, Hobbes convinced himself that he had so well "read mankind" that it would largely suffice for sovereigns to read Hobbes. Apparently eschewing the skepticism that I have attributed to him, he modestly claimed to have "put into order, and sufficiently or probably proved all the theorems of moral doctrine, that men may learn thereby, both how to govern, and how to obey." Thus almost all that is necessary for good government is that "this writing of mine may fall into the hands of a sovereign, who will . . . by the exercise of entire sovereignty . . . convert this truth of speculation, into the utility of practice" (ibid.). (Note that even this ill-considered remark recognizes the need for no less than a "converting.")

Hobbes's "hope," however, that is the success of his project of employing absolute government to increase human felicity, requires sovereigns and subjects to draw and act on several further inferences from the arguments thus far considered. The most general of these, from which Hobbes draws three subordinate inferences, is that sovereigns will limit themselves to governing primarily by law and that subjects (as such) will relate to one another and to their sovereigns first and foremost as obeyers of the civil law. (Hobbes is a theorist who urges rule primarily by law, but not a theorist of the rule of law.)

The "skill of making, and maintaining commonwealths," Hobbes says, "consisteth in certain rules, as doth arithmetic and geometry; not, as tennis-play, on practice only" (chap. 20, p. 158).[16] Arithmetic and geometry are "certain" sciences; when properly conducted they yield sums and theorems that are beyond dispute. But their certainty in this sense depends on another, namely, the clarity or "perspicuity" of the definitions that mathematicians have stipulated and from which the reasoning that leads to their conclusions proceeds. Analogously, by promulgating positive laws, sovereigns define the terms in which their subjects (again as distinct from private persons) thereafter make their "calculations." (The analogy is imperfect, though in respects that, in part, offset one another. Hobbes doesn't think that laws can be made as perspicuous as the stipulations of geometers, but sovereigns have something that geometers do not have, namely, public authority to promulgate and construe their definitions.) Thus perspicuous laws provide a settled and shared basis on which the members of a commonwealth can maintain a modus vivendi despite the mutual antagonisms, misunderstandings, and unintelligibilities that result from their individuating characteristics.

The first of the inferences subordinate to the proposition that sovereigns should rule by law, then, is that it "belongeth to . . . the office of a legislator" to make the laws as perspicuous as possible (chap. 30, pp. 255–57). The second and third such inferences can be viewed as elaborations on differences between positive laws and their model, that is, the stipulations of mathematicians. The former of these is simply a deduction from one such difference already

---

[16]In saying "not . . . on practice only," Hobbes allows that skills learned by practice and not embodied or embodiable in rules do play a role in making and sustaining commonwealths. The most important of such skills are those that he discusses (for example, in *Leviathan*, chap. 30) under the heading of public "instruction" as distinct from law. Whatever we may think of the certitude with which Hobbes presents the propositions and inferences discussed just above, as well as those of his claims that I queried in supra n. 12, on the reading I am presenting, these parts of Hobbes's argument have a problematic place in his civil philosophy.

noted, namely, that the sovereign's definitions are invested with authority and hence binding. Viewed in comparison with geometry, the point here is that law is not a system in the rigorous sense of a mathematics and hence sovereigns are advised but not obliged to maintain consistency between their new or altered laws and those they have previously promulgated. While a subject should not be punished for obeying only one of two or more laws that make mutually incompatible demands on her (as also a subject should be excused from obedience if a law is so lacking in perspicuity that it is impossible for her to know what would count as obeying it), conflicts among laws or between them and other desiderata do not invalidate or justify disobedience to any law. Hobbes refines this proposition in various ways, but in its fundamentals it is simply a corollary of his absolutism.

Together with his absolutism, the first subordinate inference might lead us to expect Hobbes to recommend extensive and encompassing legislation, to urge the sovereign to promulgate numerous laws governing many aspects of life in the commonwealth. If law eliminates or obviates the consequences of disagreement and mutual unintelligibility, why shouldn't the sovereign use it freely and widely?

In fact, however, while reiterating that the sovereign must have complete discretion concerning the number and scope of the laws promulgated, Hobbes proposes two criteria of "good laws," namely, perspicuity and "needful," and interprets them in ways that imply (albeit Hobbes himself is not invariably faithful to the implication) the desirability of narrowly limited legislation.

"Unnecessary laws are not good laws; but traps for money: which where the right of sovereign power is acknowledged, are superfluous; and where it is not acknowledged, insufficient to defend the people" (p. 256). What does Hobbes mean by "needful" and its contrary "unnecessary"? The "use of laws . . . is not to bind the people from all voluntary actions; but to direct and keep them in such a motion, as not to hurt themselves by their own impetuous desires, rashness or indiscretion; as hedges are set, not to stop travellers, but keep them in *their* way. And therefore a law that is not needful, having not the true end of a law, is not good" (ibid., emphasis added).

Words such as "direct," "hurt," and "impetuous desires" in this passage might be construed as recommending a highly active legislator, a paternalistic or even a moralistic governance. Hobbes does not rejoin directly to this interpretation, but his rejection of an inference that might seem to be licensed by his absolutism is instructive concerning it. It might be thought, Hobbes considers, that "a law may be . . . good, when it is for the benefit of the sovereign; though it be not necessary for the people; but it is not so. For the good of the sovereign and people, cannot be separated" (ibid.). Knowing as we do that the good of the sovereign qua natural person is in all likelihood different from the good of her subjects, and taken together with his revealing use of the metaphor of travelers and hedges, this caveat makes it sufficiently clear that by "needful" and "unnecessary" Hobbes means what we have by now been led to expect. Generically, those laws are needful that are essential to reduce the incidence of conditions adverse to the felicity of the individual members of the commonwealth. Equally, laws that have any other objective are unnecessary.

We also know that for Hobbes the only condition unqualifiedly destructive of felicity is death and that the condition most likely to result in premature death and otherwise to diminish felicity is civil war and violent conflict generally. We can therefore infer that the most needful laws are those that prevent or (more soberly) diminish the likelihood of the former and the severity of the latter and that the least needful are those that restrict activities unlikely to lead to war and violence. Just as prudence and reason in the conduct of private individuals are defined by reference to felicity, so needfulness and unneedfulness in law (hence prudence in the conduct of sovereigns) are defined by reference to the conditions essential to the pursuit of felicity in the commonwealth.

We do not yet have, however, a complete account of good and bad law and rule. To complete our account, and to see its place in the highly estimable civil philosophy with which Hobbes has gifted us, we need to understand how and why the two criteria of good laws are complementary.

The perspicuity of a law "consisteth not so much in the words of the law itself, as in a declaration of the causes, and motives for which it was made. This is it, that shows us the meaning of the legislator" (ibid.). Good laws, then, must have "preambles," must be accompanied by explanations of how they are to be understood. Assuming that the legislator has succeeded in making "the reason perspicuous, why the law was made," the law itself "is more easily understood by few, than many words." Why is this? Why wouldn't the clarity of the law be enhanced by elaboration and explication within as well as without it? Hobbes's answer is consonant with, if not required by, his larger philosophy, but it appears to confound the argument he is now advancing: "For all words, are subject to ambiguity; and therefore multiplication of words in the body of the law, is multiplication of ambiguity: besides it seems to imply, by too much diligence, that whosoever can evade the words, is without the compass of the law. And this is a cause of many unnecessary processes. For when I consider how short were the laws of ancient times; and how they grew by degrees still longer; methinks I see a contention between the penners, and pleaders of the law; . . . and that the pleaders have got the victory" (ibid.).

Although presented in the confident tone of advice readily followed, these remarks are less than encouraging concerning the prospects of good law. Words being necessary to the formulation and promulgation of laws, all words being subject to ambiguity and the multiplication of words therefore compounding ambiguity, the legislator's prospects of achieving perspicuity in laws are less than bright. However well the legislator has "read mankind" and mastered the science of natural justice, however satisfied she may be (in her own mind, as we might put it) with her reasons for thinking a law needful, she can have no assurance of making those reasons or the law itself clear to her subjects and hence no assurance of enhancing felicity by promulgating it. A perfect law is an impossibility, a good law—and hence a good system of laws—extraordinarily hard to achieve.

V

These deep-going complications in Hobbes's theory of governance are rooted in the fundaments of his thinking. The problematic character of *making* good law dramatizes and compounds difficulties faced by all those who must keep company with others. Placed by God in a universe that is largely devoid of meaning and in close association with other creatures who are naturally intelligible to them only in the limited respects in which they were severally created alike, each of them must *make* sense, largely if not entirely for herself and primarily by the device of arbitrary stipulation, of the universe and of those others she encounters. To the extent that she and some number of others succeed in doing these things, they must then find means, again largely by *artifice*, to communicate with one another and to order their affairs in terms of the meanings they have respectively created.

Nothing in Hobbes's analysis suggests that these things will be done easily or with steady success, and Hobbes could not have been unaware that his argument for the farfetched device of Leviathan magnifies his own conception of the difficulties.

We might stop here. We might read Hobbes's civil philosophy as ironic if not a reductio, as an argument or even a demonstration that government is far more likely to compound than to ameliorate the ineliminable inconveniences of keeping company.

Insofar as "reading" means "appropriating to my or our own purposes," something very close to this response will be hard to avoid—harder, I hope, after what follows in this text. But because even this understanding of reading is incoherent apart from some notion (however resistant to generalizable articulation) of grasping the intentions of the author and thus the senses of the text under consideration, we are, I think, obliged to recognize that Hobbes's was the more complicated intention of conveying both the possibilities and the limitations of Leviathan, the possible gains as well as the certain losses of my submitting to the rule of another who by my own lights is far more likely to be worse than better than myself.

Hobbes was a proud and buoyant man inclined to regard the human predicament as a bracing challenge, not a circumstance sickly to lament. Inasmuch as the problems of governance reflect the difficulties of all human endeavor, to take them as reasons for forgoing its possible advantages would be tantamount to forgoing the pursuit of felicity.[17] If barely possible for those of the species who have the least "worthiness," this was not a course Hobbes was prepared to accept for himself or recommend to others.[18]

[17]In theological terms, if Hobbes did not permit himself the conceit of judging the human condition to be a manifestation of God's benevolence, neither was he prepared for the impiety of imputing to God the cruelty of having altogether withheld from humankind the wherewithal of activities that She had made unavoidable for them and of arrangements necessary to tolerable success in those activities.

[18]In chapter 10 of *Leviathan* Hobbes distinguishes the "worthiness" of a person from the "worth or value; and also from his merit, or desert." Whereas all of the latter depend in one way or another "on the need and judgment of another," "worthiness . . . consisteth in a particular power, or ability for that, whereof he is said to be worthy: which particular ability is usually named FITNESS or *aptitude*" (p.

Hobbes's discussions of language and its limitations are counsels of prudence and temperance, not of despair. Nor do his applications of those discussions to law and rule discourage sovereigns from making as perspicuous as possible such laws as they judge to be needful. Every law, nevertheless, increases the number of words that must be perspicuous to large numbers of persons, few of whom can be personally known to the sovereign. In part for this reason, and because laws that are not perspicuous are "a cause of unnecessary processes" that advantage the enemies rather than the friends of the law, good sovereigns "sometimes forbear the exercise of their right; and prudently remit somewhat of the act, but nothing of their right" (*The Citizen*, chap. 6, p. 181).

Many of the elements and themes that I have been considering are, appropriately enough, compressed in Hobbes's discussions of "the greatest liberties of subjects," that is, those liberties that "dependeth on the silence of the law" (*Leviathan*, chap. 21, pp. 165–66). "In cases where the sovereign has prescribed no rule, there the subject hath the liberty to do, or forbear, according to his own discretion." Such cases are necessarily very numerous: "all the motions and actions of subjects are never circumscribed by laws, nor can be, by reason of their variety; it is [therefore] necessary that there be infinite cases which are neither commanded nor prohibited, but every man may either do or not do them as he lists himself" (*The Citizen*, chap. 13, p. 268).[19] These as it were natural or ontological limits on governance, nevertheless, do not provide a liberty wide enough for human beings as Hobbes understands them. Metaphor, exaggeration, hyperbole, and reiteration of his own arguments, rhetorically convenient borrowings of the languages of his opponents, are concatenated in underlining this point: "As water inclosed on all hands with banks, stands still and corrupts. . . . so subjects, if they might do nothing without the commands of the law, would grow dull and unwieldy; . . . Wherefore . . . it is against the charge of those who command and have the authority of making

---

79). My suggestion, to which I return below, is that he thinks some persons have more, some less, worthiness to pursue felicity under the unpropitious circumstances in which human beings find themselves.

[19]Although Hobbes does not here mention his views about the limitations of language and what might be called the "rule-skepticism" that it implies, his emphasis on the variety of actions can be read as saying that actions are too various to be encompassed, "perspicuously" or perhaps at all, by the general and prospective rules through which the sovereign is urged to govern.

laws, that there should be more laws than necessarily serve for good of the magistrate and his subjects. For since men are wont commonly to debate what to do or not to do, by natural reason rather than any knowledge of the laws, where there are more laws than can easily be remembered, and whereby such things are forbidden as reason of itself prohibits not of necessity, they must through ignorance, without the least evil intention, fall within the compass of laws, as gins laid to entrap their harmless liberty; which supreme commanders are bound to preserve for their subjects by the laws of nature" (pp. 268–69).

VI

The rhetorical exuberance of this and related passages may reveal Hobbes's (prescient) concern that he would be reputed and reviled as an enemy of liberty and the individuality that it serves; it may represent his attempt to use his eloquence to fend off a judgment that he believed unwarranted by his theory but knew would be passed on him.[20] If, as he predicted (see *Leviathan*, "A Review, and Conclusion"), his eloquence failed him in this regard, for the reasons I have assembled his conviction concerning his theory was largely warranted.

Leaving aside collectivist, communitarian, and other moralistic opponents of the felicity of individuals as the proper human end, a familiar charge against Hobbes is that his theory so isolates individuals as to exclude forms of cooperation that are salutary in themselves as well as providing needed protections against authority and power. But if it is true that Hobbes depicts human relationships as inherently competitive and risky (and to the extent that it is true—and that we are willing to indulge yet another anachronism—we might say that this is "because" Hobbes now reads much more as a postmodernist than the enthusiastic modernist he is commonly said to be),[21] it is not true that he thinks fruitful cooperation impossible for the human beings he describes. Rather, it is his view that under

[20]Cf. *Leviathan*, "Epistle Dedicatory": "For in a way beset with those that contend, on one side for too great liberty, and on the other side for too much authority, 'tis hard to pass between the points of both unwounded" (p. 5).

[21]But recall my suggestion in the Introduction that elements such as those I have been underlining, prominent as they are in postmodernist thinking, are already present in modernism and liberalism in their most attractive formulations.

the right circumstances the lives of these creatures can be steadily yet not incessantly in company rather than in solitude, moderately comfortable not poor, bracingly contentious rather than nasty, and extended not short. Whereas "there is no *deliberation* [concerning things] manifestly impossible to be changed: nor of things known to be impossible, or thought so" (chap. 6, p. 53), the master purpose of Hobbes's deliberations was to discern and diminish obstacles to such circumstances.

The appropriate objection, rather, is to those elements in his philosophical and empirical psychology that undermine his commitment to individuality. Whereas the sovereign can diminish somewhat our ruder vulnerabilities to one another, Hobbes sometimes presents the generality of people as so insidiously and pervasively dependent on others as to be all but defenseless against their merest whims. "Worth," "merit," "dignity," "desert," "honor," "glory," and the like, that is, the most important components of our power to achieve felicity, are "not absolute; but . . . dependent on the need and judgment of another." Our "true value," accordingly, "is no more than it is esteemed by others" (chap. 10, p. 73).

To be consistent with his agent-relative or voluntarist doctrine concerning evaluation (indeed with his nominalism and theory of language), Hobbes would have to say that *I adopt* or *decide* to treat as "true" your evaluations of my worth. If so, he would remain entitled to what would otherwise be his contrary acknowledgment of the tendency of "most men . . . [to] rate themselves at the highest value they can" and thereby to sustain a simulacrum of his agent-centered philosophy (ibid.). In the perspective of the deeply other-directed character of his remarks about worth and hence about all self-other relationships, however, his voluntarism and egoism become hollow and inconsequential. Aside from those (apparently few) who are at once prideful and magnanimous and who somehow remain confident of their own "worthiness," the "selves" who make evaluations and decisions concerning themselves are no better than chameleons to the others they encounter.[22] Certainly the independence, individuality, and diversity that I have claimed his theory otherwise establishes and promotes are put in serious jeopardy.

[22]Later voluntarists, especially Nietzsche, are often interpreted as taking exactly this view. The great preponderance of humankind forms a "herd" in which individuality and independence are unknown; only a tiny elite of "supermen" or "over-men" achieve and sustain these characteristics. I contest this reading of Nietzsche in Part Two.

It will help us to assess Hobbes's views about worth, as well as
provide an opportunity to say at least something about politics as
distinct from government, to consider some of his remarks about
participation in political life. "Some will say that a *popular* state is
much to be preferred before a *monarchical*; because that where all
men have a hand in public businesses, there all have an opportunity
to show their wisdom, knowledge, and eloquence . . . which by
reason of that desire of praise which is bred in human nature, is to
them who excel in such-like faculties, and seem to themselves to
exceed others, the most delightful of all things. But in a monarchy,
this same way to obtain praise and honor is shut up to the greatest
part of subjects; and what is a grievance if this be none?" (*The
Citizen*, chap. 10, p. 229).

Hobbes's answer to this rhetorical question seems to reflect but
also to circumscribe the significance of what we have found him
saying about the self and its relation to others. "I will tell you: to see
his opinion, whom we scorn, preferred before ours; to have our
wisdom undervalued before our own faces; by an uncertain trial of
a little vain glory, to undergo most certain enmities (for this cannot
be avoided, whether we have the better or the worse); to hate and to
be hated, by reason of the disagreement of opinions; to lay open our
secret councils and advices to all, to no purpose and without any
benefit; to neglect the affairs of our own family: these, I say, are
grievances" (pp. 229–30).[23]

Desires that can only be satisfied by the evaluations of others, for
example for praise and (a certain kind of) honor, although bred in
our natures, vary in intensity from person to person and are subject
to our control. We also have our "opinions" and our "wisdom," our
hatreds, and our "secret councils and advices." If these are not

[23]If we attributed to Hobbes the now widely shared view that politics always
comes along with government, these remarks could be taken to support the view
that in fact Hobbes is an antigovernment or antirule thinker. We might note in this
connection Hobbes's admission that his argument for monarchy—presumably the
form of government most resistant to politics—was the weakest part of his civil
philosophy as well as the fact that his discussions of actual monarchies, especially in
Behemoth, make it clear that they are rife with the very characteristics that he
derides in the passage above.

In what we might call its generic hostility to politics and political involvements,
the above passage does anticipate, and resonate with, similar views of Schopenhauer, James, Nietzsche, and Oakeshott. As we see below, however, their reasons
for avoiding political activities are different from Hobbes's, and they qualify their
antipolitical stances in important ways.

entirely independent of the evaluations of others, they are dependent on the evaluations of fewer others and they withstand and may even be strengthened by the adverse judgments of others. From this perspective, then, participation in politics is objectionable several times over. It maximizes our exposure to and dependence on the estimations of others; it breeds vainglory and the profitless contentions that vainglory engenders; the satisfactions it provides, being entirely dependent on the evaluations of others, are the least reliable and otherwise make the smallest contributions to our felicity; it distracts or deflects us from other activities and involvements that are both less objectionable and more rewarding. (Of course Hobbes has numerous other reasons for opposing popular government and the participation it invites.)

Whatever our reactions to Hobbes's characterizations of politics, in giving these reasons against political participation and for alternative modes and venues of conduct, he implies that we can and argues that we should reduce our dependence on the evaluations of others, that we can and should increase our independence and individuality. Along with the many other elements of his theory that are in tension with his argument concerning worth, these considerations mitigate somewhat the objection I brought against him.

They do not dispose of that objection. If his doctrine of worth were more consonant with the main bases for individuality in his theory, the theory would not make individuality hostage to the avoidance of politics (or any other mode of conduct). It would hold open and forward the possibility of individuals sufficiently robust in their self-estimations to attend to the evaluations others make of them and yet do what Hobbes otherwise says they can and must, that is make and act on their own evaluations of themselves. Individually they would be less fearful that idiosyncracy on their parts would evoke worth-denying evaluations of them, and collectedly they would be less avid to enforce what Hobbes calls (in the most obnoxious passage in his writings) "COMPLAISANCE; that is to say, *that every man strive to accommodate himself to the rest*" (*Leviathan*, chap. 15, p. 118).

Having been brought this considerable distance by the reflections of this powerful mind, it is for us to think from and beyond it. More specifically, it is for us to find ways of protecting and enhancing the already-considerable sources of individuality and diversity that his thinking provides.

Chapter 2

Sociality, Individuality, Plurality, and Politics

Enthusiasm for individuality and group or associational plurality are recurrent, if not always attentively handled, features of liberal theory and practice. Individual and group freedoms are prominent in virtually all forms of liberal doctrine; the natural and other rights that define a major mode of liberalism are usually attributed to individuals and sometimes to groups; respect for individuals and their rights is widely treated as a duty in liberal thought; numerous liberals promote individual autonomy and group self-determination as major values; and leading forms of liberalism make some form of individual consent or agreement a necessary and sometimes a sufficient condition of legitimate government.

These characteristics of liberalism are mirrored (albeit often in a darkened glass) in antiliberal thought, the single most persistent criticism of liberalism being that it is excessively individualistic and otherwise fragmenting or disaggregating. Liberalism is said by its most insistent critics to be premised on a philosophically untenable atomism and privatism, inattentive to the enmeshing and frequently determining effects of history, tradition, and culture, indifferent if not hostile to community, productive of virtue-destroying and conflict-generating selfishness, and congenitally incapable of sustaining or even accommodating authority and power and hence government and politics.

Despite the foregoing, my inclination is increasingly to think that liberalism is *insufficiently* individualistic and pluralist or at least that these elements have an inadequately grounded and otherwise insecure place in liberal thought. Sometimes out of an estimation of the "conditions" of individuality and plurality and an attendant desire to distance themselves from crudely economistic and libertarian thinking and their tendency to overlook or underestimate "externalities," sometimes (and more ominously) out of misbegotten hopes or unnerving anxieties that they share with their conservative, collectivist, and communitarian critics, liberal thinkers and publicists have adopted views and strategies that threaten to compromise those features of liberalism with which I began. Most dramatically in the name of utility, of welfare, and of the common good, but sometimes also under the rubric of concern for justice, for equality, and even for rights and autonomy, liberals have entertained and sometimes incorporated objectivist and paternalistic elements from moral philosophy, uncritical enthusiasm for the state and politics from democratic theory, and a conception of theory as properly dominant over or determinative of practice from the least-chastened passages in the history of epistemology and political philosophy. Partly because of the absence of a widely shared and genuinely robust conception of individuality and plurality, these tendencies have met with too little resistance.

Of course there are substantial countervailing tendencies within liberalism itself. Dispositionally skeptical liberals from Benjamin Constant to Isaiah Berlin have been articulate in their insistence on the centrality of individuality and plurality to liberalism and vigorous in opposing tendencies such as those to which I have just alluded. Along with amplifying the formulations of these soi-disant liberals, however, the lively continuing discourse concerning liberalism will benefit from attention to the yet more uncompromising individualisms and pluralisms of thinkers who, as with Hobbes, are not usually regarded as of liberal persuasion, sometimes rightly regarded as profoundly illiberal.

The present chapter is a modest effort of this kind. With the exception of Tocqueville, who figures briefly as a proponent of what I regard as questionable tendencies in liberalism, the thinkers to whom it responds—primarily Ludwig Wittgenstein and William James—are not promising candidates for the role of liberal thinkers. I try to show, however, that James offers a robust and in other respects estimable case for individuality and (to a lesser extent) plurality, one that is not only consonant with but contributive to liberal thinking. I neither claim nor deny that Wittgenstein was an individualist or pluralist in any moral or political sense, but I do argue that his account of mutual intelligibility and its limits is usefully complementary to James's views; I claim that it provides well-protected philosophical spaces for the individuality and plurality that James promotes while also supplying an effective antidote to the self-defeating privatism into which James sometimes falls and which is frequently attributed to the more individualistic formulations of liberalism.

I

In the opening paragraphs of the *Philosophical Investigations*, Wittgenstein ignores, one has to think willfully, main features of the account of language and meaning in Augustine's *Confessions*. Treating that work as if it propounded an early version of the referential, designative, or thing-word theory of meaning, Wittgenstein makes no mention of Augustine's insistence that earthly languages are conventional, developed out of custom and habituation, and perpetuated by authority, training, and coercion. When he learned language, Augustine says, he became able to give "utterance to my will" and to enter "deeper into the stormy intercourse of life." This gain, however, was bought at the price of "depending on parental authority and the beck of elders."[1] Later he speaks of the "signs which men have conventionally settled" (*Confessions*, p. 17) and notes "how carefully the sons of men observe the covenanted rules of letters and syllables received from those who spake before them," even to the extent of "neglecting the eternal covenant of everlasting salvation received from Thee" (p. 21).

Wittgenstein also leaves aside the centrality in Augustine's thought of the illumination that has been accorded by divine grace to humankind. Because in the earthly city that illumination is obscured by sin, the "torrent of human custom" is "hellish" (pp. 19–20) and the "intercourse" it enables "stormy" and distracting. Despite convention, training, and various modes of discipline, the meaning of our earthly words is ambiguous and often disputed; it is only in the heavenly city that univocality (whether or not expressed in language in anything like its earthly forms) will be achieved.

---

[1] Augustine, *Confessions*, trans. Edward B. Pusey. (New York: Modern Library, 1949), p. 11.

Nevertheless, this aspect of the divine privileging of humankind is necessary to our use of language. Without it, the particulars of which Augustine speaks in the passage with which Wittgenstein opens the *Investigations* would be a "blooming, buzzing confusion," would be as meaningless, both personally and interpersonally, as the notional "private languages" that Wittgenstein himself goes on to discredit.

Convention, practice, rules, training, and compulsion are prominent in Wittgenstein's own analysis of how particulars can be, and not infrequently are, "somethings" rather than "anythings" or "nothings" (*Philosophical Investigations*, I, 6). We might also wonder whether something akin to an illumination is not somewhere in Wittgenstein's own thinking. Exegetically, this conjecture is suggested by occasionally mystical sounding elements of the *Tractatus* and the *Notebooks*, particularly if those works are read in the light of information we have concerning Wittgenstein's life.[2] If there is little in his later works that directly encourages such an interpretation, we should remember that those writings insistently describe rather than explain, that the descriptions given are of examples but that the examples are not treated as "representative" in any strong sense and are typically of less rather than more widely shared meanings. (See, e.g., *Philosophical Investigations*, I, 73–74.) Given the diffidence about explanation and generalization, given the emphasis on diversity, open texture and indeterminacy, familiar philosophical considerations may prompt us to wonder whether, like Augustine, Wittgenstein isn't positing or assuming something beneath or behind convention and agreement. Without "something more" (including something that is more substantial, more determining, than what Wittgenstein calls "general facts of nature" and "the common behavior of mankind"), could we actually have meaning? Wouldn't we have the appearance of meaning but the reality of Babel?[3]

---

[2]See esp. Ludwig Wittgenstein, *Tractatus Logico-Philosophicus* (London: Routledge & Kegan Paul, 1922), 6.432–7.

[3]Cf. *Philosophical Investigations*, I, 234, and I, 346: "Would it not be possible for us, however, to calculate as we actually do (all agreeing, and so on), and still at every step to have a feeling of being guided by the rules as by a spell, feeling astonishment at the fact that we agreed? (We might give thanks to the Deity for our agreement.)" "But couldn't we imagine God's suddenly giving a parrot understanding, and its now saying things to itself?—But here it is an important fact that I imagined a deity in order to imagine this."

I consider this possibility below. But let us note immediately that nothing in Wittgenstein's philosophical work licenses a related but further speculation that might be suggested by comparisons between him and Augustine, namely, that Wittgenstein entertained the idea of a "heavenly" city in which (as we might characterize it from the present perspective) meaning would be entire and entirely shared, that is, in which nothing in any person's experience would be opaque or mysterious to herself or to others. For Augustine, in the city of God the brilliant light of divine illumination will render all and everything (except the essence of the divinity, the divine *will?*) transparent and unequivocal. In short, in Augustine's post-conversion understanding, all intersubjective meaning is a function of transcendence, and the this-worldly indeterminacy of meaning is a result of the partial character of our apprehension of or participation in the transcendental. Meaning is always partly by virtue of transcendence, and failures in or limits on meaning are always due to fallings short of the transcendental.

By contrast, if the Wittgenstein of the *Tractatus* posited a language devoid of ambiguity, one that without exception rigorously satisfied the standard *unum nomen, unum nominatum*, he insisted that such a language would have no place for those features of the world that are humanly most important (most "meaningful"). We might say that meaning in language is achieved at the cost of making experiences that are personally most meaningful (most heavenly?) mutually unintelligible. And if the later (the postconversion?) Wittgenstein found room in language and hence in social life for more of the humanly most meaningful than he managed to accommodate in the *Tractatus*, in doing so he made diversity, ambiguity, and opacity integral to that account.

In languages more familiar in social and political theory, on Augustine's conception of it, the city of God will be a genuine *genossenschaft*, a fellowship from which otherness (with the exception of merely physical separateness?) has been eliminated. If we generalized from this conception, we might say that in social as in all other respects, oneness is the norm for and the criterion of meaningfulness. Plurality and individuality in language and in sociality represent, or rather manifest (as Augustine takes the Babel story to dramatize), willfulness, deviance, and failure.[4]

---

[4]I leave aside the possibility that, as in later transcendentalisms such as Emerson's, in the quality of the relationships *among* its nondivine members, Augustine's

In the same terms (and like Augustine's description of the occluded, aporia-ridden languages of earthly cities), Wittgenstein's "forms of life" and the "language-games," "practices," and "institutions" of which they consist comprise no more than "civil societies,"[5] not *genossenschaften* or even *gemeinschaften*: the participants in these assemblages understand one another (to the extent that they do so) because there are (to the extent that there are) "agreements in judgments" among themselves. The assemblages form "wholes" within which meaning primarily, if not exclusively, occurs, but in fact there is "prodigious diversity" (cf. II, p. 224) both within and among the many such units, and the idea of a single undifferentiated whole, even the idea of a number of wholes some of which are complete or fully integrated, plays no evident role in the descriptions. Such meaning as we find is social or public as opposed to private, but sociality is characterized by diversity, not oneness, by plurality within partial and changing commonalities.

These last comparisons help to explain the impetus behind my conjecture that something like Augustine's notion of illumination plays some (perhaps unappreciated or unacknowledged) role in Wittgenstein's later thinking. As with conceptions of plenums, substrates, substances, and modes on the side of the known or the object, and as with Reason, Mind, Human Nature, and Structure, on the side of the knower or the subject, Augustinian illumination serves to explain the possibility of subsumption, categorization, and generalization and hence comprehension and intelligibility; it serves to explain how manyness can be unified into oneness, particularity into generality and perhaps universality. If the Wittgensteinian conceptions of publicness, form, agreement, knowing how to go on, rules and rule-following, and mastery of technique cannot do this work, the view he constructs out of these elements fails to achieve its objective of giving a coherent account of the phenomenon of meaning. By imputing to him a notion akin to a pervasive and partially integrating illumination, we save him from this demise. And if achieving this objective is a condition of providing a philosophical view serviceable for social and political theory (for example, one

---

city of God is no more than a *gessellschaft*, with its distinctive social character, if any, resulting from the relationship its members severally have with the divinity.

[5]Cf. *Philosophical Investigations*, I, 125: "The civil status of a contradiction, or its status in civil life: there is the philosophical problem." The German is *bürgerliche Stellung* and *bürgerlichen Welt*.

helpful in understanding sociality, plurality, and individuality and their relations to politics), then some such attribution is essential if Wittgenstein is to be appropriated for the latter purposes.

II

My own view is that Wittgenstein is fruitful concerning the topics of these reflections because he rejected all requirements of the kinds just discussed. Whatever his personal religious views may have been, he makes no mention of Augustine's belief in divine illumination because by the time of the writing of (what we have as) the *Blue and Brown Books* and the *Investigations* he had rejected the conception of linguistic possibilities that that belief informed; he leaves aside the conventionalist elements in Augustine's theory not because he objects to them in their own right but because he realized that the uses to which Augustine put them make them inseparable from that same conception. (With these elements removed from Augustine's theory, it is more plausible to regard the latter as designative in the ways Wittgenstein suggests and as betraying the difficulties that Wittgenstein thinks vitiate all designative theories.)

Wittgenstein was not a social, a moral, or a political theorist, and there is no reason to think that he rejected Augustine's ideal-cum-criterion of language and meaning out of concern for its social, moral, or political implications. He believed, rather, that in their submission to the "craving for generality" and the attendant quest for the "hidden," the "beneath," and the "essential" which they shared with much of traditional philosophizing, thinkers in thrall to that ideal had obscured and distracted us from the "ordinary," the "everyday," the mundane that are philosophy's only proper—or rather only possible—concern.

But the conception in question does have large and important social, moral, and political implications. In Augustine's version it implies that we must reject as unworthy everything that is worldly, all that fails to transcend the mundane. The plurality and individuality of the earthly city are manifestations of the sinfulness of humankind. (Cf. infra, Part Two, Section II.) In other, less- or atheological versions, the conception implies that social, moral, and political plurality and individuality are worthy (on some views are possible) only insofar as they are undergirded or underwritten by a social, moral, or political something that is, if not transcendental, universal, if not universal, general. If there never was or is not now any such unifying, meaning- and value-giving something, we are condemned to "hellish torment," to a mutually destructive chaos. If there is such a something but we fail to identify and to theorize it, we are condemned to a pervasive and corrosive angst, to an uncertainty about understanding and valorizing ourselves that can be prevented from eventuating in despair, if at all, by nothing more reliable than unthinkingness.

There's a lot at stake.

III

Wittgenstein did not base his rejection of essentialism on the claim that there *could not be* some one thing or some one integrated set of things common to all meaningful experience. (His ontological pluralism, that is, was not essentialist.) True, the descriptions he offered and the reminders he assembled dramatize plurality. For this reason, reading his work may well serve to discourage the expectation, hypothesis, or surmise that there is such a unity, that some version of monism is or will prove to be true as an empirical matter or perhaps irresistible as an ontological one.

But this tendency in his work is interwoven with a form of holism that insists not only that "meaning is *in* language" (and not, for example, in the particular things that we name or refer to with some uses of our languages) but also that language occurs in "language-games," "forms of life, and practices," that is, in ensembles or gestalts consisting of concepts, beliefs, and recurrent intentions formed and deployed according to variously interwoven elements such as conventions, rules, and widely mastered techniques. Apart from such a whole, words could "mean" (and thus things could be) "anything or nothing." Moreover, as an empirical or perhaps ontological matter, Wittgenstein acknowledged "general facts of nature," commonalities in the "behavior of mankind," and certain widespread and long-standing conventions, and he assigned each of these a special significance in his account of language and meaning. Finally, nothing in Wittgenstein's thinking is against the possibility that these several types and sources of commonality might enlarge or extend, including the possibility that they might be enlarged and extended by thinking done and action taken for that purpose.

Wittgenstein's quarrel, rather, was with metaphysical theses according to which our World or our Experience *must* be One, could not be a World or could not be intelligible Experience if it were other than One.[6] He abbreviated his arguments against such theses in presenting the metaphors of family resemblance and of a rope consisting of "the overlapping of many fibers" (*Philosophical Investigations*, I, 67): when we *look* at the experiences we in fact have, especially when we look at them from "close to," what we see is "not something common to *all*, but similarities, relationships, and a whole series of them at that" (*Ibid.*, I, 66). Once again, matters could have been and might become otherwise in these regards. Were yet-greater similarities, more commonalities, to develop, were the "series of relationships" to decline in number, the number and diversity of language-games and forms of life might also diminish. If so, it might less often happen that we could not "find our feet" with other human beings; it might become less common for "one human being" to "be a complete enigma to another" (II, xi, p. 223); a larger number of sets of rules might form "strict calculi," and generally there would be more situations in which rules would as a practical matter settle cases that fall under them; "knowing how to go on" might be less circumstantial, vary less according to "custom and upbringing" (II, p. 201).

Whatever the probability of such developments, and however beneficial or harmful their effects on human interaction (we should not assume—certainly not when thinking about the present topics—that enlargements or intensifications of commonality, even in the sense of mutual understanding, are without exception advantageous), in Wittgenstein's view no number of them would yield anything like an Augustinian illumination or transparency, a transparency, as it were, throughout and all the way down. Rather, much in Wittgenstein's later writings suggests that enlargements of the commonalities that enable mutual understanding and facilitate interaction go hand in hand with, in a certain sense bring about, obscurity and a kind of opacity.

Phenomenologically, the most common of our commonalities, the "general facts of nature," are "[s]uch facts as mostly do not strike us because of their generality" (II, xii, p. 230; cf. I, note on p. 56). But the deeper, logical or ontological, consideration is devel-

---

[6]"But it *must* be like this!' is not a philosophical proposition" (*Philosophical Investigations*, I, 599).

oped in Wittgenstein's treatment of those matters (including, but not restricted to, the general facts of nature) about which there is the greatest certainty among us, about which doubt and hence a sense of uncertainty or ambiguity are at a minimum.

Doubt and uncertainty follow, that is, presuppose, belief, presuppose acceptance of some number of facts or propositions that must "stand fast" in order for doubt to arise.[7] Nor do individual beliefs stand alone. We have seen that they (the propositions in which they are formulated and expressed) have meaning in language-games and forms of life. For reasons that immediately appear, in the discussions most pertinent here Wittgenstein sets these sociological- or anthropological-sounding notions aside in favor of the organizing concept of "system." "When we first begin to *believe* anything, what we believe is not a single proposition, it is a whole system of propositions. (Light [!] dawns gradually over the whole)" (*On Certainty*, 141). Nor is this a transient feature of our early (ontogenetic or phylogenetic) histories. "It is not single axioms that strike me as obvious, it is a system in which consequences and premises give one another *mutual* support" (142). "All testing, all confirmation and disconfirmation of a hypothesis takes place already within a system. And this system is not a more or less arbitrary and doubtful point of departure for all our arguments: no, it belongs to the essence of what we call an argument. The system is not so much the point of departure, as the element in which arguments have their life" (105).

Wittgenstein is not announcing a substantive essentialism, is not saying that there is some one system of propositions that we must, ought, or do accept. There is a great variety of such systems[8], and both deliberate and unsought changes in their contents, although seldom rapid, are familiar.[9] But Wittgenstein is inclined to think that all systems include propositions that, at any given moment and typically for lengthy stretches of time, are unsusceptible to deliberate change because acceptance of them is a condition of all thinking and acting within the systems of which they are part. "It may be . . . that *all enquiry on our part* is set so as to exempt certain propositions from doubt, if they are ever formulated." Such propositions

---

[7]Ludwig Wittgenstein, *On Certainty*, eds. G. E. M. Amscombe and G. H. von Wright; trans. Denis Paul and G. E. M. Anscombe (Oxford: Basil Blackwell, 1969), pp. 115, 160, 163, 156.

[8]See *On Certainty*, 239, for a striking example.

[9]See ibid., 96, 99, 103.

"lie apart from the route travelled by inquiry" (88). "Much seems to be fixed, and it is removed from the traffic. It is so to speak shunted unto an unused siding. Now it gives our way of looking at things, and our researches, their form. Perhaps it was once disputed. But perhaps, for unthinkable ages, it has belonged to the *scaffolding* of our thoughts" (211–12). Forming what someone with a penchant for profundity might call the "unthought," these propositions are neither true nor false, grounded nor ungrounded, justified nor unjustified. "If the true is what is grounded, then the ground is not *true*, nor yet false" (205). "The difficulty is to realize the groundlessness of our believing" (166).

Although the "unthought" is an element in all thinking, there is reason to think that it will bulk largest—but loom smallest—where certainty, not doubt, where agreement, not uncertainty or dispute, are commonly experienced. The unthought is not unthinkable. Letting propositions A, B, and C "stand fast," we can question propositions D, E, F; and so forth. But there is no impetus to such questioning where not only D, E, and F but A, B, and C and a large array of further propositions grounded in or interwoven with them are generally regarded as both unambiguous and true. The "grounding propositions" are obscured from view; they stand, as it were, in shadows cast by the propositions of which they are the grounds. And where agreement has obtained for "unthinkable ages," the shadows may have become so dark that we can no longer "see" what we think.

In such circumstances our "consciousness" might be described as "happy."

IV

The Hegelian suggestion is of course mine, not Wittgenstein's. We know that Wittgenstein was fiercely individualistic in some matters and strongly nationalistic in others. But in his philosophical work he never explicitly valorized the shifting mélange of commonalities, pluralities, and individualities depicted by his descriptions of our ordinary language (and of the sociality to which that language is integral and of which it is both enabling and disabling). If there is a tendency in his later work to emphasize the range of possibilities enabled by our forms of life (and hence also a certain blandness), and if he insistently combated the confusions engendered by mis-begotten philosophizing, we do not learn whether he welcomed or lamented, accepted or stood against, the interacting and fluctuating medleys of certainty and doubt, luminosity and obscurity, which I claim his works summon to our attention. Nor did he ask concerning the bearing of these experiential admixtures on political life or of the latter on the former.

For these reasons, and because Wittgenstein's work is widely (albeit absurdly) regarded as representing the increasingly unwelcome method of proceeding from our language to our world, it may advantage our reflection to turn to a thinker who, in addition to influencing Wittgenstein, attempts to make good some of these deficiencies while developing a view closely akin to the one I have been discussing.

Whatever might be thought of the emphasis I have placed on diversity and indeterminacy in Wittgenstein, no one could complain against an interpretation of William James that stressed these themes. If his "radical empiricism" was a corrective to the atomistic or "dust-heap" theory of world and of mind that he found in the British empiricists, it was much more insistently an antidote to the poisons of Hegelian and neo-Hegelian idealism and the "block universe" that they promoted. James may have worried too little whether his "felt connections" could make the flow of individual consciousness into a "stream," whether those consciousnesses are not so irreducibly other to one another as to leave no alternative to solipsism, and whether the varieties of religious, aesthetic, and moral experience are not on his account so great as to yield cacophony not polyphony, Babel not language, chaos not a multiplicity of diverse groups and societies. But he leaves us in no doubt that he relishes plurality and individuality, despises uniformity and conformity. Better discord or even disintegration than a dreary commonality. Perhaps better to avert one's glance from the issues just mentioned than to risk reinforcing the already too-powerful integrationist, vitality-diminishing tendencies in our culture and its societies.

In "What Makes a Life Significant" James recalls a "happy" week spent at Chautaukua Lake, a place that "spread before" him "the realization—on a small, sample scale, of course—of all the ideals for which our civilization has been striving: security, intelligence, humanity, and order."[10] On "escaping" from the "enclosure" (*Writings of William James*, p. 648), however, he caught himself "quite unexpectedly and involuntarily saying, " 'Ouf! what a relief!' " (p. 647). Later in the essay he mildly chastises himself for this reaction: he had almost certainly been blind to the plentitude of joys, sorrows, and ideals that animated the participants in the "serious and studious picnic" that he had attended. But he is convinced that the qualities he had overlooked were despite, not because of, the "achievements" of this "Sabbatical city." In its "flatness and lack of zest," Chautaukua was no less than "unspeakable." Worse, the characteristics there displayed in etched miniature were showing up well beyond its confines. Our "social process . . . seems everywhere tending toward the Chautauquan ideals" (pp. 648–49).

James's conviction that there was, that there must be, diversity and individuality beneath the glassine surface of the Chautauqua community rested on the most persistent and diversely articulated elements of his thinking. He did not think that he could conclusively refute the possibility of an unqualified holism such as was posited by the idealists, but he argued that so much of our experience tells against it that the hypothesis of a pluralistic universe is the only defensible metaphysical position. For the same reasons, even the best supported of our empirical generalizations and ontological propositions must carry the qualifier "ever not quite." He accepted the primacy of the knower over the known, but denied on both epistemological and theological grounds the possibility of an all-knowing knower. Because he also followed Hume's assimilation of knowledge to strongly held belief and insisted on the primacy of largely unpredictable will in belief formation, in both its intra- and interpersonal dimensions his theory of knowledge and philosophical psychology were pluralistic in ways akin to Nietzsche's perspectivalism. Along with his doctrine that experience includes "felt connections" among particular perceptions and sensations, his emphasis on the role that concepts in fact play in our thought and action was one of his main disagreements with the empiricisms of Locke and Hume. But insofar as he had a philosophy of language, he seems to have thought that all concepts are both originally and

[10]William James, *The Writings of William James*, ed. John J. McDermott (New York: Modern Library, 1968), pp. 646–47.

ultimately after the fact, that is, are assigned to experiences that in every sense other than the trivially terminological are what they are without regard to language. Finally, in his moral psychology and metaethics he was a voluntarist, holding both that the valuable is that which some person or persons desire and that words such as *good* and *evil* are, as we have seen Hobbes put it, "ever used with relation to the person that useth them: there being nothing simply and absolutely so; nor any common rule . . . to be taken from the nature of the objects [to which the words refer] themselves."

I will document very little of this reportage concerning James's views. Insofar as it is accurate, it is an implication of those views that an abundant pluralism, including—or rather especially including—diverse and shifting individualities, is a prominent and almost certainly an ineliminable characteristic of our natural and social condition. It does not follow, however, that these characteristics will be generally recognized or that they will be so much as accepted by those who do recognize them. To the extent that James entered the lists of technical philosophical argumentation, much of his work was directed against idealists such as Hegel, Bradley, and Royce who thought that they had discerned an actual unity in the apparent heterogeneity of experience or had convinced themselves that unity at some level or in some sense of the term was a condition of full or genuine intelligibility. No small part of this argumentation, however, and a yet-greater part of James's tireless lecturing and writing for wider audiences, defended his view that plurality and individuality are better than unity and commonality; that plurality and individuality should be encouraged and enhanced, celebrated and cherished rather than tolerated, regretted, or diminished. Often romantic, not infrequently elitist, occasionally antinomian to the extent of calling into doubt the possibility of intelligibility and sociality themselves, the congestion of thoughts comprising James's works sounds no less than a paean to individuality and plurality.

Melding the foregoing "is's" and "oughts" to articulate a "pluralism somewhat rhapsodically expressed," James remarks, "Not unfortunately, the universe is wild—game-flavored as a hawk's wing" (p. 135). In its social, moral, and religious dimensions, James would have preferred it yet "gamier" on the palate. He nods to the idea that moral principles must be universalizable, but he treats it as important primarily as a solvent of merely habitual thinking (p. 120), and the most general moral notion that I have found in his works would hardly appeal to the more celebrated proponents of universalizability: "Take any demand, however slight, which any creature, however weak, may make. Ought it not, for its own sole sake, to be satisfied? If not, prove why not. The only possible kind of proof you could adduce would be the exhibition of another creature who should make a demand that ran the other way. The only possible reason there can be why any phenomenon ought to exist is that such a phenomenon actually is desired. Any desire is imperative to the extent of its amount; it *makes* itself valid by the fact that it exists at all." (p. 617). Abstractly, this axiology-cum-metaethic leaves open the question whether desires converge or diverge, whether nature, culture, and history, have produced or will yet produce extensive commonalities or complementarities among the desires that human beings actually form. As we have seen, James not only allows of the possibility that the latter will occur but discerns and laments a powerful tendency toward them in his own society and culture.

Why, then, should this tendency be regretted and resisted? There are two familiar considerations that James occasionally mentions but that are at most subsidiary to his thinking. One of these is the empiricist idea abbreviated in John Stuart Mill's phrase "experiments in living." James certainly favored a wide variety of life-styles and practices, and no doubt thought that there was some sense in which an abundant diversity in these regards is instructive as well as vitalizing. But rejecting as he (usually) did the notion of moral truth, he scorned the notion that "experiments" could progressively diminish the diversity that *ought* to remain by disqualifying some moral views and practices and confirming others. Another is the notion that diversity is "functional" or "productive" from a societal, cultural, or civilizational standpoint, that by, say, stimulating or releasing individual or group energies and abilities it moves the whole or collectivity to a higher level. It is clear that for James uniform or homogeneous societies are worse than heterogeneous ones; but he understands this to be a judgment about the distribution of qualities over an aggregation of discrete individuals and groups and about the effects of that distribution on the interactions among individuals and groups. In Michael Oakeshott's terms, he is expressing a collec*ted* judgment, not a judgment about a collec*tivity*.[11]

[11]See Michael Oakeshott, *On Human Conduct* (London: Oxford University Press, 1975), p. 87.

Here are some of the elements of James's more affirmative view: "Whenever a process of life communicates an eagerness to him who lives it, there the life becomes genuinely significant. Sometimes the eagerness is more knit up with the motor activities, sometimes with the perceptions, sometimes with the imagination, sometimes with reflective thought. But, wherever it is found, there is the zest, the tingle, the excitement of reality; and there *is* 'importance' in the only real and positive sense in which importance ever anywhere can be" (*Writings of William James*, p. 631).

"Life," "eagerness," "zest," "tingle," "excitement." These and virtues (or rather *virtus*) of the martial or "strenuous" life such as strength, vigor, and courage are the qualities diminished by the cruder forms of coercion and compulsion, stifled by the softer but more insidious despotisms of Chautauqua and Chautauqua-like societies, flattened or dimmed by the "great cloud-bank of ancestral blindness weighing down upon us" (p. 646). Owing to the prevalence of these forces, and because he acknowledges the intensely personal, sometimes uncommunicable, character of the perceptions, feelings, and thoughts that lend eagerness to one's life, James saw few prospects for heightening the "sensibilities" and "responsiveness" necessary to having these experiences ourselves and to appreciating their occurrence in one another. Certain writers, for example Robert Louis Stevenson, Wordsworth, Whitman, Emerson, and above all Tolstoy, are themselves exceptionally *receptive* and have the gift of conveying the intensity of their experiences to others. Reading these authors and vigorously combating all attempts (most often made by philosophers) "to substitute . . . clean-shaven systems for that exuberant mass of goods with which all human nature is in travail" (p. 622) may have some valuable effects. "But how can one attain to the feeling of the vital significance of an experience, if one have it not to begin with? There is no receipt which one can follow. Being a secret and a mystery, it often comes in mysteriously unexpected ways" (p. 640).

James does have prescriptions to make. Answering his own question whether desires *ought* to be satisfied, he insists that the "result" of the "considerations and quotations" he has advanced concerning "importance" is the following set of categorical imperatives: we are "absolutely" forbidden "to be forward in pronouncing on the meaninglessness of forms of existence other than our own"; and we are "commanded" to "tolerate, respect, and indulge those whom we see harmlessly interested and happy in their own ways, however unintelligible these may be to us. Hands off: . . . It is enough to ask of each of us that he should be faithful to his own opportunities and make the most of his own blessings, without presuming to regulate the rest of the vast field" (p. 645).

James's is not a narcissistic and naively realist view that promotes "authenticity" or "self-realization." We are not to peer inward in the hope of discovering our perdurant true or genuine or higher self and then act so as to express that self or to bring our false, inauthentic, or lower self into consonance with it (or fail to do so and sink into shame or self-disgust). In something like Michael Oakeshott's terms (see *On Human Conduct*, esp. pp. 70–78), on James's view we do not "disclose" a preexisting self to ourselves and others; we "enact" and more or less continuously reenact our selves as we perceive and feel, think and act. As with everything of which our "world" consists, the self is made and remade, not found. "Other sculptors, other statues from the same stone! Other minds, other worlds from the same monotonous and inexpressive chaos!"[12]

For closely related reasons, James rejected all forms of transcendentalism, that is, all views according to which the meaningfulness or vitality of our experience is a function of the extent to which we apprehend or become one with a something larger or greater than ourselves. The "worlds" of the passage just quoted are "embedded" in nothing more or other than an "inexpressive chaos." "My world is but one in a million alike embedded, alike real to those who may abstract them" (*Writings of William James*, p. 73.) As much as he admired Walt Whitman's poetry ("ejaculations—things mostly without subject or verb, a succession of interjections on an immense scale" [p. 637]), he objected that Whitman "abolishes the usual human distinctions, . . . loves and celebrates hardly any human attributes save those elementary ones common to all members of the race. . . . He felt the human crowd as rapturously as Wordsworth felt the mountains, felt it as an overpoweringly significant presence, simply to absorb one's mind in which should be business sufficient and worthy to fill the days of a serious man" (pp. 637–38). As with other experiences among the many varieties of religious experience that he catalogued, he recognized the sense of ease and fluency, of

---

[12]*Writings of William James*, p.73. In more technical terms than James himself uses, his "stream of consciousness" psychology suggests a theory of personal identity akin to David Hume's and to those articulated in recent years by Robert Nozick and Derek Parfit.

"at-homeness," that Whitman, Wordsworth, and other transcendentalists seek and sometimes find. But if these are goods, they are bought at a high price. Acquiring them puts us "in a sort of anaesthetic state in which we might say with Walt Whitman, if we cared to say anything about ourselves at such times, 'I am sufficient as I am.' This feeling of the sufficiency of the present moment, of its absoluteness,—this absence of all need to explain it, account for it, or justify it,—is what I call the Sentiment of Rationality."[13] Gratifying as it may seem when we are overtaken by it, this "sentiment" stills what is most important in life. "All feeling ... depend[s] ... not on simple discharge of nerve currents, but on their discharge under arrest, impediment, or resistance. Just as we feel no particular pleasure when we breathe freely, but a very intense feeling of distress when the respiratory motions are prevented,—so any unobstructed tendency to action discharges itself without the production of much cogitative accompaniment, and any perfectly fluent course of thought awakens but little feeling; but when the movement is inhibited, or when the thought meets with difficulties, we experience distress. It is only when the distress is upon us that we can be said to strive, to crave, or to aspire."[14]

In this respect, and recognizing the numerous and important differences between them, Whitmanesque transcendentalism shares too much with the various philosophical idealisms that James relentlessly combated. Although eschewing their absurdly abstract intellectualism, it is like them in effecting a "monstrous abridgement of life." We each of us may occasionally refresh ourselves "by a bath in the eternal springs" to which these views beckon us; but every

[13]William James, "The Sentiment of Rationality" in *The Will to Believe* (New York: Dover Publications, 1956), p. 64.

[14]Ibid. The first part of this passage anticipates, as does much in what I later discuss in Nietzsche, the Heideggerian notion of "an excess of Being over Experience." Earlier in the essay he makes a related but logical point, one akin to an argument of Wittgenstein's discussed above. Even "when all things have been unified to the supreme degree, the notion of a possible other than the actual may still ... prey upon our system. The bottom of being is left logically opaque to us, as something which we simply come upon and find, and about which (if we wish to act) we should pause and wonder as little as possible." Because neither the philosopher nor anyone else can "exorcise this question, he must ignore or blink it, and, assuming the data of his system as something given ... simply proceed to a life ... based on it." But this ineliminable contingency, this among the "bounds of thought," is not a matter for regret: "There is no doubt that this acting on an opaque necessity is accompanied by a certain pleasure" (p. 73).

"man" who is "entire" will soon flee from their "insipid spacious-
ness" into "the teeming and dramatic richness of the concrete
world." ("Sentiment of Rationality," p. 69). "Transcendentalism,"
James wrote sardonically, "has two editions of the universe—the
Absolute being the edition *de luxe*."[15] Life in the deluxe universe "is
sure to put on a narrow, close, sick-room air. Everything sentimen-
tal and priggish will be consecrated by it." In it the "rough, harsh,
sea-wave, north-wind element" is "banished because it jars too
much on the desire for communion." Acknowledging that some
"will keep insisting on the reason, the atonement, that lies in the
heart of things, and that we can act *with*," there will be (he hoped)
others adamant for "the opacity of brute fact that we must react
against" ("Sentiment of Rationality," pp. 89–90).

V

The martial, agonal, even Dionysian elements in James's personal
ideals will be disturbing to many. But in my view their predominant
tendency is to affirm and strengthen rather than cancel or compromise the genuineness of his commitment to individuality and other
forms of diversity. James's open disdain for "the herd of nullities
whose votes count for zero in the march of events" (p. 100) may
have been disobedient to his own "command" to "respect" "those
whom we see harmlessly . . . happy in their own ways," but he
expected like treatment from those who reciprocated his scorn and
seems otherwise to have been more faithful to his "hands off" rule
than most of us who profess allegiance to something like it.

Given James's conviction that "zest" and "eagerness" occur only
or mainly when we "act against" something that is resistant to us,
the presence of a diversity of competing and conflicting views and
interests becomes a strongly contributive, if not a necessary, condition of the realization of his own ideals. Alternative and especially
opposing points of view are not to be suffered, abided, or tolerated
out of benevolence, altruism, or any other self-diminishing or self-
abnegating "principle"; they are to be sought, encouraged, promoted in order to sustain the circumstances necessary or strongly

[15]Ralph Barton Perry, *The Thought and Character of William James*, 2 vols.
(Boston: Little, Brown, 1935) vol. 2, p. 384.

conducive to one's own thriving. Properly understood, moral principle, social policy, and individual and group interest can conjoin, reinforce, and complement, concatenating to the conclusion that individuality and (albeit less certainly) other forms of social, moral, and political plurality are indispensable to a "strenuous" life, a life of eagerness and vitality.

Leaving aside most of the specifically philosophical questions posed by James's views, the following (closely connected) issues remain: (1) Do James's views support plurality in senses additional to individuality? (2) Are those views antithetical to sociality? (3) Can we find in, or bring to, James's theory a conception of politics that complements or otherwise advantages our responses to (1) and (2)?

There are reasons to say that, in his own understandings and intentions, James's pluralism privileges individuality at the expense of group or associational multiplicity and diversity. Because the universe itself, in its opacity to our understanding and its recalcitrance to our intentions, is a worthy protagonist to "men" of "energy," it is too much to say that social, moral, or political plurality are indispensable to James's ideal. Abstractly, the humanly lonely struggle of a Sisyphus with his earth and his gods would seem to be enough to make his life "significant" and worth his living.[16] Dramatizing its often deeply privatized character, this among James's views at once manifests some of the most attractive elements in his thinking and gives urgency to the hesitations I just expressed.

In approaching these questions, we should first note respects in which the views I have been discussing are compatible with and perhaps conducive to a richer and more vigorous group life—and at least to that extent to sociality—than James himself may have envisioned.

It is clear that James is not a holist, an organicist, or a corporationist *à la* a Gierke, a Maitland, or a Figgis, a Durkheim, Mauss, or Dumont. (For discussion of these and other theorists of pluralism, see infra, Chap. 3.) He does not think that groups are made or given

---

[16]Although quite prepared to countenance and to admire suicide under a variety of circumstances, the "wisdom of Silenus" that Hannah Arendt elevated to no less than the outlook to beat had no appeal for James. Our world is not made for us or us for it in the sense of there being a natural or an easy consonance between its purposes and ours; but its very resistances to us constitute a setting appropriate to the modes of self-enactment that James thought most important to us.

by nature or by God, that they are logically, metaphysically, or ontologically prior to individuals, and he certainly does not think that individual desires, interests, and purposes should as a matter of course be subordinated to the integrity, the objectives, or the needs of groups and group life. If we advert once again to an Oakeshottian conception, on Jamesian assumptions groups will be regarded as "enterprise associations," that is, will consist of a number of individuals "related in the joint pursuit of some imagined and wished-for common satisfaction" (Oakeshott, *On Human Conduct*, p. 114).[17] The satisfactions sought by members of associations of this type "may be anything recognizable as a substantive condition of things imagined and wished-for as the outcome of human activity. That it is a chosen relationship follows from it being association in terms of a common [i.e., a shared] want: two or more agents may be joined in seeking a common satisfaction only in virtue of a choice on the part of each. This choice may be revoked, and if [so,] . . . the relationship lapses. An agent need not have expressly enrolled himself by a deliberate act, but . . . it is a relationship from which an agent may [properly, if too often not in fact] extricate himself by a choice of his own" (p. 115). Decisions about how to pursue the purposes of such associations are made "collectedly" and "are only contingently connected with the common purpose or interest concerned; they are not deducible from the choice to be associated in pursuit of it and they cannot be recognized by the associates as their own merely in virtue of that choice" (ibid.).

In a comment that at once consolidates the Jamesian character of the conception and signals a part of the objection I am addressing, Oakeshott observes that association in this mode "is often . . . identified as a community of wills" (ibid.).[18] Given the will-driven and hence deeply agent-relative character of James's account of beliefs and values, if groups form at all they will certainly be unsta-

[17]The difficulties I am trying to identify can be partly delineated by noting that for Oakeshott the pursuit of such satisfactions in enterprise associations is primarily in the mode of self-disclosure rather than of self-enactment but that the latter (which in Oakeshottian terms is the mode of action that James privileges) as much as the former presupposes a shared, mutually authoritative "vernacular of moral self-discourse." See *On Human Conduct*, pp. 70–78. In its most pronounced formulations, James's privatism excludes the possibility of such a vernacular.

[18]Owing to his own (Hobbesian) views concerning the will, Oakeshott characterizes this identification as "somewhat hazardously" made and prefers "community of choices." As will become clear in Part Two, I see no reason to follow him in this respect.

ble, very likely transient if not evanescent. Certainly there is nothing in James's thinking that guarantees a plurality of social or political groups. If, with the English pluralists from Maitland to Cole and Lindsay as distinct from the American pluralists from Bentley to Truman and Dahl, we insist on a metaphysically or ontologically embedded and hence assured pluralism, James's stress on individuality will make his views seem inadequate and perhaps dangerous.

Among the countervailing tendencies to these features of James's thought are his faith that the natural (but not the moral) world lets itself be sorted by us into "kinds" (pp. 102–93, 92–3, 116) and his admission that "habit" reinforced by socialization and education produces commonalities of conception, disposition, and evaluation. Insofar as he recognizes that some affirmative commonality or complementarity of interest or objective is necessary as a basis for groups and group interactions (or for sociality in any form), these elements in his thinking may do something to provide it.

It would be a distortion, however, to place great weight on either of these views. James regarded the first as providential, that is, both fortunate and inexplicable, a circumstance without which we could not think or act at all but one which we cannot understand and hence cannot deliberately create or sustain (see esp. pp. 92–93). And as we have already seen, he regarded habit and most of the effects of socialization as regrettable and to be combated wherever possible.

In this as in other respects, he thinks we would do better to reckon on the agonal disposition to "act against" resistance and opposition. Just as war is the most effective impetus to energetic but coordinated action on the part of entire societies, so the most effective means of uniting the energies of large segments of a populace (assuming there are occasions on which it is appropriate to do so) is to seek "moral equivalents" to it. Following the same line of thought, more narrowly localized or otherwise domain-specific competitions, clashes, and conflicts can bring numbers of individuals into association without sacrificing or compromising their individuality. Although not likely to remain stable over extended periods of time (and hence—if this were a concern—not apt to become "factions" in James Madison's sense),[19] groups formed out of these

[19]Skeptical, if not antagonistic, toward the notion of a common good or public interest, James had no reason to exercise himself concerning this Madisonian problem. Nor does he worry himself much about religious, ideological, or other forms of group fanaticism.

kinds of dynamics can stimulate and may sometimes give enhanced expression to the energies and abilities of the individuals who compose them.

Reminiscent as it is of the American theory of *political* pluralism mentioned above, this account of the banding and disbanding of individuals into and out of groups suggests that interjection of a more emphatically political conception into James's (for the most part extrapolitical) thinking might counter or diminish the privatizing tendencies in his thought. I return to this possibility, primarily as articulated by Tocqueville, by way of concluding this essay. But whether impelled or characterized by competition and conflict or cooperation and consensus, whether recognizably political or otherwise, group relationships must be, in part, relationships of mutual intelligibility or comprehension. The actions of numbers of people who are unfathomable to one another may come together to produce consequences that they severally recognize or not, intend or seek to prevent, welcome or regret, and so forth, but some measure of mutual intelligibility is a necessary condition of groups and group activity. One of the charms of James's thinking is his relish for cases in which this condition goes unsatisfied. Can we preserve this relish in ourselves while overcoming his sometimes indifference and sometimes resistance to theorizing cases in which the condition is partly satisfied? Can we have the relish without the charm? Having turned to James in search of a complement to Wittgenstein, turnabout will be fruitful play.

Thoughts, James insists in his early *Principles of Psychology*, are "found in personal consciousnesses," in "minds, selves, concrete particular I's." "Each of these minds keeps its own thoughts to itself. There is no giving or bartering between them. No thought even comes into direct *sight* of a thought in another personal consciousness than its own. Absolute insulation, irreducible pluralism, is the law. It seems as if the elementary psychic fact were not *thought* or *this thought* or *that thought*, but *my thought*, every thought being *owned*. Neither contemporaneity, nor proximity in space, nor similarity of quality and content are able to fuse thoughts together which are sundered by this barrier of belonging to personal minds. The breaches between such thoughts are the most absolute breaches in nature" (p. 23).

For James, these are not matters of merely professional psychological or philosophical interest. While no psychology "can question the *existence* of personal selves," it can distort and diminish them: indeed, the "worst a psychology can do is so to interpret the nature of these selves as to rob them of their worth" (ibid.) Perhaps in part because he valorized it so positively, James never relinquished his near, if not actual, solipsism, contenting himself with entering the kinds of ad hoc qualifications to it that we have encountered above.

On a widely received and partly correct understanding of his later philosophy, Wittgenstein contends that the passages I have just quoted from James are incoherent in the strong sense that they deny suppositions of what they most want to affirm, namely, that the "thoughts" of individuals are intelligible or meaningful—are "somethings" not "anythings or nothings"—to those who "own" them. Brutally abbreviating a complex and subtle argument, meaning or intelligibility is exclusively a public or social or group phenomenon in that it requires a minimum of two persons who share standards or criteria the satisfaction of which makes perceptions, thoughts, and feelings, *this* perception, *this* thought as opposed to any other or none. Whatever we might want to say about "nature," if or insofar as there are "breaches" between the experiences of one person and all others, that person herself has and can have no thoughts, feelings, or perceptions (Wittgenstein, *Philosophical Investigations*, esp. I, 243–315, 348–412; II, xi, pp. 220–29). If or insofar as James was—and we are—justified in thinking that individual's have these experiences, to that extent his radical privatism is discredited.

If we accept Wittgenstein's arguments, does it follow that we must do without the "relish" and the protections for individuality that James found in and hoped for from his privatism and solipsism? A first point here is that my summary of Wittgenstein (along with much of the literature concerning him) is misleading in deflecting attention from the fact that his account of the conditions necessary to meaning or intelligibility is also and equally an account of the conditions of meaninglessness or unintelligibility. That account presumes itself, presumes that the propositions of which it itself consists are meaningful and that they are meaningful *because* they satisfy the conditions that it itself makes the necessary conditions of meaning. That is, identifications of instances of meaninglessness are always and necessarily parasitic on identified (to our satisfaction) instances of the meaningful, but instances of the latter enable identifications and valorizations of the former. To adapt a familiar (and necessarily only partly successful) metaphor, standing on the deck of the ship (some would say clinging to the frail bark) of meaning that we have built and thus far managed to keep intact, we can locate and welcome or regret unmeaning in and about us. Understood in this way, Wittgenstein does nothing to jeopardize the "meaningless" or the possibility of the special challenge and savor of acting against "it."

Less heady than speculations about "the meaningful" versus "the meaningless" are those Wittgensteinian points discussed earlier. Never *entirely* meaningful (whatever that might mean), our thinking and acting are distributed along a host of continua that move from (for example) the fluently articulated and readily grasped to the uncertain, the confusing, and the bewildering. In James's sense of the distinction, acting *with* and acting *against* are equally possible at all points on all of these continua, this being a matter of variable disposition and valorization, not of impossibility or necessity. Our "world" was not made for us even in the Jamesian sense of being made or making itself opaque to us such that we can act against its opacity. The worlds that we have thus far made for ourselves include (along, no doubt, with much that they exclude) this and many other possibilities.

VI

Our present possibilities include looking to politics either to enhance or to diminish sociality, individuality, and plurality as well as contesting attempts to use politics for any of these purposes. Although the theorists with and against whom I have mainly tried to think in this essay are for the most part silent concerning these possibilities, as I read them their works are compatible with them.

In *Democracy in America* (to which I restrict myself among Tocqueville's works) Tocqueville sets out a fourfold taxonomy of forms or modes of sociality that encompasses the main possibilities implicit in the foregoing discussion. The three most widely discussed of these are the traditional or aristocratic societies that Tocqueville thought were being destroyed by equality and democracy, the destructive form of secularized, simple egalitarian, resentment-laden democratic society that he feared was emerging in France, and the more complex, pluralistic, and freedom-sustaining democracy that he thought he had found in embryonic form in North America. The fourth is what we might call the "antisociability sociality" that he observed in the American West and especially the American Southwest. To the extent that we can translate James's thinking into these categories, elements of the first—very differently estimated—may be discerned in his hostile comments about habit and "ancestral blindness," the second is reminiscent of "Chautauqua society," and the fourth is what Tocqueville thought and many others will think the all but certain resultant of privatistic, agonal, individuality *à la* James.

Having abandoned hope of rescuing traditional (aristocratic) society from the democratizing forces of history, Tocqueville looked (regretfully) to the third of these modes to make the second tolerable and to avoid the utterly repugnant (to him) fourth. The interest here lies in his argument that politics and political activity are essential for these purposes, particularly those parts of his argument according to which politics intensifies processes of group formation and activity (including those processes most consonant with other elements of James's thought and weakly validated by James), and thereby qualifies and confines individualism and its excesses.

Pausing for a moment to put Tocqueville's anguished reflections into Wittgensteinian terms, in his own very different diction the French thinker specifies necessary conditions of mutual intelligibility and hence of sociality and affirms that they are satisfied—perhaps all too well—in the emergent democratic societies and polities. "Without . . . common belief no society can prosper; say, rather, no society can exist; for without ideas held in common there is no common action, and without common action there . . . is no social body. In order that society should exist . . . it is necessary that the minds of all the citizens should be rallied and held together by certain predominant ideas; and this cannot be the case unless each of them sometimes draws his opinions from the common source and consents to accept certain matters of belief already formed."[20]

In the "new states of the West and Southwest" these conditions

[20] Alexis de Tocqueville, *Democracy in America*, ed. Phillips Bradley, 2 vols. (New York: Vintage Books, 1957), vol. 2, p. 9. Cf. vol. 1, p. 73: "As all persons must have recourse to certain grammatical forms, which are the foundations of human language, in order to express their thoughts; so all communities are obliged to secure their existence by submitting to a certain amount of authority, without which they fall into anarchy. This authority may be distributed in several ways, but it must always exist somewhere." These passages may be usefully compared to Nietzsche's notion of a "law of agreement." See infra, Part Two, Sections II and III.

remain unsatisfied. "Society has no existence" (*Democracy in America*, vol. 1, pp. 53–54) and we are presented with no more than "an agglomeration of adventurers and speculators" with no "force, independent of legislation and of the men who direct it" by which "the state can be protected and society be made to flourish" (p. 211). Representing "democracy arrived at its utmost limits," these "settlements," in what later came to be called—with a good deal more ambivalence than Tocqueville could manage—the Wild West, "founded offhand and as it were by chance" (pp. 53–55), displayed the worst, Tocqueville thought, we have to fear from ourselves.

By contrast, "in [much of] the United States the majority undertakes to supply a multitude of ready-made opinions for the use of individuals, who are thus relieved from the necessity of forming opinions of their own. Everybody there adopts great numbers of theories, on philosophy, morals, and politics, without inquiry, upon public trust; and if we examine it very closely it will be perceived that religion itself holds sway there much less as a doctrine of revelation than as a commonly received opinion" (pp. 11–12).

Fending off the debased and destructive chaos of untrammeled individualism (of self-interest wrongly understood), these rarely reconsidered commonalities and certitudes also enable, or rather encourage and facilitate, a numerically abundant pluralism at the level of "civil society." "Americans of all ages, all conditions, and all dispositions constantly form associations. They have not only commercial and manufacturing companies . . . but associations of a thousand other kinds, religious, moral, serious, futile, general or restricted, enormous or diminutive. The Americans make associations to give entertainments, to found seminaries, to build inns, to construct churches, to diffuse books, to send missionaries to the antipodes; in this manner they found hospitals, prisons, and schools. If it is proposed to inculcate some truth or to foster some feeling by the encouragement of a great example, they form a society. Wherever at the head of some new undertaking you see the government in France, or a man of rank in England, in the United States you will be sure to find an association" (ibid., vol. 2, p. 114).

Although qualified if not compromised by the fact that it is a manifestation of their weakness as individuals, this proclivity of Americans might be enough to "long preserve their wealth and their cultivation" (such as the latter is), and without it "civilization itself would be endangered" (p. 115). But if the "consciousnesses" of these denizens of the American civil society is indeed "happy" in the Hegelian sense, it is not likely to remain happy in any other. Neither the pluralism nor the combination of it and its enabling conditions is enough to preserve liberty or the genuinely diverse pluralism necessary to liberty. Rather, this very combination presents an unprecedented threat to diversity and liberty. There is indeed a "hum" or "buzz" of activity; that is, the activities are repetitious in the extreme. The equal civil rights turn out to be "rights of indulging in the same pleasures, of entering the same professions, of frequenting the same places; in a word, of living in the same manner and seeking wealth by the same means" (p. 100). The "passions" of Americans have "a sort of family likeness," which "soon renders the survey of them exceedingly wearisome. This perpetual recurrence of the same passion is monotonous; the peculiar methods by which this passion seeks its own gratification are no less so" (p. 240). As with James's strongly analogous estimation of the Chautauqua society, Tocqueville thought that the "remark I here apply to America may indeed be addressed to almost all our contemporaries. Variety is disappearing from the human race; the same ways of acting, thinking, and feeling are to be met with all over the world" (ibid.). And because genuine diversity is essential to liberty, rather than having found "the means of independent life," Americans and their ilk may "simply have discovered (no easy task) a new physiognomy of servitude" (p. 13).

In sharp contrast to James (who had more than a little admiration for the adventurers of the Wild West), however, Tocqueville rejected the idea that individuals, importantly out of their own resources, could resist the "tyranny of the majority" and its relentless demands for conformity and submission. He would almost certainly regard James as a proponent of individual*ism*, of a view that in his judgment is at once a chief product of, and one of the strongest supports for the new servitude, not a friend of the "independence" and individual*ity* that Tocqueville favored. In his judgment the latter are impossible to achieve or to maintain under conditions of isolation, whether of the physical variety manifest in the Western states or the more subtle but insidious type characteristic of most of the rest of America and increasingly of France. In democratic as opposed to aristocratic societies, independence can be achieved and maintained only by persons who, accepting a grammar and a set of authoritative beliefs and values that enable mutually intelligible thinking and acting, "act in concert" (p. 13) with some and against others of their fellow *citizens*. As the last term indicates (and as will be underlined for us as readers of Hannah Arendt by the quoted phrase), independence or individuality requires *political* activity.

Relying on a distinction that requires scrutiny, Tocqueville looked to politics rather than government to check these tendencies and to invigorate independence and diversity. Unlike their aristocratic and monarchical predecessors, democratic governments have no independence from civil society. Expressing and implementing the social consensus, they more often strengthen than combat the powerful pressures for submission and unthinking conformism. The various governments proliferated by the American founders, for example, rarely act against majority tyranny. "The plan was [nevertheless] a wise one" because it "infuse[d] political life into each portion of the territory in order to multiply to an infinite extent opportunities of acting in concert for all of the members of the community" (ibid.).

There is something of a mechanical and otherwise unsettling quality to Tocqueville's account of the processes by which the political activity that develops around governments fosters independence. In addition to providing opportunities, the "infusing" of political life "makes" citizens "constantly feel their mutual *dependence*" (ibid., emphasis added). "Local freedom [to act in concert] . . . brings men together and forces them to help one another in spite of the propensities that sever them" (p. 111), thereby counteracting the separation and consequent vulnerabilities that are, paradoxically, produced by democratic sociality. As the mechanical metaphors suggest (and as later appropriations of them by American theorists of political pluralism affirm), these processes do not have the high moral tone sometimes attributed to or hoped for from democratic citizenship. Government is not itself an agency that promotes independence, but instituting it teaches citizens "to think of their fellow men from ambitious motives; and they frequently find it, in a manner, their interest to forget themselves" (p. 110). "Pride must be dissembled; disdain dares not break out; selfishness fears its own self" (ibid.). In short, democratic politics are not a school of moral virtue, but they give lessons in the vitally important skills of accommodating to others in order effectively to pursue self-interest rightly understood. A citizenry that learns and applies these lessons, Tocqueville thinks, can hope to fend off both governmental and social tyranny, thereby opening spaces for thought and action of an estimable character.

Sociality, Individuality, Plurality, and Politics

It is arguable that the plausibility of Tocqueville's argument concerning politics and political activity has been enhanced since he advanced it. In diagnosing pervasive social control and the ways in which it is abetted and intensified by democratic government, Tocqueville (and James, except in respect to the role of governments) anticipated themes that are prominent and persuasively advanced in critical social and political thinking in our own time (perhaps most especially in the work of Michel Foucault). And his contention that the mutual accommodations and dependencies and aggregated force of political association are the most effective means of protecting individuality, plurality, and hence liberty in democratic, modern, or late-modern societies, while no doubt in need of elaboration, adaptation, and specification, is cogent and perhaps now circumstantially compelling.

Although for the most part presented as instrumentally necessary to objectives conceptualized as independent of it, Tocqueville's argument for political activity sometimes takes on the character of the expression and promotion of an ideal, of something valuable— perhaps supremely so as in Arendt and so-called participationist democratic theories—in its own right. To whatever extent such activity impedes tyranny or social control or protects liberty or individuality, those who engage in it are made better by doing so. So viewed, in the unlikely event that the members of a society converged on and sustained their uncoerced commitment to the ideal, those of us who are skeptical or antagonistic regarding it, aside from offering them such arguments as occur to us against it, should adopt, and urge on them in respect to us, James's "hands off" rule concerning their arrangements and activities.[21]

In the instrumental form in which I presented it above, Tocqueville's argument depends importantly on his distinction between politics and government and particularly his claim that we can act politically, act as *citizens*, without thereby enhancing the already-great (in his estimation too great) authority and power of government to reinforce social consensus and enforce social conformity. In Jamesian terms, it depends on the possibility of acting against government without acting with it and so as to strengthen its capacity to prevent us from acting against it. It would be absurd altogether to deny such a possibility. But neither Tocqueville's conceptual distinc-

---

[21]For further and somewhat differently nuanced discussion of related issues, see infra, Part Two, esp. Section V.

tion nor the day-to-day differentiations that acting on it would require are as clear as his argument assumes. As Aristotle taught us, citizenship is an office in, or rather of, government. Citizenship is therefore a conceptual impossibility apart from government, and in fact it is usually created and distributed by a government. Accordingly, to act as a citizen is in part to discharge the duties or fulfill the responsibilities established and defined by an entity that, on Tocqueville's view, those holding that office should be trying to act against. Tension between acting against that which one is acting within is a familiar feature of institutional settings and is often managed more or less successfully. The issue, again, is not the possibility of what Tocqueville forwards, but what goes with it and hence is also promoted when it is given the privileged standing and significance that Tocqueville's theory accords to it. Given widespread acceptance of government and its immense and immensely dangerous authority and power, the complicity of citizenship and political activity with them cannot be sufficient reason to denigrate the one or to eschew the other; it is more than sufficient reason to be wary of political theories that deflect us from alternative ways of fostering individuality and plurality while endeavoring to maintain such sociality as is necessary to them and otherwise pleasing to ourselves.[22]

William James was pleased to think of himself as a "happy-go-lucky anarchistic sort of creature" (*Writings of William James*, p. 457). Distinguishing him from anarchists and all of the many others given to solemnity concerning politics and government, as political theorists we may be inclined to regard this self-characterization as exposing a carelessness that jeopardizes (as does, it might be argued, Wittgenstein's neglect of political questions) his otherwise admirable affirmations of individuality and plurality. Without attempting to address the circumstantial questions, we might, however, consider two alternative possibilities. The first of these, already partly sketched, is that the reach for politics and hence government to protect and enhance individuality might be counterproductive. By augmenting the authority and power of the form of association that is encompassing and compulsory (the mode of "relationship from which an agent may [*not*] extricate himself by a choice of his

[22]I have developed the themes of this paragraph in "Citizenship and Authority: A Chastened View of Citizenship," chap. 3 in *Toward a Liberalism*.

own"), we may strengthen the forces of homogenization and normalization that we seek to combat. By forgetting our selves, dissembling our pride, and suppressing our disdains so as to be able to act with others, we may extend and intensify our dependencies and diminish our capacities to act apart from and against them.[23]

The second possibility is that the above judgment about James betrays our own perhaps less than fully recognized hesitations about individuality and plurality, our fear that if not controlled by government and politics (or moral community or divine or otherwise transcendental illumination), they encourage speculation and adventurism, license vulgarity and degradation, engender disorder and conflict, make life in this our city of the earth a hellish torment. We—perhaps especially we liberals—must take care that our sometime lamentations about the discipline and normalization we experience are not ways of concealing from ourselves a desire on our parts to seize the commanding heights that only government and politics provide and from them to impose on others and perhaps on ourselves a discipline that may be different, may be better, but is every bit as much a discipline.

A thinker who regards politics rightly understood as "a mode of human relationship . . . as rare as it is excellent" (Oakeshott, *On Human Conduct*, p. 180) has amplified these conjectures in a manner that gathers a number of the themes of this chapter and these reflections more generally. For reasons partially considered early in this chapter, individuality, plurality, and politics presuppose a "vernacular language". "That there should be many such languages in the world, some perhaps with familial likenesses in terms of which there may be profitable exchange of expressions, is intrinsic to their character. This plurality cannot be resolved by being understood as so many contingent and regrettable divergencies from a fancied perfect and universal language of moral intercourse (a law of God, a utilitarian 'critical' morality, or a so-called 'rational morality')." That every such language "should be spoken more or less exactly and with varying degrees of grace or clumsiness, and that there should be near-literates and fraudulent verbalizers; that it should be subject to change, that neologisms should make their appearance, and that antique expressions should survive in its interstices; that it

---

[23]Cf. the discussion of Hobbes's notions of "worth," "worthiness," and "complaisance" at the end of chap. 1, *supra*.

should sometimes be unequal to the occasion and that it should not only be liable to corruption but also commonly corrupt—none of these circumstances is at all remarkable: they are the vicissitudes common to all vernacular languages" (pp. 80–81).

Nor should we be surprised that from time to time attempts are made to remedy these defects, including by resort to the authority and power of government and politics. "Human beings are apt to be disconcerted unless they feel themselves to be upheld by something more substantial than the emanations of their own contingent imaginations. This unresolved plurality teases the monistic yearnings of the muddled theorist, it vexes a moralist with ecumenical leanings, and it may disconcert an unfortunate who, having 'lost' his morality (as others have known to 'lose' their faith), must set about constructing one for himself. . . . But it will reassure the modest mortal with a self to disclose and a soul to make who needs a familiar and resourceful moral language (and one for which he may hope to acquire a *Sprachgefühl*) to do it in and who is disinclined to be unnerved because there are other such languages to which he cannot readily relate his own" (ibid.).

Chapter 3

Individuality, Plurality, and Liberalism

At what we might call the arithmetic core of their meanings, *individual* (particular, single) and *plural* (two or more) are conceptually interwoven. *Plural* and hence a plurality requires countable and hence individualizable entities, and *individual* makes a distinction only if there are two or more such entities. In this elementary— but also elemental—sense, descriptive and evaluative theories of individuality and plurality are mutually dependent and complementary, not opposed or contrary one to the other.

Perhaps influenced by these considerations, various social and political doctrines, especially versions of liberalism, aver that in fact individuality and plurality are complementary and often synergetic phenomena. The diversity of perspectives, beliefs, purposes, and styles that individuality involves are possible bases or starting points for a plurality of groups and associations, perhaps even cultures and traditions;[1] for its part, a plurality of the latter may stimulate,

---

[1]A newcomer to the neighborhood with an enthusiasm for tennis but no partners takes to hitting tennis balls against a wall of the local school. Seeing her do this, another resident in the same plight approaches to propose a game at the somewhat deteriorated municipal court. The game attracts the attention and interest of others, leading to an active tennis club, which also builds a swimming pool, a badminton court, and starts a child-care center.

What if my tennis enthusiast has just arrived not in a neighborhood in which tennis is widely known and accepted but in a culture unfamiliar with it? Familiar with it but regarding it as frivolous and self-indulgent? Acceptant of it for men but decidedly not for women? As different as initial and perhaps continuing reactions to her wall volleying would certainly be, perhaps. . . .

support, or otherwise enable individuality.[2] On this understanding, which I call complementarism, theories or practices that promote either individuality or plurality at the expense of the other would appear to diminish or even jeopardize both.

At the level of generality at which I have thus far stated complementarist views, the support they offer to values prominent in liberalism should make them attractive to anyone of a liberal persuasion. They are certainly to be preferred to monistic, organicist, and strongly communitarian doctrines that deny the reality or disdain the worth of everything—particularly of individuals and their individuality—less than "the whole." Their merits relative to more insistent forms of individualism is a more complicated matter that will occupy us as we proceed. Perhaps, however, there are forms of individualism, liberal or otherwise, as foolish as its holistic antagonists allege, so foolish as to mimic holism by denying the reality of anything but individuals or the possibility that groups and societies, traditions and cultures, can contribute to individuality. If so, it is easy to think of reasons for setting them aside in favor of an understanding along the lines sketched above.

So far so good. But the numerous more particular formulations from which the foregoing is an abstraction identify and valorize individualities and pluralities in terms that are more substantive, more concrete, than those I have thus far used. These identifications and evaluations are likely to be controversial in themselves and to be in the service of yet more sharply contested theoretical and practical purposes. Perhaps more important here, there are difficult questions concerning the conditions under which individuality and plurality are possible or are likely to flourish. Disagreements prevail even where there is wide acceptance of the complementarist view

---

[2]Two newcomers to a community with an active tennis club are pressed to join. Newcomer Able overcomes her theretofore reclusive and otherwise reticent disposition and becomes an active player with an unusual style of play, as well as a distinctive participant in social life centering on the club. Reacting against what she experiences as unwelcome pressure, newcomer Baker refuses to join, and the encounter prompts her to begin writing introspective poetry that is opaque but beguiling to the cloistered writing group with which she occasionally meets.

It is unlikely that many of the inhabitants of the city of Kandahar will have opportunities to join tennis clubs, much less likely that women inhabitants of that city will do so. But then there was a time when there was no such thing as the game of tennis, later times when it was unknown or known but unplayed over most of the globe. . . .

that individuality and plurality, insofar as they are present, are interwoven and often complementary. Briefly reviewing a few of the divergent views familiar in recent political theory will help us to get our bearings as we try to think about these issues.

Group theorists in the tradition of Otto von Gierke, J. N. Figgis, and Louis Dumont might agree with the statements I made above, but they identify individuals as parts of groups or other entities larger than individuals and they treat individuating characteristics as functions of group life (or as pathologies resulting from the breakdown of group life) and as properly subordinate to the latter. The plurality they promote means a multiplicity of cultures, groups, and associations, only secondarily and derivatively of individual personalities; plurality and individuality can be complementary but only insofar as individuality is consonant with group life. On the political and jural theory yielded by this formulation, the primary concern of politics, the state, and law is to recognize, respect, and otherwise foster groups and group life; the state and its law relate to, and treat of, individuals primarily if not exclusively through the medium of the groups to which individuals belong.[3] Although efforts have from time to time been made to incorporate these ideas into liberalism, most liberals have been suspicious of their corporatist and anti-individualist tendencies.

A partly contrasting example is provided by American political pluralists such as David Truman, Robert Dahl, and their numerous followers in American political science. Perhaps influenced by an ontology (deriving from John Dewey's pragmatism?) considerably more relaxed in its holism than Gierke's or Dumont's, but in any case more concerned to remedy defects in competing accounts and assessments of American political life than with philosophical controversies, writers in this school have largely avoided abstruse issues about whole-part relationships, about the moral, jural, or other "personality" of groups. Observation shows, they argue, that the primary agents or actors in the political process (at least in the

---

[3]J. N. Figgis, *Political Thought from Gerson to Grotius* (New York: Harper, 1960) and *The Divine Right of Kings* (London: Cambridge University Press, 1914); Otto von Gierke, *Political Theories of the Middle Ages* (London: Cambridge University Press, 1951), and *Natural Law and the Theory of Society: 1500 to 1800* (Boston: Beacon Press, 1957); Louis Dumont, *Homo Hierachicus* (Chicago: University of Chicago Press, 1980), *Essays on Individualism* (Chicago: University of Chicago Press, 1986).

United States) are neither discrete, unorganized individuals nor antagonistic classes or strata, but the large and fluctuating array of groups and associations that sometimes compete, sometimes cooperate, with one another in "pressuring" governments to serve their interests and promote their objectives. Although conceding that the internal organization of the larger and more permanent of these groups sometimes works to the disadvantage of some of their own members, for the most part theorists of this school treat the groups they study as voluntary in that the groups form because of recognition of shared interests and individuals retain membership in them depending on their own judgments whether their interests are thereby best served. Although sometimes allowing that groups may achieve a disproportionate or otherwise objectionable influence on public institutions and policies, proponents of this version of pluralism have been as skeptical of notions such as a common good or a public interest as they have been resistant to ideas of false consciousness and true or objective individual interests. Against von Gierke and later corporativisms, on pluralism of this variety the state recognizes and relates directly to individuals as such in that it accords them a set (however large or well secured) of constitutionally established individual rights. However, insofar as proponents of this view manifest a concern to promote individuality, they rely primarily on access to competing voluntary associations to enable and encourage it. It would be too much to say that individuals and their individuating characteristics are banished or permitted to disappear from the theory, but they figure in it chiefly as elements or factors in intragroup dynamics.[4] In part for this reason, and despite the self-identification of many American pluralists with liberalism or liberal democracy, critics have frequently treated this form of pluralism as antiliberal.[5]

There are a number of variants of complementarism that tilt toward individuality rather than a multiplicity of groups and asso-

[4]David B. Truman, *The Governmental Process* (New York: Alfred Knopf, 1957); Robert A. Dahl, *A Preface to Democratic Theory* (Chicago: University of Chicago Press, 1956), and *Pluralist Democracy in the United States* (Chicago: Rand McNally, 1967).

[5]Grant McConnell, *Private Power and American Democracy* (New York: Alfred Knopf, 1966); Theodore J. Lowi, *The End of Liberalism* (New York: W. W. Norton, 1969); J. Roland Pennock, *Democratic Political Theory* (Princeton: Princeton University Press, 1979).

ciations. This tendency is sometimes discernible in John Locke and in other early versions of liberalism influenced by Protestant theology, and it can be glimpsed in Hobbes and other seventeeth-century thinkers (protoliberals?) who incorporated nominalism and other forms of philosophical skepticism into moral and political thought. It is pronounced in the thinking of Benjamin Constant and in Constant's admirer Isaiah Berlin; it is a recurrent, albeit insecure, element in the liberalism of John Stuart Mill as well as in those parts of the thinking of liberals such as John Rawls and Ronald Dworkin that stress the voluntarist or agent-relative character of conceptions of the good. A more powerful version, which includes features prominent in the group theories already discussed but also elements of the radical individualist thinking of writers such as Friedrich Nietzsche, is presented in the professedly antiliberal reflections of Michael Oakeshott.

At the epistemological and metaphysical level, Oakeshott effects a distinctive melding of holism and a pluralism that aims to secure both individuals and entities larger than individuals but less than the whole. Coherence being his criterion of intelligibility and hence also of the "satisfactoriness" of experience, he holds that *the idea of* an encompassing and fully coherent whole is necessary to identifying and comprehending anything and everything less than it. This idea, however, can never be realized in fully concrete form. All but our strictly philosophical thinking occurs within "modes" of experience that are "arrested," and philosophical thinking pursues enhanced or augmented coherence primarily by identifying the presuppositions of experiences that are intramodal.[6] In parallel fashion, "theorizing" (Oakeshott, *On Human Conduct*) the "practical" mode of experience consists in delineating and interrogating the presuppositions of those identifications that give partial (but for practical purposes often serviceable) intelligibility to individuals, groups, practices, law, traditions, and the other elements that compose practical experience. None of these elements would be intelligible apart from the mode of experiences that they together constitute, but also and equally that mode and its (partial) coherence consist entirely of those elements and the relationships among them.

In addition to giving closer attention to philosophical issues than

[6]Michael Oakeshott, *Experience and Its Modes* (London: Cambridge University Press, 1933).

is usual in the other versions of pluralism discussed thus far, Oake-shott's theory differs from them in the pride of valuative place it accords to individuality. Oakeshott's idealist epistemology and metaphysic features the coherence of entities larger and more complex than individuals, and his antirationalism[7] foregrounds the traditions and practices, the customs, conventions, and vernaculars without which thought and action are, on his view, impossible. His greatest admiration, however, is for those (few) persons who appropriate these invariably ambiguous resources for the "enactment" and reenactment of their selves and their lives; his greatest scorn is for the "individual manqué" and the "anti-individual" who are indistinguishable parts of a "mass" the leading characteristic of which is unremitting and destructive resentment of individuality (*On Human Conduct*, especially Essay III). Individuals would be incomprehensible to themselves and to others apart from traditions and societies, and individuality is difficult if not impossible in the absence of a plurality of practices and groups; but ensembles of these elements that lack a diverse and vigorous individuality are insipid, derisory, and often dangerous to themselves and to others, while those that are actively antagonistic to individuality are deserving of our scorn and may properly arouse our fears. Accordingly, the one form of human association that is not and cannot be fully or even substantially voluntary, the politically organized society called the state, must not be conceived and conducted in any of the numerous ways that augment the anti-individuality all too prominent in the Western tradition, ought to be conceived and conducted so as to protect and to foster individuality.

In promoting self-enactment and in his apprehension that political and other forms of associational life are often antagonistic to it, Oakeshott's work features ideas that are most forcefully developed in thinking that is usually regarded as non- or even anti-liberal. His notion of self-enactment and his conception of the major threats to it are strongly reminiscent of ideas of William James and of Nietzsche, of existentialists from Soren Kierkegaard to Jean-Paul Sartre, of Henry David Thoreau and Ralph Waldo Emerson, certainly of Hannah Arendt. His conviction that plurality and individuality, at their occasional or rather their infrequent best, are complementary differentiates him from the thinkers just mentioned, but he is as

[7]Michael Oakeshott, *Rationalism and Politics* (London: Methuen, 1962).

aware as any among them of the likelihood of conflicts between plurality and individuality, and he is as insistent as any of them that individuality is what matters.

I

What explains the persistence of differences such as these among views most of which are broadly complementarist in character, and between them and those who regard all forms of complementarism as naive if not dangerous? In part, the answer to these questions lies in difficulties and conflicts that are widely recognized as endemic to the individuality-plurality relationship but differently identified and estimated in competing theories.

The most prominent of these difficulties in the literatures of political and social theory and science are those commonly discussed in the languages of force and power, tyranny and imposition, deception and manipulation. On the one hand, neighborhood and avocational associations, families, unions, and corporations, churches and schools (each of these frequently aided and abetted by governments) demand conformity and submission from individuals who resist those demands as best they can. On the other, bullies and dictators, patriarchs and bosses, evangelizers and pedants force their preferences on the individuals and groups around them while malcontents and misanthropes veto potentially fruitful endeavors or impede them by withholding their needed participation and contributions. When these tendencies are pronounced, either pluralism in the sense of a multiplicity of powerful groups and associations diminishes individuality or aggressively selfish individuals weaken associational life (or both).

The languages in which such conflicts are most commonly described manifest the belief that the conflicts are readily enough understood and that (from a complementarist standpoint) the appropriate response to them is to devise means or mechanisms that protect and strengthen, relative to their antagonists, the element in the individuality-plurality relationship that is currently faring least well. If unions are oppressing and stifling the independence and individuality of their members, then adopt right-to-work legislation; if corporations are tyrannizing over their employees, then strengthen unions and regulate the workplace; when domineering or rebarbative individuals obstruct or hold to ransom political parties or neighborhood or avocational associations, then adopt membership requirements and procedures such as cloture rules and majority voting. And so forth.

Let us assume that there are societies whose understandings and practices are for the most part consonant with, and hence provide evidence supportive of, the complementarist view of the individuality-plurality relationship. If we also assume that these societies endorse some version of that view as against uncompromising forms of prescriptive holism or individualism, it will follow that in them the bulk of the work of adjusting relationships and managing conflicts will be done by local fine-tuning of the kinds I have mentioned. To these highly pragmatic activities, moreover, general theorizing concerning individuality and plurality is unlikely to make more than a modest contribution.

Something like this stance, including a certain element of complacency about practice that is not infrequently associated with doubts about the value of general theory, is evident in what I called the American school of political pluralism. Although most versions of this theory allow that American practice is marred by serious imperfections, they present it as basically satisfactory and pretty much able to keep itself in that condition. Aside from any intrinsic intellectual interest that theorizing about matters such as these may have, the perspicuous and orderly account that pluralist theory claims to give of practice is of practical value mainly as an antidote to or prophylactic against false but potentially disruptive or delegitimating doctrines such as elitism, Marxism, and communitarianism.[8]

---

[8]By contrast, group personality and corporativist theory from von Gierke and Figgis to Louis Dumont is animated by the belief that modern thought and practice generally has fallen into an atomistic individualism destructive of group life. For most of these thinkers, the antidote to this vicious tendency is available in premodern or non-Western theory and practice, but diachronic and synchronic studies are necessary to revive awareness of and appreciation for them. Extending the comparison to other views sketched above, these critical diagnoses and prescriptions partly overlap with, partly diverge from, Oakeshott's (and in similar ways Constant's and Berlin's) assessments. Although he has written very little concerning the United States, Oakeshott agrees that the individualism (as opposed to individuality) prominent in the "Modern European State" is antagonistic to genuine plurality as well as to individuality. By contrast with von Gierke, Figgis, and Dumont, however, he regrets this characteristic and the emergence of the "masses," which he thinks go with it, chiefly because it is destructive of individuality.

We could not accuse any of these thinkers of the complacency I attributed (no

Under the assumptions just set forth, this stance has something to recommend it. Certainly there is little reason to think that a general theory of the individuality-plurality relationship could direct practitioners of that relationship in their continuing efforts to maintain complementarity among its components. More generally, it is arguable that something like those assumptions and some version of this stance may be a condition of all instances of, and hence all but the most dismissive or antagonistic theorizing about, individuality and plurality. Recurring to my starting point, if "individual" and "plural" are conceptually interwoven, evidence that in fact the one necessarily or always drives out the other would support the conclusion that both are impossible or impossible to sustain for any extended period. If so, complacent- or defensive-sounding reactions against theoretical challenges to the complementarist view may be grounded in something more worthy than false or happy consciousness, may be the appropriate response of critical and self-critical theorists. Whatever else it should or shouldn't involve, self-critical theorizing about a topic makes itself ridiculous if it is negligent of the conditions of its own continued possibility.

These normative and metatheoretical cautions will require further consideration below. We cannot, however, let such cautions— or the fact that I am conducting this reflection in a society in which complementarism is something of an article of faith—deflect our attention from difficulties that may be deeper and yet less readily manageable than the conflicts considered thus far. If problems of the latter kind remain despite awareness of conflicts on the part of the individuals and groups involved in them, the difficulties that remain to be considered consist (generically) of limitations on awareness and understanding of self and other, limitations that may circumscribe or destroy the possibilities for complementarity (but may thereby advantage individuality or plurality?).

II

The challenges to complementarism that are conceptually most continuous with the more benign of the understandings already

---

doubt unfairly to some among them, certainly to Dahl) to the American pluralists. Although upholding the possibility and promoting the realization of complementarism, in their judgment individuality-plurality relationships in their societies are seriously diminished by conflicts and tensions such as those I am discussing.

considered contend that, in fact and perhaps necessarily, power sufficient to diminish individuality or plurality (or both) always concentrates in the hands of despotic individuals, of an elite or class, of an ethnically, religiously, or linguistically homogeneous group. If individualities and other forms of diversity persist, they are of kinds that are peripheral in that they do not threaten the position of the dominant persons or groups. As before, on this account both the dominating and the dominated know that this is the case, but the latter are unable to resist or supplant the former. However we may assess the most general formulations of these propositions, it is undeniable that they accurately describe much of what goes on in human affairs. Nor is it obvious that the kinds of fine-tuning mentioned above will be effective against such concentrations of power.

Also as before, and leaving aside the possibility, distant at best, that a prescriptive theory might convince those in power voluntarily to relinquish their positions of dominance, general theorizing about individuality and plurality will be of use to the participants in such a circumstance only to the extent that it yields tactical guidance, guidance as to the most efficacious use of their resources in what is perfectly well understood to be a struggle for and against power. The primary need of participants is not for the truth or knowledge, the insight or understanding, that theory claims or aims to provide; it is for the weapons necessary to fight a war. Theories of class, elite, and hegemonic power that purport to provide, by theorizing, remedies for it underestimate the very phenomenon to which they direct our attention.

Perhaps, however, there is another, less directly practical, contribution that theory can make.

Both cooperation and conflict, both mutually gratifying complementarity and the most one-sided domination, presuppose substantial self- and mutual understanding on the part of those who are party to the relationship. This being the case, the very prevalence of cooperation and conflict in human affairs may explain the tendency of otherwise sharply divergent views to take the presence of such understandings for granted. Would attention to this shared but seldom-examined assumption help us to assess the disagreements we are considering?

In the literatures directly pertinent to our topic, such attention is most frequent in thinkers pessimistic about the likelihood of fruitful cooperation and complementarity, inclined to view relationships in their societies as systematically diminishing all or most of the individuals and groups involved in or affected by them. From Jean-Jacques Rousseau to Alexis de Tocqueville and Karl Marx, from Max Weber, Sigmund Freud, and Nietzsche to Erving Goffman and Michel Foucault, we have heard that our institutions and our practices are structured in ways that none among us knowingly or intentionally brought about and few if any of us understand; that our thinking and acting within the confines of these settings and arrangements is suffused and largely controlled by assumptions of which we are at best dimly aware. Some of our most treasured convictions—for example, that our political, economic, and social arrangements were made by us or are subject to remaking by our own decisions and choices, that our beliefs are held and our actions taken for good reasons, that we are sometimes constant, sometimes wavering in our judgments, sometimes agree, sometimes disagree with one another but that we understand ourselves and one another—are for the most part illusory. And not far below the surface of our societies, just beneath the superficial or even epiphenomenal diversities that some of us celebrate and others of us lament, there is a dreary uniformity that is all the more deadening because it is unrealized by us.

From this latter perspective the pervasiveness of complementarism—in liberalism and elsewhere—has to be regarded as a symptom of one of the worst diseases that afflict our thinking. And the least treatable form of that disease is complacency and the dismissive attitude toward theorizing commonly associated with it. If or to the extent that our condition is as these radical critics portray it, complacency is the last thing to which we are entitled, and theorizing concerning the deepest of our assumptions about individuality and plurality is among our most urgent needs.[9]

III

The least disputable of the limitations on our self- and mutual understandings concern our capacities to sustain awareness of any-

[9]We might say that the radical critics I mentioned are united in rejecting G. W. F. Hegel's claim—the quintessential claim of the quintessential complementarist—that theorizing is now unnecessary because Reason has already triumphed within and among ourselves and our practices.

thing approaching the full range of the assumptions and beliefs that inform our judgments and intentions and hence the actions we take. However we may have arrived at the various items making up our array of beliefs, in altering that array and in drawing on it to form and act on intentions, we necessarily leave unexamined many of the beliefs of which it consists. Let us consider anew and attempt to follow out the leads given by a salient example of this view.

"When we first begin to *believe* anything, what we believe is not a single proposition, it is a whole system of propositions. (Light dawns gradually over the whole.)" "It is not single axioms that strike me as obvious, it is a system in which consequences and premises give one another *mutual* support." "All testing, all confirmation and disconfirmation of a hypothesis takes place already within a system. And this system is not a more or less arbitrary and doubtful point of departure for all our arguments . . . [it is] the element in which arguments have their life" (Wittgenstein, *On Certainty*, 141, 142, 105).

If we are tempted to read these passages as constituting a manifesto of philosophical holism, perhaps of some species of social or political organicism or corporativism, we must realize that they are part of a larger view according to which the systemic character of our believing and thinking, the very quality that gives them life and strength, also diminishes our capacity to assess and adjust, reconsider and revamp, indeed to summon to our own and to one another's awareness, many of the elements of which the system has at any time come to consist. "It may be . . . that *all enquiry on our part* is set so as to exempt certain propositions from doubt, if they are ever formulated." Many of our beliefs "lie apart from the route travelled by inquiry." "Much seems to be fixed, and it is removed from the traffic. It is so to speak shunted unto an unused siding. Now it gives our way of looking at things, and our researches, their form. Perhaps it was once disputed. But perhaps, for unthinkable ages, it has belonged to the *scaffolding* of our thoughts" (88, 211–12). "If the true is what is grounded, then the ground is not *true*, nor yet false." "The difficulty is to realize the groundlessness of our believing" (205, 166).

By comparison with a number of the other formulations that (from at least Immanuel Kant forward) are responsible for the wide influence of views of this kind, in the altered perspective in which we are now viewing it, Wittgenstein's version might be called moderate

Individuality, Plurality, and Liberalism

in character. On his account, the "unthought" may, here and now, be psychologically or even ontologically inaccessible to us, but it is not logically or epistemologically before or beyond our thinking. Although all certainty and all doubt, all reflection and judgment, presuppose that some beliefs "stand fast" (115, 160, 163, 156) as we form and act on, assess and revise others, it is not impossible that new circumstances will prompt us to question those that had previously gone unconsidered—even if for "unthinkable ages."[10]

Nor is Wittgenstein's argument a skepticism in the dogmatic form of a denial of our capacity to arrive at warranted beliefs, beliefs that pass the tests or satisfy the criteria appropriate to deciding whether to hold them. The passages I have been quoting, rather, are part of an argument that certitude concerning our beliefs, while never warranted ("grounded") in the supposititious, superstrong sense of being incorrigible or invulnerable to the very possibility of cogent questioning or dispute, is sometimes adequately warranted, sometimes not. Indeed they are part of an argument that has been styled complacent or conservative because of its affirmation that we often do know how to go on, that the combination of our native capacities and the languages, practices, and institutions that have developed among us enables (of course it does not guarantee) mutual intelligibility, successful attempts at action, and so on. Nor is there any reason to doubt that this going on can and does include forming, revising, and acting on conceptions of oneself and of others, noticing and responding to similarities and differences, entering into agreements and disagreements, and generally engaging in the kinds of thinking and acting of which human relationships commonly consist. In these respects, and despite the qualifications we have already encountered and will consider in more detail, Wittgenstein's investigations not only support the possibility of complementarism but identify ways in which individualities and pluralities stimulate and support one another (compare notes 1 and 2 supra, this chapter). We might go further and say that his reflections promote the

[10]In order to write a check and subtract the amount on the ledger I must "hold constant" the system of banking, of numbers, of addition and subtraction, I must assume the durability of paper and of writing in ink, the postal system and everything that it depends on, and so forth through a very long list. But there are those who reflect about and otherwise attend to these components of actions such as mine, and even the familiar act of writing a check *might* prompt me to join their company.

stance toward the possibility of complementarism that I entertained at the end of Section II of this chapter.

The charge of complacency is badly misdirected if it accuses Wittgenstein of anything like the generally approving and optimistic attitudes toward extant political, social, and moral practice that I attributed to the American pluralists. Nothing in Wittgenstein's work suggests that individuals or groups are or will be gratified by the conceptions they form of themselves and others, by the character of the relationships that develop among them, by the outcomes of their actions and attempts at action. The characteristics that Wittgenstein identifies as sometimes enabling self-understanding and mutual intelligibility are consistent with relentless tyranny and intractable conflict, with extensive, intensive, and fruitful cooperation, with substantial dispersion and mutual indifference.[11]

It is true that much of Wittgenstein's later work is directed against philosophical doctrines that (wittingly or otherwise) have induced disillusionment and even despair in some quarters by insisting on criteria of "meaning" and "truth," "knowledge" and "understanding," "validity" and "justification," that cannot be satisfied. In dissolving these misconceived requirements, he clearly intends to provide reassurance against the most unqualified and unnerving forms of skepticism, solipsism, and nihilism, and he may bolster confidence in the ordinary procedures, the homely everyday standards, that those requirements are intended to discredit and to replace. No one closely acquainted with Wittgenstein's zigzag, maddeningly complex writings, with his often immediate problematizing of the very notions on which he himself has just relied, could believe that it was any part of his intention to engender generalized complacency in his readers. Nevertheless, a main reason for the kind of theorizing that Wittgenstein called *philosophical* (or at least what Wittgenstein himself identified as a main impetus to his own "philosophical investigations") is such facts as the following: "We do not *command* a clear view of our use of our words." The "aspects of things that are most important for us are hidden because of their simplicity and familiarity. (One is unable to notice something—

---

[11]Familiarity with the substantial and growing biographical materials available concerning Wittgenstein will hardly encourage the thought that he was approving of or optimistic concerning the state of political, social, or moral affairs in his own time. Aside, however, from brief remarks such as his characterization of his times as "in . . . darkness" (*Philosophical Investigations*, Preface), Wittgenstein's philosophical works largely avoid these topics and issues.

because it is always before one's eyes.) We fail to be struck by what, once seen, is most striking and powerful" (*Philosophical Investigations*, I, 122, 129). We become "entangled in our own rules" and fall into the kinds of contradictions that lead us to say such things as "I didn't mean it like that." "The civil status of a contradiction, or its status in civil life: there is the philosophical problem" (I, 125). Accordingly, a stated objective of his philosophizing is to "assemble reminders" of what we are ignoring or have overlooked or forgotten and thereby to provide a kind of "therapy" that can "unt[y the] knots in our thinking."[12] Whatever Wittgenstein's estimation of the probability of success in these activities, his evident belief that they are possible qualifies his views concerning the limitations on our thinking and acting. This and related qualifications that will be considered below constitute a major dimension of his thinking, a dimension that, again (and by contrast with the other investigators of the "unthought" that I gestured toward above?), affirms the *possibility* of complementarity and complementarism.

Close attention to the actual uses of our words and the standards of intelligibility and understanding actually employed in our practices and activities, then, can dissolve puzzles and paradoxes, enhance confidence, and diminish tendencies to angst. But it may also heighten awareness of ways in which our languages and practices (along with and in part due to the ways in which they are serviceable for us) are incomplete and indeterminate, opalescent, opaque and occluded, are of the ambiguous, the dissonant, and the incomprehensible in our experiences of ourselves and others. In short, Wittgenstein's analyses of the conditions necessary to the self- and mutual intelligibility that are (I am thus far assuming) presupposed by individuality and plurality can also be read as identifying circumstances under which those conditions are not and perhaps cannot be more than partially satisfied.

We have already seen that for Wittgenstein many of our most firmly fixed beliefs (whether held individually or, more frequently, shared more or less widely) are obscured from our view by the further beliefs for which they provide the "ungrounded grounds." Insofar as these most firmly fixed elements of thought include our

[12]Ludwig Wittgenstein, *Zettel*, ed. G. F. M. Anscombe and G. H. Von Wright, trans. G. E. M. Anscombe. (Oxford: Basil Blackwell, 1967) 452. For purposes of this discussion I deliberately de-emphasize Wittgenstein's view that much of his philosophical work was occasioned by the confusions generated by previous philosophers. I assess this aspect of his view in *Toward a Liberalism*, esp. chap. 1.

beliefs about the similarities and differences between ourselves and others, we comprehend the relationships and interactions that those beliefs inform primarily to the extent that we have a grasp of the overall system or web or gestalt of beliefs of which they form a part. It is difficult and in various circumstances impossible for us to break into, as it were, the system so as to attend to its various parts. To this extent, the results of Wittgenstein's investigations can be said to circumscribe the possibilities for complementarity and complementarism.

(Do his reflections therefore promote a more skeptical stance toward the possibilities for individuality, plurality, or both? If liberalism presupposes these possibilities, do his reflections cast doubt on its tenability? Or is it possible that the very circumscriptions and qualifications that he identifies advantage individuality and plurality? Do they give us reason to qualify the assumptions with which I began and the connected view that both individualities and pluralities flourish best when there is complementarity among and between them? Are they consonant with and supportive of those differentiating and perhaps mutually isolating agent-relative and voluntarist elements that some liberal thinkers have taken from theology and philosophy and that I forward below? No on the first two counts, Yes on the others.)

"Our language forms an enormous system. And *only* within *this* system has a particular bit the value we give it" (*On Certainty*, 410, emphasis added). "'I set the brake up by connecting up rod and lever.'—Yes, given the whole of the rest of the mechanism. *Only* in conjunction with that is it a brake-lever, and separated from its support it is not even a lever; it may be anything, or nothing" (*Philosophical Investigations*, I, 6, emphasis added). Accepting, that is, thinking and acting within, these systems or mechanisms, games, gestalts, or webs is not a defect or failure. "And that something stands fast for me is not grounded in my stupidity or credulity," not "hastiness or superficiality," not something done "out of thoughtlessness" (*On Certainty*, 235, 358, 657). "But it isn't that the situation is like this: We just *can't* investigate everything, and for that reason we are forced to rest content with assumption. If I want the door to turn, the hinges must stay put" (343).[13]

[13]"My *life* consists in my being content to accept many things" (*On Certainty*, 344). "What has to be accepted, the given, is—so one could say—forms of life" (*Philosophical Investigations*, II, xi, p. 226).

Assuming for the moment that the perimeters of such entities or units are clearly delineated (an assumption that will have to be qualified below), these pronouncements carry implications and consequences of some moment for the concerns of this essay. Consider: "If someone wanted to arouse doubts in me and spoke like this: here your memory is deceiving you, there you've been taken in, there again you have not been thorough enough in satisfying yourself, etc., and if I did not allow myself to be shaken but kept to my certainty—then my doing so cannot be wrong, even if only because this is just what defines a game." Faced with such challenges, indeed, "I find it quite correct for someone to say 'Rubbish!' and so brush aside the attempt to confuse him with doubts at bedrock." Equally, however, "I hold it to be incorrect if he seeks to defend himself (using, e.g., the words 'I know')" (497, 498).

Suppose that "we" who are "guided . . . by the propositions of physics" meet a people who "instead of a physicist . . . consult an oracle. (And for that we consider them primitive.) Is it wrong for them to consult an oracle and be guided by it?—If we call this 'wrong' aren't we using our language-game as a base from which to *combat* theirs?" Or yet closer to home:

> But what men consider reasonable or unreasonable alters. At certain periods men find reasonable what at other periods they found unreasonable. And vice versa.
>
> But is there no objective character here?
>
> *Very* intelligent and well-educated people believe in the story of creation in the Bible, while others hold it as proven false, and the grounds of the latter are well known to the former. (336)[14]

Of course most senses of "combat" presuppose some degree of mutual understanding, some overlap or consilience among the language-games of the combatants. Thus if combat is possible, couldn't we also give our adversaries reasons for our views? Indeed, "wouldn't I give him *reasons*? Certainly; but how far do they go? At the end of reasons comes *persuasion*. (Think what happens when

---

[14]Very intelligent and well-educated people believe in liberalism, socialism, and communitarianism, in supply-side economics, conspiracy theories of the assassination of John F. Kennedy, the right to abortion on demand, the deterrent effect of the death penalty, the harmfulness of eating red meats, the efficacy of psychoanalysis, while others hold these beliefs to be proven false, and the grounds of the latter beliefs are well known to those who hold the former ones.

missionaries convert natives.)"[15] And as we may well be reminded by the example of missionaries, "where two principles really do meet which cannot be reconciled with one another" by reason, persuasion, or even combat, "then each man declares the other a fool and a heretic" (609, 612, 611)—and acts on that declaration.

Language-games, forms of life, and the various less encompassing "systems" in which thought and action occur enable mutual understanding and various modes of cooperation and conflict among those party to them. In the setting of the shared beliefs, rules, and conventions that constitute such a system, we sometimes even "say of some people that they are transparent to us." The very features of language-games that enable such relationships and interactions, however, also diminish or disable these possibilities between or across the boundaries of the games. "It is, however, important as regards this observation [of transparency] that one human being can be a complete enigma to another. We learn this when we come into a strange country with entirely strange traditions; and, what is more, even given a mastery of the country's language. We do not *understand* the people. (And not because of not knowing what they are saying to themselves.) We cannot find our feet with them" (*Philosophical Investigations*, II, xi, p. 223).

Nor are the experiences of opacity, occlusion, and even stark incomprehensibility restricted to encounters with distant or otherwise unfamiliar traditions and forms of life. "I believe that every human being has two human parents; but Catholics believe that Jesus only had a human mother. . . . Catholics believe as well that in certain circumstances a wafer completely changes its nature, and at the same time that all evidence proves the contrary. And so if [G. E.] Moore said 'I know that this is wine and not blood' Catholics would contradict him" (*On Certainty*, 239).[16]

Do the "Wittgenstein" and the "Moore" of this passage understand the "Catholics" that figure in it? The former two, we can presume, have frequently encountered and very likely have had explained to them not only these particular beliefs but the larger set

[15]Thinking the thought that Wittgenstein here recommends might be assisted by attention to works such as Tzvetan Todorov's *The Conquest of America* (New York: Colophon-Harper & Row, 1984).

[16]As through much of *On Certainty*, Wittgenstein's reference to Moore is primarily to the latter's "In Defence of Common Sense," chap. 2, in G. E. Moore, *Philosophical Papers* (London: George Allen and Unwin, 1959).

of tenets of which the doctrines of immaculate conception and transubstantiation are parts (we can presume this because the beliefs are, and for a long time have been, prominent in the traditions and culture in which "Wittgenstein" and "Moore" had their upbringing and lived their lives). That set of beliefs, we can also presume, includes numerous items that "Wittgenstein" and "Moore," whether or not they regard them as religious beliefs, fully accept (for example, the set of beliefs enunciated by Moore in the paper cited in note 16). By these far-from-negligible criteria the answer to my question is yes. As Wittgenstein says in a related context: "In one sense, I understand all he says—the English words 'God', 'separate' etc. I understand. I could say: 'I don't believe in this', and this would be true, meaning I haven't got these thoughts or anything that hangs together with them."[17]

Yet these particular beliefs of the "Catholics" seem to contradict beliefs about which "Wittgenstein" and "Moore" are entirely certain; indeed, they seem to contradict beliefs that are among the "grounds" of much else that "Wittgenstein" and "Moore" believe (240). On this view, even if "Wittgenstein" and "Moore" understand what we might call the propositional content of the beliefs of the "Catholics," they could understand how the "Catholics" *could* accept those beliefs only if they gave up much of what they themselves now believe, only if they were "converted" to the system of beliefs that the "Catholics" accept and think within.

There are numerous cases in which I not only do stand firm against the beliefs of others—including others in the community or communities of which I am part and with which I identify—but am justified in doing so in that everything in my system of beliefs supports—no, *requires* my doing so.[18] Am I then also justified in claiming that I understand the views I am rejecting? The sentence that completes the paragraph just quoted reads: "But not that I could contradict the thing"; and Wittgenstein then considers the

---

[17]Ludwig Wittgenstein, *Lectures and Conversations on Aesthetics, Psychology, and Religious Belief*, ed. Cyril Barrett (Berkeley: University of California Press, 1967), p. 55. See the editor's preface for the cautions necessary in relying on the materials presented in this book.

[18]Cf. *On Certainty*, 667. It is perhaps worth underlining that these of Wittgenstein's discussions are askew of much of the debate currently conducted in terms of dichotomies such as holism-atomism, communitarianism-individualism, embodied-disembodied or encumbered-unencumbered selves.

objection " 'Well, if you can't contradict him, that means you don't understand him. If you did understand him, then you might.' " To which he responds: "That again is Greek to me. My normal technique of language leaves me. I don't know whether to say they understand one another or not" (*Lectures and Conversations*, p. 55).

Let us pause to consider whether we have reached points on which there is convergence between these parts of Wittgenstein's thinking and views concerning individuality and plurality that have for some time been widely accepted in numerous modern Western societies and that are regarded by many as essential to any form of liberalism. Religious beliefs and believing, it is widely held, are categorially different from beliefs and believing of other kinds. As it is sometimes put, religion is at least partly a matter of faith or deep conviction, not of knowledge or even of belief in the ordinary sense of a view I hold because of evidence or argumentation and that is more or less readily susceptible to revision or rejection. This is one of a number of reasons why attempts to promote or to impose uniformity of religious belief and practice fail to achieve their objectives as they engender intractable conflict and inflict grievous harms. And for many it is for the same reasons that there must be toleration of a wide diversity of religious beliefs and practices. In this regard, plurality and perhaps individuality are, in a deeper-than-usual sense of the expression, faute de mieux.

It is a further point—further both to the commitment to toleration that I cautiously attributed to modern Western societies and to the passages I have quoted from Wittgenstein—to claim that proponents of differing religious beliefs often do not understand one another. Beginning with the former, it is widely thought that tolerance presupposes understanding sufficient for disapproval as distinct from bare recognition of difference or incompatibility.[19] Just as, on this view, we cannot "tolerate" that which we think good or right, neither can we be tolerant (or intolerant) of that about which we are unable to form a judgment or make an assessment. Is this insistently judgmental, even censorious, character of our thinking about toleration partly responsible for the grudging, regretful, even sour quality often characteristic of relations marked by tolerance? If

[19]For critical discussion of this view, see Joseph Raz, *The Morality of Freedom* (Oxford: The Clarendon Press, 1986), esp. chap. 15.

so, what would be the practical consequences of a more radical view (whether or not it is Wittgenstein's) according to which often or even for the most part we have no more than partial understandings of religious confessions other than our own? Would such a view engender or permit a stance more supportive of religious diversity than mere tolerance of it? A more generous and in that sense a more liberal doctrine of religious freedom?[20] Or would recognition of the limitations on our understandings engender anxieties so unnerving as to make mutual tolerance—hardly to be despised—impossible for us?

It is clear that Wittgenstein regarded religious beliefs and believing (or beliefs and believing that are genuinely religious, as we should perhaps say) as marked by certain characteristic features. For example, in religious matters "you don't get . . . the form of controversy where one person is *sure* of the thing, and the other says: 'Well, possibly'." "There hasn't been opposed to those who believe in Resurrection those who say 'Well, possibly'." "This is partly why one would be reluctant to say: 'These people rigorously hold the opinion (or view) that there is a Last Judgement.' 'Opinion' sounds queer." "It is for this reason that different words are used: 'dogma', 'faith'." "We don't talk about hypothesis, or about high probability. Nor about knowing." "In a religious discourse we use such expressions as: 'I believe that so and so will happen,' and use them differently to the way in which we use them in science" (*Lectures and Conversations*, pp. 56–57). Sometimes a person gives "up a practice when he has seen that something on which it depended is an error, but . . . this is not how it is in connection with the religious practices of a people and what we have here is *not* an error."[21]

These passages affirm an assumption tacitly at work in the discussion thus far, namely, that we sometimes understand or misunderstand religious thinking and acting in the sense that we identify or misidentify them *as religious*. Moreover, in understanding that

20Cf. José Ortega y Gasset: "Liberalism . . . is the supreme form of generosity; it is the right by which the majority concedes to minorities and hence it is the noblest cry that has ever resounded in this planet." Regrettably, this "cry" is now largely stifled. "The mass . . . does not wish to share life with those who are not of it. It has a deadly hatred of all that is not itself" (*The Revolt of the Masses* [New York: W. W. Norton 1932], pp. 83–84).
21Ludwig Wittgenstein, *Remarks on Frazer's "The Golden Bough,"* quoted in Peter Winch, *Trying to Make Sense* (Oxford: Basil Blackwell, 1987), p. 109.

religious discourse is usually characterized by a certain configuration of characteristics and the absence of a number of others that are typical of science, mathematics, and so on, we do more than classify or categorize. Identifying thoughts and actions as religious is integral to engaging with and otherwise relating to them. Our identifications carry with them expectations and criteria of judgment that inform and guide us as we "go on" with our religious (and our antireligious) activities.

Let us combine this claim with remarks considered earlier in which Wittgenstein says that we often understand many of the individual words and propositions that occur in religions that we do not accept, and perhaps understand yet more of the discourse of religions that we accept wholly or in part. Bringing these elements together has the effect of replacing the (philosopher's?) dichotomy "understand/don't understand" with a diverse and unstable array of possibilities that includes understanding in some respects but not others, various combinations of understanding and misunderstanding, not knowing whether we understand, and mixtures of certainty and uncertainty as to whether the notions "understanding" and "misunderstanding" have any application in the circumstances in which we find ourselves. My apparently univocal question Do "Moore" and "Wittgenstein" understand the "Catholics"? masks many different questions, some of which make little or no sense; when unpacked, my "question" has many different answers or none. (Hence the "answers" have a diversity of implications for judgment and action vis-à-vis religion.)

Wittgenstein effects this and like substitutions throughout the entire domain of believing and doubting, judging and assessing, agreeing and disagreeing. Contrary to the assumption that I have been making, Wittgenstein's "unit of analysis" concepts—system, culture, form of life, language-game, and practice—do not differentiate sharply distinct domains of thought and action. Perhaps because "God" and the other concepts characteristic of religious discourse "are among the earliest learnt" (*Lectures and Conversations*, p. 59), Wittgenstein is confident that we are, or at any rate often are, able to recognize and relate to religious beliefs and practices. Nevertheless, "different connections would make [a set of statements] into religious beliefs, and there can easily be imagined transitions where we wouldn't know for our life whether to call them religious beliefs or scientific beliefs" (p. 58). (Creation science?) But this situation, so far from being unique to or even distinctive of religion, is characteristic of all our language-games.[22] Like the concept of game from which it might be viewed as a projection, "language-game" itself (and hence religion, logic, politics and all other language-games) is a family-resemblance term, one that gathers a number of phenomena with recognizable and for some purposes salient similarities but no single common element or set of elements that is the necessary and sufficient condition for its correct use. The absence of such a commonality, and of the univocality and certitude that some philosophers who hanker for commonality believe it would make possible, is not a defect, does not disable our ordinary, routine, unhesitating uses of the concept.[23] But it does mean that sometimes we will "not know for our life" whether to call something a language-game, a game, a religious or scientific belief, *and so on* (*Philosophical Investigations*, I, 65ff).

In various combinations and intensities, such mixtures of luminosity, transparency, and fluency with opacity, hesitation, and doubt obtain through the entire inventory of the concepts we have, have had, and might come to have, through all of the thinking and acting that we do in and with these concepts. Not only is it "a matter of course for me to call this colour 'blue' " but "there is in general complete agreement in the judgments of colours made by those who have been diagnosed normal [e.g., not color blind]" (I, 238; II, xi, p. 227). But equally, any number of considerations can be assembled to "show the indeterminateness in the concept of colour or again in that of sameness of colour."[24] "Just try—in a real case—to doubt

---

[22]Of the Wittgensteinian categories, "language-game" is perhaps the most appropriate for thinking about religion in modern Western societies. One might use the usually more encompassing "form of life" in thinking about, say, medieval European Christianity or Islam in contemporary Iran. But the observations that follow apply to all of the "unit of analysis" concepts that Wittgenstein employs.

For further and wider discussion of religion and its relationships with "other" modes of thinking, see infra, Part Two, Sections II and V.

[23]"The more narrowly we examine actual language, the sharper becomes the conflict between it and our requirement [i.e., the connected requirements of commonality, univocality, etc.]. (For the crystalline purity of logic was, of course, not a *result of investigation*: it was a requirement.) The conflict becomes intolerable; the requirement is now in danger of becoming empty.—We have got on to slippery ice where there is no friction and so in a certain sense the conditions are ideal, but also, just because of that, we are unable to walk. We want to walk: so we need *friction*. Back to the rough ground!" (*Philosophical Investigations*, I, 107).

[24]Ludwig Wittgenstein, *Remarks on Colour*, ed. G. E. M. Anscombe, trans. Linda L. McArister and Margarete Schättle. (Berkeley: University of California Press, 1978) I, 17. This work assembles a large array of considerations that support the generalization I quote above.

someone else's fear or pain" (*Philosophical Investigations*, I, 303; cf. I, 391). But equally: "I am sure, *sure*, that he is not pretending; but some third person is not. Can I always convince him? And if not is there some mistake in his reasoning or observations? 'You're all at sea!'— we say this when someone doubts what we recognize as clearly genuine—but we cannot prove anything" (II, xi, p. 227).

> It is certainly possible to be convinced by evidence that someone is in such-and-such state of mind, that, for instance, he is not pretending. But 'evidence' here includes 'imponderable' evidence. . . .
> Imponderable evidence includes subtleties of glance, of gesture, of tone.
> I may recognize a genuine loving look, distinguish it from a pretended one (and here there can, of course, be a 'ponderable' confirmation of my judgment). But I may be quite incapable of describing the difference. And this not because the languages I know have no words for it. For why not introduce new words?—If I were a very talented painter I might conceivably represent the genuine and the simulated glance in pictures." (II, xi, p. 228)

And so on.

There is no doubt that Wittgenstein had an abiding interest in religion and its place in our forms of life. Along with reflecting about its distinctive characteristics, however, in the passages considered above he is using religious examples to call attention to characteristics that obtain in respect to *all* knowing and believing, *all* thinking and acting, characteristics that sometimes enable and enrich, sometimes circumscribe and prevent, mutual understanding and the kinds of interaction that it makes possible. On his readings of the forms of life, language-games, and practices with which his investigations were concerned, what I (but not Wittgenstein) have called the conditions of complementarity are sometimes satisfied, sometimes not; most often they are satisfied in some respects, not satisfied in others. If we want to find out where, when, and to what extent they are satisfied, his advice, succinct in the giving, arduous in the following, is "don't think, but look!" (I, 66).

IV

Let us recall in somewhat enlarged terms some of the issues and disagreements that prompted us to examine Wittgenstein's investigations. Here are some of the more striking claims advanced by those who profess to have "looked" at individuality, plurality, and related matters in modern Western societies. (1) Whether forced or otherwise, the members of these societies are compressed or are congealing into a mass of unthinking look-alikes among whom individuality and plurality are no more than marginal possibilities. There are many shared beliefs and values, numerous and insistently enforced conventions, norms, and expectations, but these work against, not for, plurality and especially individuality. (Tocqueville, Thoreau, William James, Nietzsche, Weber, Ortega y Gasset, Arendt, Goffman, Oakeshott.) (2) These societies have dispersed or are steadily fractionating into an atomized and anomic array of individuals and insular groups among whom mutual understanding is for the most part impossible. Individualism and other forms of idiosyncrasy and parochialism are rampant, but they breed frustration and despair, suspicion and antagonism, not fulfillment, mutual appreciation, or cooperation. (Emile Durkheim, Dumont, Leo Strauss, contemporary communitarians such as Charles Taylor, Robert Nisbet, Ivan Illych, Alasdair MacIntyre.) (3) Some of these societies present a gratifying mix of commonality, individuality, and plurality, which is, or with relatively modest modifications could become, the basis for a fruitful combination of cooperation and competition. (American pluralists, Marx in his more optimistic moments, much liberalism from John Stuart Mill, if not from John Locke, to Rawls and Richard Rorty.)

These sustained, self-consciously developed accounts are reflections of beliefs that present themselves, in various combinations, in the views of those who "look" in the sense (perhaps closer to the one Wittgenstein had in mind) of "keeping their eyes open" as they go about the activities of every day. (1) As members of these societies we are constrained and oppressed by an intrusive state and its bureaucracy, by the tyranny of the majority, of the rich or the poor, of the multinational corporations or the military-industrial complex, the media, the dominant gender or race, or of some other more covert or for other reasons less readily identifiable hegemon (2) Crime, substance abuse, and many other forms of deviance and degradation are rampant; laxity and self-indulgence are manifest in the refusal of parents to parent, of teachers to teach, of workers to work and managements to manage, of governments to govern with an eye to anything more than the present moment or the preservation of their power. (3) These societies are basically satisfactory;

certainly they are to be preferred to all the historical and contemporaneous alternatives.

Wittgenstein neither arbitrates among these sweeping generalizations-cum-evaluations nor attempts to settle the numerous more delimited points of disagreement and dispute out of which grand controversies of these kinds arise. His investigations direct our attention to the features of our experience that produce and sustain these divergent accounts and assessments of it, but the suppositions behind his advice to look, not think, strongly suggest that resolving the disagreements falls less to philosophers or theorists than to all of us as participants in social and political life.

Should it be among our objectives to resolve them? Or are there respects in which individuality, plurality, or both are protected or otherwise advantaged by these diversities and conflicts? Does (would) concern for individuality and plurality press us, as liberals or otherwise, to be "critical" as "far down" and as "far out" as is possible for us, down or out far enough to find or create greater common ground?

From Socrates's animadversions concerning the unexamined life through Hegel's celebration of Reason to Jürgen Habermas's promotion of undistorted communication, much in our tradition returns affirmative answers to these questions. Self- and mutual understanding—what Charles Taylor thinks of as clairvoyance concerning our beliefs and values and their harmony or disharmony with both our deepest or truest selves and with the norms, mores, and aspirations of our society and our culture is or should be our ideal.[25] We should regard opacity and occlusion in the same ways that we look on ignorance and irrationality, that is, as defects to be remedied where possible, deficiencies that should be regretted where they cannot be eliminated.

Although hardly characteristic of Wittgenstein himself, these aspirations are not generally, certainly not categorically, disqualified or discredited by his investigations. However, along with his assiduous efforts to clarify this, that, and the next of our confusions, he denies that the unthought in our thinking prevents us from "going on," suggests that the groundlessness of our believing, the indeter-

---

[25]Charles Taylor, *Hegel and Modern Society* (London: Cambridge University Press, 1976), esp. pp. 160ff., and *Philosophical Papers*, 2 vols. (London: Cambridge University Press, 1986), vol. 1, esp. essays 1, 2, and 4; vol 2, esp. essays 5, 7, and 8.

minacy in our rules, the often enigmatic character of others and indeed of our selves are sometimes essential to our doing so.

Should we go further than he did and say that limitations on our self- and our mutual understandings provide protections for and otherwise enhance individuality and plurality? As to the first point, there is indeed reason to think that the hinges that are most likely to stay put so that I or we can act (and therefore possibly enact and reenact myself or ourselves) are those of which I am unaware or aware that I *must* let stand as they are if the door of action is going to turn.[26] On the second and yet more provocative point, if you (they) do not understand me (us), or do not know whether you understand me or not, your ability to enter into my affairs, certainly your capacity to do so skillfully and especially insidiously, is diminished. Argumentation, persuasion, command and other forms of authoritative direction, and even coercion presuppose some degree of mutual understanding; even successful manipulation requires understanding on the part of the manipulator, *mis*understanding on the part of the manipulated. Of course territorial and other boundaries, property and other rights, law, morality, politics, and the conventions of polite conduct all afford protections—among other

[26]The first of these formulations ("unaware") is close to Oakeshott's in *Rationalism in Politics* and to more general doctrines about the role of "prejudice" in thought and action from Edmund Burke to Hans Georg Gadamer. The second ("aware that I *must* let stand") has many affinities with Oakeshott's treatment (*On Human Conduct*, Essay I) of the distinction between the theorist whose task is constantly to interrogate the presuppositions of her understandings and who is thereby disabled from action and the practitioner who treats the identifications and understandings of which her thinking now consists as diagnoses and prescriptions, that is, as invitations to action rather than to further theorizing. The latter also resembles Hannah Arendt's concern that the injunction "stop and think" stills the impulse to action (see esp. *The Life of the Mind*, 2 vols. [New York: Harcourt, Brace, Jovanovich, 1978], vol. 1). On all of these doctrines, thinking in the sense of unremitting questioning of the beliefs and understandings that we have thus far acquired is a siren's song to which we often must—willfully—close our ears if the life of action is to continue. Is this why these thinkers are widely regarded as antiliberal and even illiberal? Can liberalism accommodate these views? Can it do so to a yet greater extent than I have suggested some versions of it have already done so?

It is striking that contemporary proponents of self- and mutual clairvoyance and rationality in ethics such as Charles Taylor and Alasdair MacIntyre also promote community and solidarity, values previously forwarded by conservative thinkers such as Edmund Burke, Joseph de Maistre, and François Chateaubriand, who thought they could be sustained only where the ultimately mysterious character of the human condition was not only accepted but cherished.

things they afford—against these influences and intrusions. But these arrangements and institutions, in addition to being variable in their efficacy and making substantial demands on the resources of those they are intended to protect, can be efficacious only to the extent that they themselves restrict and indeed intrude. By contrast, when we stand to one another's beliefs as Wittgenstein described his (?) relation to certain of the beliefs of Catholics, then we are at a loss regarding the particulars of those beliefs and hence regarding one another insofar as we hold and act on them. We identify the beliefs as such, and one another as holders of beliefs, on the basis of aspects of one another that we do understand, and we can act with and against one another in these respects. But because the beliefs in question do not mesh, join, or even meet, we can act neither with nor against one another in respect to them.

Let us briefly consider some yet headier and perhaps more disconcerting possibilities that have been explored and even promoted by thinkers far more explicit than Wittgenstein in their desire to protect and enhance plurality and especially individuality. In seeking an assured basis for that species of individuality that they called "tranquillity" (*ataraxia*), the Pyrrhonians among both ancient and early modern skeptics (Sextus Empiricus, Michel de Montaigne, Pierre Bayle, David Hume) found inadequate (or overly demanding of efforts and other resources to maintain) the cultivated indifference to others promoted by much Stoicism and (later) by reclusives and misanthropes such as Rousseau (in some among his many moods!) and Thoreau. The skeptics relied, rather, on the protections provided by the impossibility of knowing the truth or falsity of what they and others believed. Even if we can understand one another's beliefs in the senses that Wittgenstein says he can understand the beliefs of the Catholics, recognition of the impossibility of determining the truth or falsity of those beliefs eliminates the only (as it were) objective or even fully exchangeable justifications for acting on our own and against others' beliefs. Sextus, Montaigne, and Hume among others, and Hobbes in respect to religious beliefs, promoted these views in the hope of stilling or calming the destructive dogmatisms, enthusiasms, and fanaticisms generated by convictions of the truth of my or our views, the falsity of yours.[27] More

[27]Because they do not discredit my *belief* that my views are superior to yours (or, in Hobbes's case, the propriety of the sovereign establishing and requiring public acceptance of a single religious—and in some respects moral—view), as thus far

important, they and later writers influenced by them let their skeptical dispositions—and their reasons for valorizing what they hoped would be the consequences of wide cultivation of like dispositions—extend from the content of our beliefs to our believing itself and thereby to that whole range of our understandings of one another that are concerned with our believing and our acting on our beliefs. Rejecting the view that we hold our beliefs because of something apart from us and in principle accessible to all of us, that is, because of properties of the subjects or objects of our beliefs (e.g., the properties that make the beliefs true), they explained the phenomenon of believing in terms of attributes of those who hold beliefs. They and their successors in this regard then summoned for this explanatory purpose attributes to which, on their view, persons other than those holding the beliefs have restricted access and sometimes no access, for example, the individual person's passions or desires, or her unconscious; the traditions, conventions, language, and so forth, of the community or group; the "standpoint" or "consciousness" of the class or caste.

In the first form discussed, acceptance of a skeptical outlook largely deprives others of the possibility of refuting my beliefs and hence of the *justifications* for actions vis-à-vis me that may be provided by evidence or argumentation showing that my beliefs are false. On the extension of skepticism just outlined, you are also unable or little able to understand why I hold my beliefs, how I came to hold them. It follows that the *possibility* of your acting skillfully and efficaciously to alter my beliefs is diminished, if not eliminated. Your actions or movements may, in fact, affect my beliefs and those of my actions informed by those beliefs, but they do so more by chance than by your design.

These limitations on the very possibility of mutual access and influence (as distinct, again, from limitations deliberately created and sustained by me or by us) were greatly extended by later writers, some of whom are successors to earlier skepticisms. One particularly far-reaching extension (which ended if it did not begin

---

described these arguments could be said to promote toleration of the type that involves disapproval of the beliefs or practices tolerated. The extensions of skepticism considered in the further discussion above, however, move toward the kind of "beyond toleration" position briefly adumbrated in Section III of this chapter and discussed further in Part Two, infra.

in a dogmatic albeit a domain-restricted skepticism) can be understood in (roughly) the following manner: If meaning in the sense in which we say that language and other signs are meaningful is a function of truth and falsity (depends on the truth-evaluableness/falsifiability of the propositions that purport to be meaningful), then skepticism about truth and falsity provides the much thicker insulation of mutual meaninglessness. Logical empiricism adopted this theory of meaning, and those members of this school of thought who were also robust emotivists (for example, A. J. Ayer and Moritz Schlick) combined it with the claim that the "propositions" distinctive of ethics, aesthetics, and religion are not truth-evaluable and hence are meaningless. On this alarming view we are, in the most literal sense, meaningless to one another throughout the entire axiological realm, have access to and can deliberately influence one another only to the limited extent that we understand the psychological states that our (pseudo)propositions "evince."[28]

Whether or not the emotivists regretted these enormous circumscriptions on mutual intelligibility (if regret is an evaluative term, they would have to have held that it would be meaningless for them to *say* they regretted them),[29] there are no signs of regret concerning the conclusions, which are analogous to those of the emotivists in their unqualifiedly voluntarist or agent-relative character, reached by say, William James, Søren Kierkegaard, or the Jean-Paul Sartre of *Being and Nothingness*. Nor is regret a pervasive feature of those postmodernist doctrines that have assaulted the enlightenment ideals mentioned earlier by insisting on an *inpensee* irremediably beneath or apart from our thinking, on the radically indeterminate, aporia- and caesura-ridden character of our "texts" and "text-analogues" and so forth, that is, on the various ways in which our claims to mutual intelligibility are delusive, if not vain, conceits.

Lurking and sometimes explicit in these several views are variants of the idea that I initially drew out of some of Wittgenstein's observations, namely, that opacity creates spaces protective of individuality and plurality, makes it difficult and sometimes impossible for those who are other to individuals or groups to know or understand them well enough to diminish their distinctiveness by acting with or

---

[28]A. J. Ayer, *Language, Truth, and Logic* (New York: Dover, 1946), esp. chap. 6; Moritz Schlick, *Problems of Ethics* (New York: Dover, 1962).

[29]Cf. Wittgenstein, *Tractatus*, and "A Lecture on Ethics," *Philosophical Review* 74 (January 1965).

against them. If individuality means that, in fact, there are individuals who in some or all of their thought and action (as well as in their physical makeup) are not assimilated or assimilable to, commensurate or commensurable with, one another, then on these doctrines individuality is an ineliminable feature of the human condition.

Reactions to the views I have sketched (perhaps including the tendency to ignore or deflect attention from these elements in Wittgenstein's thinking) leave no doubt that this is an idea that is deeply disturbing to many. Nor are these reactions surprising. Few would deny that in fact we often fail to understand one another; and the claim that in important respects we cannot but fail to do so is familiar enough among the philosophically inclined. But the further proposition that these limitations should be protected, welcomed, and even cultivated challenges the soaring aspirations I mentioned earlier—and much more. It would appear that to accept this proposition is to reject, in the name of the value of individuality and perhaps of certain forms of plurality, not only manifestly unrealizable ideals of entire, opacity-excluding mutual transparency but the very doctrine that I and numerous others have treated as a main support for individuality and plurality. For those who accept this proposition, most versions of complementarism are enemies, not friends, of individuality, quite possibly of plurality.

V

We are on, or rather over, the brink of absurdities that I have been trying to avoid from the first words of this chapter.

Pressed very hard, the view that there is not (or should not be) *any* mutual intelligibility makes (would make) individuality and plurality at once unavoidable and impossible, thereby falling into incoherence. If my or our distinctiveness, in all but the most crudely physical respects, owes nothing to, is unknowable by, and hence is impervious to others, then, humanly speaking, it is invulnerable, guaranteed. Individualities and pluralities are not achievements, they are divine or natural facts, unalterable by humankind.[30] All of

---

[30]Or, on the Kantian version, synthetic a priori truths, truths that reason must accept, cannot alter.

the apparent cases of individuality- or group-destroying impositions, oppressions, and controls are and must be illusory.[31] But
equally, individuality and plurality are impossible because neither
term draws any distinction. Even if I could know, realize, or somehow experience my own characteristics, my inability to know or
understand the characteristics of anyone else would prevent me
from regarding my self as distinctive, from viewing myself as characterized by individuality. And assuming that we can know our
characteristics as a culture, society, or group, our inability to understand the characteristics of any other such entity would prevent us
from regarding ourselves as one among a plurality of entities.[32]

The (fraternal) twin of this absurdity is the view that there is (or
should be) no opacity or mutual unintelligibility among us because
in all but physical respects we are (should make ourselves, or otherwise become) one with one another, form an internally undifferentiated whole or wholes that is or are fully intelligible to us. Here
individuality and plurality in the sense of diversities within the
whole appear to be rendered impossible while their opposites, oneness or unity, are made necessary. Once again, however, the distinctions or contrasts on which the cogency of these claims depend have
been conceptually obviated.

From a Wittgensteinian standpoint, the attempt to press as hard
on notions like opacity as I have tried to imagine defeats itself
because it presupposes the very thing that the attempt purports to
question or to deny, that is, *some* mutual intelligibility.[33] This does

---

[31]Thus, pressed not quite so hard in this direction, these considerations yield
blindness to or complacency concerning some of the ugliest moments in human
experience. Retreating to what Isaiah Berlin calls the Inner Citadel, I close my eyes
to, or look with indifference on, the worst that others do not only to my family and
friends but to me. See Isaiah Berlin, *Four Essays on Liberty* (London: Oxford
University Press, 1960), esp. pp. 135–41. I return to this point below.

[32]In short, pressing very hard on the reality or desirability of mutual unintelligibility (or, as we see just below, their opposites) is one of the ways in which
theorizing about individuality and plurality can make itself ridiculous. Although I
attempt to give it a Wittgensteinian rendering, the paragraph above can be viewed
as a gloss on Rousseau's discussions of the state of nature in his *Discourse on the
Origin and the Foundations of Inequality among Men* and his *Essay on the Origin
of Languages*.

[33]Trying to question mutual intelligibility is itself a language-game that presupposes shared beliefs, rules, and so forth; the notion of "simple" or "atomic" entities
(e.g., internally undifferentiated individuals or groups) on which the activity de-

not mean that mutual intelligibility, or any particular distribution of intelligibility and unintelligibility, is divinely or metaphysically guaranteed to us; it only means that some such intelligibility is presupposed by the activity of thinking about the extent to which we are and are not, should seek to be or to avoid becoming, intelligible to one another.[34]

Setting these absurdities aside helps us to see that the attitudes and reactions toward intelligibility and unintelligibility that are familiar among us are as variable as the distributions of the two. As Wittgenstein's discussions would suggest (are intended to reflect?), we sometimes sanctify and worship that which is beyond our understanding, sometimes contemn and attempt to obliterate it. In some settings familiarity, obviousness, and transparency breed indifference and contempt; in others they are sources of reassurance, of comfort, and of contentment. Some people and some groups are assiduous in their efforts to disclose themselves fully to and to engage regularly and deeply with numerous others; they dislike and distrust the unknown and the uncertain, the protective and the private, the reclusive and the exclusive.[35] Others seek to sustain and to cultivate the latter conditions and qualities, viewing disclosure as display and theatricality, regularity and predictability as monotony, exposure as vulnerability, engagement as mutual intrusion, cooperation as dependency and diminution. More commonly, perhaps, individuals and groups manifest one of these outlooks in some of the domains of their activities, quite different ones in others.

As the last observation (and indeed much of what I have considered in this essay) suggests, it is deeply implausible to think that one

---

pends is meaningful only by comparison with some notion of a complex entity; the activity presupposes a logically "private" language; and so on through a considerable number of the main elements of Wittgenstein's thinking.

[34]The creatures about whom Rousseau speculated and who figure in the more robust versions of the Babel story are not metaphysical impossibilities, but such speculation and story telling is possible only for those among whom there is mutual intelligibility. It is well to remember, however, that Rousseau also anticipated Wittgenstein's view that the very conditions and characteristics that allow us to engage in mutually intelligible speculation, story telling, and so forth, also limit our understandings of our own and one another's performances.

[35]Among the remarkable features of the thinking of Hannah Arendt is that she promotes self-disclosure and mutual involvement, disdains the private, but treasures the uncertain, the unknown, and the mysterious.

or another of these patterns or modes is categorically or even generally to be preferred to the other. Thinking and acting within the conditions necessary to both, preferring one to the other, are matters of practical (that is, of circumstantial) judgment. There has been, however, a tendency—including a tendency within complementarism and liberalism—to favor the first of the two patterns I sketched, a resistance and not infrequently an antagonism toward the second. In the (liberal?) spirit of countercyclical pedagogy, let us therefore take somewhat further our exploration of the advantages and disadvantages of the latter.

There is no denying the risks, including those to individuality and plurality, involved in embracing and promoting mutual indifference, misanthropy, and isolation. Having disabused us of the self-defeating versions of this program, Wittgenstein himself signals some of the dangers here when he observes that people who find themselves at a loss with one another—and who can't or don't want to ignore one another altogether or in the respects in which they find one another incomprehensible—often call one another fools and heretics. This brief but pregnant observation reminds us that various heavier-handed kinds of impositions remain possible, under some circumstances are made easier and hence more likely, by limitations on mutual understanding. Where we are as brute facts to one another, ressentiment, fear, anxiety, and even certain unthinking forms of disdain and megalomania sometimes prompt us to behave toward one another in the brutal ways all too characteristic of our conduct toward animals and our natural environment generally.

Typically, these impositions are more costly, inefficient, and hence self-limiting than forms of interaction and influence that benefit from some degree of mutual understanding. Any number of political thinkers (perhaps most elegantly David Hume) have emphasized, for example, that political rule based entirely on brute force is not so much as a possibility; rule relying heavily on force is certain to be ineffective and likely to be short-lived in that those exercising it will soon be forced to give way to others. Perhaps more relevant here, it is arguable that such impositions, whether political or otherwise, are less damaging to individuality and plurality than modes of influence and control that work, as it were, through the beliefs, values, and judgments of those influenced and controlled. To the extent that my individuality or the distinctiveness of our group, society, or culture consists of my or our desires and interests, of the beliefs and values I or we hold, of the dispositions and aptitudes I or we have cultivated, impositions of these kinds may leave individuality and plurality intact.

Of course, these qualities can be eroded and sometimes destroyed by the infliction of prolonged pain and suffering, by subjecting individuals and groups to compulsions and restraints that prevent them from acting on their beliefs and values, from putting their aptitudes to use.[36] Along with bearing in mind the resources needed to make and sustain such impositions on any very large number of people, we want to distinguish as well as we can between the effects of physical impositions and those of the terror, indoctrination, manipulation, and so forth that commonly accompany them, and we do not want to forget those who have sustained and even heightened their individuating characteristics despite imprisonment and other forms of confinement and constraint, torture and severe physical deprivations. Nevertheless, and whatever might be the most effective means of preventing and combating such evils, we certainly do not want to pretend them away or to be careless concerning them.

The individualities and pluralities that we have encountered in Wittgenstein are in the setting of various degrees and forms of commonality and mutual understanding. The beliefs and values, aptitudes and dispositions, that I and we acquire and develop are formed and altered as I or we encounter (directly and vicariously) the thoughts and actions of others. How I or we respond to those encounters is itself in varying degrees understandable by myself (ourselves) and others.

To the extent that we understand that we do not understand these responses, or even understand that we do not know whether our notions of understanding get any foothold concerning them, it is open to us to regard them as loci of individuality and plurality and to look on them with either favor or disfavor, with relish and delight, or with fear and loathing. (If we do not understand even this much, the matter, as Hobbes somewhere wryly says, "arises not for deliberation.") As with reactions to other phenomena that we call

[36]Cf. Elaine Scarry, *The Body in Pain* (New York: Oxford University Press, 1985).

mysterious, which of these responses this or that person or group makes may itself be among the most mysterious of our experiences.

To the extent that we understand more than this, additional and more differentiated possibilities may present themselves. Understanding that you believe X but not why you believe it, I may distance myself from you generally or in respect to this among your beliefs. Or I might approach very close indeed, might be so attracted by your belief that I want to become as one with you in holding and acting on it, or so affrighted by it that I want to extirpate your belief and, if necessary, you. Which of these and the very large number of other attitudes I adopt and courses of action I take will be influenced by many considerations in addition to my assessment of your belief.

•

The figure transcribed by this chapter approximates a circle. Examination of the conditions of complementarity has confirmed and extended the understanding that individuality and plurality are conceptually interwoven. Nor has our examination discountenanced the complementarist expectation that, existentially, individualities and pluralities will often be mutually enhancing. I have nevertheless ended a little apart from where I began. I have done so because (as in the otherwise quite different discussion of Hobbes in Chapter 1)[37] I found reason to think that both individuality and plurality can be advantaged by circumstances often judged to be incompatible with or uncongenial to them, disadvantaged by conditions that influential versions of complementarism affirm and promote.

For reasons mentioned at intervals through the chapter and reiterated in somewhat different terms just above, the considerations I have adduced and the conclusions I have reached resolve few, if any, of the moral and political issues encountered in the course of the reflection. The only doctrines that I have claimed to invalidate defeat themselves without my help, and my attempts to delineate possibilities and desirabilities have been in terms much too general to settle questions of action or policy.

There may, however, be a modest upshot along the ideological— and to that extent the practical—dimension that I have tried to

---

[37]Insofar as it is cogent and convincing, the argument in this chapter concerning mutual opacities and unintelligibilities is a partial, but quite deep, response to Hobbes's doctrines of "worth" and "complaisance" or accommodation to others.

maintain. In foregrounding and valorizing not only difference, separation, and incompatibility but indeterminacy, opacity, and incomprehensibility, I have urged favorable consideration of features of
human affairs that have no better than an insecure place in liberal
thinking, that are accorded much greater prominence in doctrines
and outlooks widely regarded to be illiberal. But if liberalism does
value individuality and plurality, and if these features of human
affairs protect and enhance them, then the porous and fluctuating
ensemble of ideas that we call liberalism would be the better if it
were more accommodating to, more welcoming of, them.[38]

[38]Antagonism toward (fear of?) indeterminacy and opacity is one of the reasons
that group theories such as those of von Gierke and Dumont, and communitarian
theories that insist on deeply situated and harmonized selves, have difficulty sustaining a place for individuality. Suspicion of these features of human affairs also does
something to explain the implicit tension between individuality and plurality in
forms of pluralism that officially reject corporativism and the notion of group
personality but nevertheless treat individuals and their characteristics as functions
of intragroup dynamics. Finally, a certain underestimation of ambiguity and mutual
incomprehensibility may help to explain the almost heroic (certainly the powerfully
willful) character that thinkers such as James and Nietzsche, Oakeshott and Arendt,
must attribute to those who achieve and sustain individuality. For James and
Nietzsche, individuals must continuously fight off the pervasive demand for conformity powerfully imposed by the "herd." Oakeshott and Arendt agree with this. But
the former, like James and Nietzsche, diminishes the difficulty by treating the
messages and intimations that I receive from others and from the traditions and
conventions of my society as invariably ambiguous, as *requiring* interpretation.
Each of us can, and all too many of us do, go very far in surrendering this
interpretive task to others, but this fault or failing dramatizes what it cannot alter,
namely, that it is I who has surrendered myself to others. By contrast, Arendt can be
said to deepen the difficulty by locating the meanings of my "actions" entirely in the
responses of others to them, in the stories that others tell about what I do. In this
respect, and despite her unremitting antagonism toward him, Arendt adopts the
least estimable aspect of Hobbes's thinking.

PART TWO

VOLUNTARISM, INDIVIDUALITY, AND LIBERALISM

I   *Voluntarism and Voluntary Conduct*

A variety of views that might be styled "voluntarist" are integral to liberal theory and practice. Examples are suggested by the preference of many liberals for a negative conception of freedom and the tendency of those of this persuasion to rank the protection of freedoms so conceived at or near the top of their list of values. This conception of freedom presupposes the viability of distinctions between voluntary action and compelled, coerced, or manipulated movement or behavior. As evidenced by their hostility toward arrangements and understandings such as slavery, authoritarian government, puritanism, and paternalism, these liberals typically affirm these distinctions and accord great value to voluntary action. Again, voluntarism in this sense seems to be endorsed and promoted to the extent that liberal thinkers propose consent as the basis of legitimate government, champion agreement and contract in the realm of civil society, and seek to foster spontaneity, autonomy, and diversity in their societies. Views such as these underline the affinity between a certain version of voluntarism and the enthusiasm for individuality that intermittently characterizes liberalism, but they also support forms of social and political pluralism that many liberals have regarded as complementary to individuality, especially preference for voluntary rather than compulsory organizations and associations (volunteer rather than conscripted armies, open as opposed to closed shops, unrestricted enrollment and loosely organized versus cell- or cadre-type political parties), and to efforts to foster and sustain a diverse and fluctuating array of private associations. In some quarters views such as these have given impetus to the more specialized doctrine of "volunteerism," the doctrine that a variety of services and activities is better provided or organized by nongovernmental agencies and paid for by charitable contributions rather than by taxation.

Liberalism has no monopoly on these commitments and not all liberals share the beliefs I have mentioned. It is hard to see how any political or moral thinking could dispense entirely with a distinction such as that between action and coerced behavior. More than a few self-designated liberals have embraced notions of positive freedom that authorize intrusion and control, and some among them deny that freedom has any special place in liberal thought or practice. Pluralists who are widely regarded as illiberal (corporativists, syndicalists) nevertheless promote a diversity of substate groups and associations, while some liberals with a particular ardor for individuality are suspicious of the subordinating effects of group memberships and involvements. And so forth.

More generally and notwithstanding these points of disagreement, it has been characteristic of liberals to think of individual human beings as capable of developing desires and interests, objectives and purposes that are in some meaningful sense their own, of forming beliefs and intentions that are partially distinctive to themselves, and of making personal choices and taking actions on the basis of these. Whatever the means by which liberals have sought to protect and promote these qualities, doing so has been among their favored projects. Articulated in the works of its leading theorists from Adam Smith, Benjamin Constant, and Immanuel Kant through T. H. Green and John Stuart Mill and up to Isaiah Berlin and John Rawls, and manifested more widely in commitments and policy preferences such as those I have mentioned, voluntarism in the sense I have thus far discussed has been a prominent feature of liberalism and, for me, one of the major attractions of liberal thought and practice. The sometimes critical comments that follow are meant to qualify and augment, not to reject, voluntarism in this sense.

In the version I have sketched, the core of voluntar*ism* is insistence on the human capacity for and a generalized preference in favor of voluntary conduct when the latter is construed primarily by contrast with notions like compelled or coerced bodily movements and manipulated, programmed, or otherwise externally induced or controlled behaviors. Because these distinctions are frequently drawn and this valorization widely accepted, from an ideological and political standpoint voluntarism in this sense, and hence this dimension or element of liberalism, may appear commonsensical and even bland.

As we see in much of what follows, this impression—especially of blandness or a certain anodyne quality—is strengthened when the ideas thus far discussed are compared with more contentious doctrines that are also called, indeed more frequently called in philosophical literatures, voluntaristic. This comparison, however, will be more instructive if we first recall disagreements that continue to surround voluntarism in the form it has most often taken in liberalism itself.

Extensive philosophical discussion has not produced a generally accepted analysis of the notion of action. Theorists at what might be regarded as one extreme of the philosophical spectrum analyze "action" exclusively in terms of notions such as desires formed, beliefs held, intentions and purposes framed and adopted, and reasons that connect these with one another and to the decisions or choices that immediately precede the action. They construe all of these notions as categorially distinct from the concepts appropriate to analyzing events for which sufficient causal explanations can in principle be given. Whereas events of the latter kind (which include numerous movements of and processes that occur within human bodies) cannot but take place given the causal forces that produce them, *attempts* at action occur or do not at the discretion or choice of the agents whose attempts they are, and actions themselves occur in this way unless the movements necessary to them are prevented by other agents or agencies.

On the other hand, while on this view actions are not causally explainable, they are held to be for the most part understandable to and assessable by persons other than those whose actions they are. Human beings who are not severely diseased or demented are regarded as desire- and belief-forming, intentional, purposive, and more or less rational. To the extent that individuals use these capabilities and are partly apprised of the considerations that have informed the actions of other persons, they are typically able to comprehend and to make pertinent responses to one another's actions. Prominent in much liberalism, this feature of the analysis of action, and hence of voluntary conduct, requires critical scrutiny.

On this philosophical view, the concept of action and the doctrine of voluntarism are conceptually and theoretically secure. Liberals who accept this view, accordingly, can occupy themselves with sorting actual events into these categories, with protecting desirable or permissible actions against illegitimate efforts to prevent or frustrate them, and with identifying and effecting such limitations on action as are mandated by justice, by political stability, or by other requirements of moral and political life. In their more self-congratulatory moments, liberals claim that they have had considerable success in these efforts and hence that, as a generalization, voluntary conduct is appropriately prevalent in liberal societies.

Both the philosophical and ideological views just sketched are widely and often sharply contested. Determinists, causalists, and behaviorists at or toward the other philosophical extreme accuse proponents of the above view of shrouding human beings and their affairs in mystery. Gratifying as it may be to think of ourselves as unmoved movers, as sui generis and perhaps even self-subsistent agents, succumbing to this temptation excludes both self- and mutual understanding. Although the anticausalists profess to sustain these latter desiderata, they do not realize that we understand something just insofar as we are able to explain how it came about, what would change it, and so forth. Concepts such as desire and belief, intention and purpose, will and act must either be rendered in causal/behavioral terms or set aside as obstacles to clear and rigorous thinking (and hence also as impediments to improving on the human condition).[1]

Analogues to—perhaps in some cases applications of—these alternative philosophical views are discernible in prominent antiliberal ideological positions. Left critics of liberalism, for example, while often claiming to share the liberal belief in the possibility of voluntary conduct and the liberal aspiration to enhance oppor-

---

[1]More carefully delineated intermediate positions in this debate will concern us below, but the account—admittedly colored—thus far given outlines positions that have been prominent since ancient philosophy and remain so today. See, for example, Alan Donagan, *Choice: The Essential Element in Human Action* (London: Routledge & Kegan Paul, 1987). Donagan argues quite passionately for a version of the position first sketched above, with equal passion against all versions of causalism in respect to human action. He claims that the crucial issues in the philosophy of action, and the essentials of what continue to be the major contending positions concerning them, are already articulated in Plato's *Phaedo*.

tunities for it, object that liberals underestimate the prevalence and the subtlety of forces that make such conduct difficult and often impossible for many members of professedly liberal societies. Out of whatever reasons or motives, liberals tend to attribute consent, choice, or at least uncoerced acceptance to what are in fact instances of compulsion, manipulation, and indoctrination. It is for this reason, these critics argue, that liberals have been resistant to the kinds of ideological and political mobilization and discipline that, here and now, are necessary to counteract such forces and thus approach the voluntarist ideal. The conservatives and communitarians on liberalism's ideological Right, on the other hand, while usually proclaiming allegiance to "true" freedom and "genuinely" voluntary conduct, contend that liberalism leaves people too much to their own inadequate devices, depriving them of needed help in dealing with the irrational and often conflicting forces that operate within them and leaving them unprotected against the worst of the more powerful others. Against these liberal proclivities, they urge us to think of ourselves as parts of social or cultural wholes, and they seek to locate us in hierarchies of status and authority or to enmesh our thinking and acting in intricate and encompassing webs of norms and rules. Genuinely voluntary conduct is possible, but only for persons who are "situated" in a society or culture with these characteristics.

In part due to these criticisms, liberalism has for some time been on the defensive. And perhaps because the objections in question converge as challenges to the understanding of voluntarism thus far discussed, liberals have frequently responded by altering that understanding and sometimes by questioning their own commitment to it. Confronted with the charge that voluntary conduct as they have understood it is either impossible or unlikely to be better than narrowly distributed in societies of the kind they admire, they have revised their estimations of the resources and forces working for and against such conduct and adjusted the concept itself to allow that conduct can be, or can in time become, voluntary because of changes effected in persons who attempt it or the circumstances in which it is attempted. Poverty and unemployment; poor diet, medical care, and education; racial, sexual, religious, and other forms of discrimination; manipulation and control by elite media, educational, corporate, union, partisan political, and like forces—all of these are treated not as obstacles and difficulties with which those who confront them must more or less regularly contend but as forces reducing those persons and their movements or behaviors, over a wider or narrower domain, to resultants of conditions and forces that operate on them. Accordingly, a variety of programs and policies—political, governmental, social, economic, religious, psychotherapeutic, and so forth—are instituted to alter these conditions, counteract these forces, and thereby to restore or to elevate these persons to the status of agents engaging in voluntary conduct.[2] An assumption informing both the diagnoses and the prescriptions is that those who make them understand the members of their society well enough to know that they are disabled from action by the conditions and forces, will be enabled for it (or made better off by some other philosophically or ideologically appropriate criterion) by the policies and programs adopted to alter and counteract them.

This circumstance, and particularly the fact that much of the debate within and about liberalism explicitly or tacitly questions its understanding of and commitment to voluntarism, does indeed suggest attention to that notion. Perhaps it is true that prevalent liberal construals of voluntary conduct invite and enable obstacles to it and to realization of the values associated with it.

It is, however, worth considering whether a more rather than a less robust or insistent form of voluntarism is the appropriate response. Is it possible that (as, using other dictions, I have been suggesting in earlier chapters) liberals share too much with their causalist and behaviorist opponents? Perhaps their frequent insistence on the rational, reasonable, mutually intelligible character of action itself serves to make voluntary conduct vulnerable to control and to diminution? Do liberal attempts to augment these characteristics of action serve rather to enhance the possibilities for intrusion and manipulation? If so, are there alternative formulations that would diminish these vulnerabilities and at the same time serve related liberal objectives? Idle as it would be to think that reflection concerning these possibilities could of itself fully deliver liberalism from its difficulties, it is not impossible that such a reflection could enlarge somewhat the prevailing sense of alternatives.

[2]Welfare liberalism and the welfare state.

II   *Voluntarism and Will*

A. Theological Voluntarism: Divine Will as the Redoubt of God and the Freedom of Humankind

> God is in no way a debtor to anyone.
> —William of Ockham

As a somewhat technical theological term, "voluntarism" was first used and is still often used of doctrines that make will as opposed to reason the primary characteristic of God. In a familiar albeit severely abbreviated formulation of this view, God is and does by Her will not because Her being and doing accord with any requirement prior to or otherwise independent of Her will. Most particularly, God is not reason (or Reason) and She does not act by the canons of rationality or reasonableness. As distinct from what is often implied when we speak of the human will and especially of willfulness on the part of one another, for the theological voluntarists this was not to say that God's being and doings are irrational or in some other sense arbitrary. Their argument, rather, was that "reason" and "rational," "irrational," "arbitrary," and the like are inappropriate to characterizing and assessing God and Her actions.

We should nevertheless notice at once that there is one critical respect in which these characterizations of God operated in much the manner of our attributions of will and willfulness to one another, namely, to diminish or even to deny the possibility of understanding, assessing, and otherwise gaining what we might call access to the individuals and actions to which will and willfulness are attributed. With the partial exceptions of the respects in which God has chosen to reveal Herself directly to humankind in Her holy word, on the strong voluntarist view the bases of or reasons for Her decisions and actions are beyond human comprehension; humankind's yearnings to understand God are futile and (on major versions of the doctrine) its claims to do so are manifestations of sinful pride. Needless to say, for thinkers of this persuasion such further notions as judging God and Her actions, certainly of acting on those judgments with the purpose of affecting God's decisions and actions, are yet more absurd and odious.

Theological voluntarism was first developed by medieval and early-modern theologians such as Augustine, John Duns Scotus, William of Ockham, and Martin Luther; it was largely endorsed by fideists such as Montaigne and Pascal (and in part by Hobbes); and it was later adopted in a yet more radical form by Kierkegaard and his followers. In some cases influenced by these theologians, a number of nineteenth- and twentieth-century "secular" thinkers, including Arthur Schopenhauer, Friedrich Nietzsche, William James, Jean-Paul Sartre (in some of the many moments of his thinking), Hannah Arendt, and Michael Oakeshott, adopted (or reoccupied, as Hans Blumenberg puts it) strongly analogous doctrines concerning human beings. Finally, in recent years philosophical psychologists and philosophers of action such as Roderick Chisholm, Anthony Kenny, Brian O'Shaugnessy, and Jennifer Hornsby, working in a philosophical tradition that had for the most part rejected the notion of the will as figmental and obscurantist, have attempted to reinstate it in their accounts of human action.

In a manner reminiscent of the reactions of Ockham, Luther, and Kierkegaard against the theological rationalisms of Anselm, Aquinas, and Hegel, nineteenth- and twentieth-century secular voluntarists rejected and sought to supplant the philosophical rationalisms of Kant, Hegel, and Bradley, of Locke, Bentham, and Mill. And much as Duns Scotus, Ockham, Luther, and Kierkegaard regarded the theological orthodoxies that they contested as demeaning of God, so the secular voluntarists insist that Enlightenment rationalisms diminish as well as distort humankind. The theological voluntarists sought to restore the majesty of God by insisting that She is and does as She sees fit and that humankind has access to Her exclusively by Her leave and on Her terms. In this comparison (the validity of which varies from thinker to thinker), the secular voluntarists attribute to humankind the qualities and characteristics that their theological predecessors and counterparts reserved to God. They attempt to restore and indeed to enhance the standing or dignity or self-estimation of human beings by insisting that we human beings are—or could become—what each of us chooses to make ourselves by our own acts of will; and they further insist that in important respects each of us can thereby set the terms on which others of our kind can understand, judge, and otherwise gain access to us. If effecting this restoration would diminish the possibilities for mutual understanding, cooperation, and the like, it would also enhance freedom and dignity (or as Nietzsche would have it, health and strength, joy and self-containment).

What could these admittedly disturbing ideas possibly contribute to liberal thought or practice? An objection to considering theological voluntarism for this purpose, which I discuss below, is that a strict separation between theology and politics is fundamental to liberalism. If these stronger versions of voluntarism are so much as residually theological in character, liberalism must eschew them. A second objection that requires response at this juncture is that all but the most recent of the secular voluntarists I have listed either regarded themselves (or are usually, and for many good reasons, regarded as) enemies of liberalism. The elitism that is so pronounced among them, the antirationalism if not irrationalism that they appear to promote, the hostility of most of them not only to democracy but to constitutionalism and the rule of law, are all antithetical to liberalism. These features of their thinking, moreover, seem to be inseparable from the primacy they accord to will.[3]

These considerations do weigh heavily against regarding Schopenhauer and Nietzsche, James or Sartre, Arendt or Oakeshott, as liberals, certainly against substituting them for, say, Kant or Constant, Mill, Rawls, or Berlin as thinkers to whom we look for considered articulations of liberal ideas and ideals. The question before us, however, is not whether liberals should become Nietzscheans or Jamesians, Ockhamites or Kierkegaardians, in some all-in or all-out sense (never mind that neither the ideas of these thinkers nor our appropriations of them are sufficiently of a piece to permit of this possibility); rather, it is whether liberal theory and practice might be strengthened, or (more soberly) its currently prominent difficulties somewhat ameliorated, by greater receptivity to elements that are distinctively prominent in these and like-minded thinkers. A

---

[3]Kindred objections are sometimes made against the theological voluntarists. When they restrict themselves to discussion of God and the relation of humankind to God, their emphasis on the power and mystery of divine will consigns human beings to a submissiveness that, insofar as it is so much as possible, is slavish and demeaning. And when they project from that conception in treating of the church, the political community, and other intrahuman relationships, they adopt views all too close to those later adopted by the secular voluntarists. I argue below that these objections are well taken as regards, for example, Augustine and Luther, much less so concerning, say, Ockham, Montaigne, and Hobbes.

major purpose of this reflection is to essay an affirmative answer to this question.

An early but qualified example of theological voluntarism is provided by Augustine, particularly in those parts of his thinking that are concerned with the theodicy problem. If (1) God is omnipotent and (2) there is evil in the universe, does it not follow that (3) God is responsible for evil? Augustine's sometime friends the Gnostics and Manicheans acknowledged (2) but avoided the unacceptable (3) by positing sources of evil that God cannot eliminate or control. Acknowledging (2) but having come to believe that any qualification of (1) is contrary to scripture, Augustine was obliged to reject the Gnostic and Manichean solutions as an affront to God. In order nevertheless to avoid (3), he argued that evil was due to human choices, to human exercise of the freedom of will that God had accorded to humankind.

In Augustine's intention, this argument is less than complimentary to humankind, but the more immediate objection to it is that it does not resolve the difficulty to which it is addressed.[4] If God is omniscient and omnipotent, thus foreseeing and able to prevent the sin and evil that result from human free will, why did She grant it to Eve and Adam to begin with and why has She not since withdrawn or annulled it? Whether because he was less confident of the human capacity for fidelity to God than later and stricter theological voluntarists, because of the considerable residue of neo-Platonism in his thinking, or because of the sinful pride of which he frequently accused himself (he evidently had one hell of an ego), Augustine was neither above nor beneath attributing reasons to God or offering reasons on Her behalf. When or as these reasons gave out, his "answer" was that these questions are beyond the human ken. For those graced by God with Christian faith, it suffices to believe that God is mysterious will and that it is God's will that human beings be at liberty to sin. Those not thus blessed will speculate and wrangle—fruitlessly or with a yield of bitter fruit.[5]

[4]Cf. Nietzsche: "The [Greek] gods justified human life by living it themselves— the only satisfactory theodicy ever invented" (*The Birth of Tragedy*, trans. Francis Golffing [Garden City, N.Y.: Doubleday Anchor, 1956], p. 30).

[5]Augustine's most extensive treatment of these questions, on which the above remarks primarily rely, is in *De Libero Arbitrio Voluntatis*, trans. as *St. Augustine on Free Will* by Carroll Mason Sparrow (Charlottesville: University of Virginia Studies, 1947).

Notwithstanding the inconsistencies and even hybris that doing so might be thought to attribute to him, we can construe Augustine's turn to voluntarism as an attempt on his part to come to the aid of a God beset by Her human creations. Despite the combination of God's revelations and Her command that otherwise human beings simply honor and obey Her, human beings have formed and held tenaciously to gross misunderstandings of Her. Where possible, Augustine corrects mistaken views; where not, he insulates God against those errors and puts the blame for their consequences where it belongs. Hans Blumenberg does not mince words in this regard. Augustine's "justification" of God was "accomplished at the expense of man, to whom a new concept of freedom is ascribed expressly in order to let the whole of an enormous responsibility and guilt be imputed to it." "The burden [Augustine] placed on man is . . . only a side effect of the unburdening of his God."[6]

For reasons to be discussed more fully below, the element of hybris involved in Augustine's position is inherent in theological voluntarism (just as a certain self-privileging and even self-aggrandizement necessarily accompanies what we will see is the importantly self-circumscribing stances of strong forms of secular voluntarism such as Nietzsche's). But we can accept Blumenberg's characterizations and yet insist (as Blumenberg himself does) that Augustine's fellow human beings were the addressees of his teaching. Living where and when he did, Augustine could hardly have avoided invoking God's authority. And while he himself would have been outraged (bewildered?) by the suggestion that he constructed his conception of God to serve his human purposes (as outraged as he would be by the suggestion that he thought God needed his assistance), viewing his conception in this way will help us to decide whether his and yet more robust theological voluntarisms are serviceable for our moral and political purposes. If there are grounds on which to hold that God is will, not reason, and/or if God is honored and protected by our taking that view of Her, are there grounds for thinking of ourselves in the same way? Would we honor, enhance, or provide a measure of protection to ourselves by taking that view of one another?

[6]Hans Blumenberg, *The Legitimacy of the Modern Age*, trans. Robert M. Wallace (Cambridge: Massachusetts Institute of Technology Press, 1983), pp. 133, 134.

133

I argue below that theological voluntarism allows of and has sometimes returned affirmative answers to these questions. But Augustine himself, while more than prepared to think of human beings as willful, could scarcely countenance the idea that he thereby honored or protected them. In glorifying God and God's will, he clearly meant to deprecate earthly humankind and to condemn its willfulness as sinful pride. Rather than revel in the liberties that God had permitted them, human beings should scorn their present selves and their earthly circumstances and look ahead to their union with God in the heavenly city. Owing to his insistence on the immense disparity between the divine and the human will, Augustine's voluntarism is a recipe not for human self-esteem and individuality but for self-abnegation and self-disdain, for submission not only to God but to the earthly authorities that God has ordained.[7] And if Protestant Augustinians such as Luther can be called individualists because of their emphasis on the direct or immediate character of the relationship between each person and God, as both a doctrinal and a temperamental matter they otherwise shared Augustine's low regard for the merely human will and its works.

Between Augustine and the fourteenth- and fifteenth-century nominalists and voluntarists who formulated the *via moderna*[8] in theology, scholastic theologians had greatly augmented the "rationalist" elements in conceptions of God, of humankind as made in the image of God, and of the relationship between God and humankind. Modernists such as Duns Scotus, Ockham, and Nicholas of Autrecourt were "Augustinian" in viewing these developments,

[7]It is almost as if human beings would be the better if they were more rational when this means less willful. But if Augustine frequently laments and indeed excoriates the irrationality and perverse willfulness in worldly human affairs, his every complaint against human nature threatens to become a criticism of its Creator. Thus his own position requires that he urge human beings simply to accept that it is God's will that they now are as they are and to look ahead to the vastly improved condition that She has prepared for them.

Cf. Schopenhauer: In studying Augustine one "experiences something analogous to the feeling of one who tries to make a body stand whose centre of gravity falls outside it; however he may turn it and place it, it always tumbles over again" (*The World as Will and Idea*, trans. R. Haldane and J. Kemp [Garden City, N.Y.: Dolphin Books, Doubleday, 1961], p. 416n).

[8]For a brief but pertinent account of this school or tendency, see Heiko A. Oberman, "*Via Antiqua* and *Via Moderna*: Late Medieval Prolegomena to Early Reformation Thought," in Anne Hudson and Michael Wilks, eds., *From Ockham to Wyclif* (Oxford: Basil Blackwell, 1987).

with their incorporation of the pagan thinking of Aristotle into Christian theology, as unconscionable magnifications of human reason at God's expense. Thus they developed a theological voluntarism that was purer and more insistent than Augustine's own. By contrast with Augustine, however, some of them were prepared to extend something like their high estimations of the will of God to the wills of God's human creations.

For William of Ockham, the divine will "relates necessarily to no object but its own essence. Therefore it relates contingently to anything else."[9] This means that, as with the "created [i.e., the human] will" but as distinct from "natural causes," the divine will, "existing for some time prior to t_1, at which time it causes [x], can freely and contingently cause or not cause [x] at t_1," (Ockham, *Predestindation*, p. 76.) As Marilyn McCord Adams explains, Ockham agreed with John Duns Scotus that both the divine and the human will contrast with natural causes in "having a capacity for opposite objects or opposite acts. Both hold . . . that the will is naturally prior to its acts in that the acts depend for their existence on the existence and causal efficacy of the will.[10] . . . And both [hold] . . . that when the will acts, it actualizes its capacity for one act to the exclusion of the other" (ibid., pp. 24–25).[11]

---

[9]William of Ockham, *Predestination, God's Foreknowledge, and Future Contingents*, trans. Marilyn McCord Adams and Norman Kretzmann, 2d ed. (Indianapolis: Hackett, 1983), p. 83.

[10]Adams adds "but not vice versa" (ibid. pp. 24–25). But if "vice versa" means the possibility that the will "depend[s] for its efficacy on the existence and causal efficacy of the acts," I do not grasp the idea she seems to be entertaining.

[11]Being omnipotent, when the divine will "actualizes its capacity for one act" it also necessarily brings about the state of affairs intended by that act. The human will is efficacious in bringing about the act it has "chosen" or "elected" but not necessarily the further state of affairs that the agent seeks to bring about by taking the action in question. Depending on how we construe "capacity," this interpretation might suggest that both Duns Scotus and Ockham regard the notion of a failed *attempt* at human action—a failed attempt at attempting, as we might put it—as self-contradictory. You can prevent me from raising my arm, perhaps prevent me from willing to do so, but if I have formed such a will, no one and nothing can prevent me from attempting to raise it.

This question remains very much with us. "A photographer asks an actor to lift his arm at t_1 precisely (when the bell rings), and the 'take' is vital. At t_1 the actor hears the bell; at $t_1 + .001$ sec. an impulse starts down the arm; by $t_1 + .01$ it has almost reached the muscles; at $t_1 + .01001$ a special apparatus that is being worked at a distance by a gang of anti-social scientists destroys that neural impulse. Accordingly, the muscle fails to contract, the arm fails to move, the photographer swears at

By comparison with Duns Scotus and especially with Aquinas and the orthodoxy he represented, however, Ockham radicalized the contingency and hence the mysteriousness of both the divine and the human will. For Duns Scotus, "Christians believe" that God acts contingently in the sense that it is in God's power "either to act or not to act, . . . [and] to act in time or to act instantaneously."[12] For the "subtle doctor," however, "self-knowledge" as well as "self-love" are of the "essence" of God, and God's self-knowledge or "intellect" is "necessary and is prior by nature to the existence" of the things it knows and wills. "Otherwise he [God] would not act perfectly, for knowledge is the norm which regulates his work. God, therefore, has previous distinct knowledge, either actual or at least habitual, of everything that he can make" (Scotus, *Philosophical Writings*, p. 61). God's knowledge of the universe (as it "existed" in, or as, God's idea or simply in, or as, God?) antedated the act of will by which She created the universe.

As a part of its unstated but manifest claim that human reason can comprehend what we might call the ontological structure of God's acting, this formulation suggests that God's will is conditioned and hence limited by Her knowledge of Herself, that She could not form or act on a will in respect to "objects" that She did not antecedently know and hence could not create an object by a sheer act of will. The mystery of God's originating, creating, acting will is diminished by looking behind it to God's knowledge.[13] Ockham sometimes writes as if he agrees with Duns Scotus's account of God's omniscience but that his doing so poses no difficulty for his belief in the omnipotence and mystery of God's will. "There is no process or priority or contradiction in God such that the divine intellect at one instant does not have evident cognition of future contingents and at another instant does have [such cognition of

---

the 'star'! The empirical but vitally important question is: did the 'star' try to move his arm?" (Brian O'Shaughnessy, *The Will: A Dual Aspect Theory*, 2 vols. [Cambridge: Cambridge University Press, 1980], vol. 2, p. 265.) Later we see that O'Shaughnessy equates willing and attempting or rather willing and striving or trying.

[12]John Duns Scotus, *Philosophical Writings*, trans. Allan Wolters (Indianapolis: Hackett, 1987), pp. 80–81.

[13]The human will is doubly limited, i.e., by its own knowledge within the confines set for it by God and by God's knowledge-cum-will for it. We understand the human will by looking to the knowledge (or at least beliefs) that at once inform and limit it, and for, Duns Scotus (but not, as we see below, for Ockham) we explain it by looking to God's knowledge-cum-will.

them]. For to say that the divine intellect receives any perfection from something else would be to posit an imperfection [in the divine intellect]" (Ockham, *Predestination*, p. 89). Equally, however, "the will of God is omnipotent and not capable of being obstructed" (p. 13, quoted by Adams from Ockham's *Commentary on the Sentences*).

In order to obviate the apparent conflict between these claims, Adams argues, Ockham distinguished between God's "antecedent" and Her "consequent" disposing will. Prior to creating the universe,[14] God's knowledge encompassed Her antecedent will and its objects eternally, that is, God knew, distinctly and forever, what Her antecedent disposing will had been and would be and thus knew the objects of that will. Having created the universe, God knows Her own consequent disposing will to the extent of that creation. What Her further consequent disposing will would be, however, what that will would be as regards matters not yet encompassed in their particularities in Her creation, was and is a contingent matter about which certain knowledge was and is impossible for God. "When something is determined contingently, so that it is still possible that it is not determined and it is possible that it was never determined, then one cannot have certain and infallible cognition based on such a determination. But the determination of the divine will in respect of future contingents is such a determination. . . . Therefore God cannot have certain cognition of future contingents based on such a determination" (Ockham, *Predestination*, p. 49).[15] God must await

---

[14]The antecedent/consequent distinction is within the category of the "disposing" as opposed to the "revealed" will of God and requires understanding of the related distinction between God's "*potentia absoluta*" and the "*potentia Dei ordinata*." The *potentia absoluta* refers "to the total possibilities *initially* open to God, some of which were realized by creating the established order of the universe," i.e., through the *Dei ordinata* and hence revealed will (Oberman, "*Via Antiqua* and *Via Moderna*," p. 450).

[15]On the strictest view of the contingency of the original creation, the creation ex nihilo, this formulation would seem to deny God's foreknowledge of Her creation. It is a further question whether God knew her intentions for the universe prior to creating it. If we combine Elizabeth Anscombe's view that our intentions are known to us without observation with Donald Davidson's view that all actions are intentional under some description, we could say that God *acted* in creating the universe only if God knew Her intentions for it. On this understanding, contingency enters with respect to whether, or the extent to which, God is successful in achieving Her intentions through Her actions. Just as we sometimes say of ourselves that we know in advance of our actions what we intend to bring about by them but only find out afterwards what we have actually done, so God knew what universe She intended to create but had to await events to learn what She had actually wrought. Cf. "And

events, both the events to which She responds and the event that is the "upsurge"[16] of Her own will in respect to those events.

Among the numerous matters at issue here is predestination and, more generally, the relation between the divine and the human will. If God's consequent disposing will is unobstructable, and if She has certain and eternal knowledge of Her consequent as well as Her antecedent disposing will, then (for example) Peter's own will played no part in his denial of Christ, he deserves no reprobation, and neither Christ's death nor any other divine or divinely ordained act is necessary for his redemption. "For I ask whether . . . the determination of a created will necessarily follows the determination of the divine will. If it does, then the [created] will necessarily acts {as it does,}[17] just as fire does, and so merit and demerit are done away with. If it does not, then the determination of a created will is required for knowing determinately one or the other part of a contradiction regarding those {future things that depend absolutely on a created will}." Ockham comes down unequivocally in favor of the latter view, hence against Duns Scotus's account of the relationship between God's knowledge and God's will, but hence also in favor of an account of human will that allows it to act independently of the consequent disposing will of God. "For the determination of the uncreated will does not suffice, because a created will can oppose the determination {of the uncreated will}. Therefore, since the determination of the {created} will was not from eternity, God did not have certain cognition of the things that remained {for a created will to determine}" (Ockham, *Predestination*, p. 49).[18]

God saw everything that he had made, and, behold, it was very good" (Gen. 1, *The Reader's Bible* [London: Oxford University Press, 1951]), p. 7.

[16]This is Jean-Paul Sartre's term (*surgir, surgissement*) for the actions or expressions of the *Etre-pour-soi*, "being-for-itself," that is, for the feature or characteristic of human beings that most closely approximates what other strong voluntarists call the will. See *Being and Nothingness: An Essay in Phenomenological Ontology*, trans. Hazel E. Barnes (Seacaucus, N.J.: The Citadel Press, 1956), esp. pt. 2. If I understand Sartre's view, he intends "upsurge" to exclude agential intentionality or at least knowledge thereof. Later I consider O'Shaughnessy's view that there are actions that are intentional under no description but that all actions involve the will and that the agent always knows her will.

[17]Materials in {}s are insertions in Ockham's text by the editors.

[18]In *The Life of the Mind*, Hannah Arendt treats Duns Scotus as the preeminent philosopher of the will in the Western tradition (see vol. 2, p. 31 and esp. pp. 120ff.). Her discussion, however, entirely ignores Ockham and disagreements between Duns Scotus and Ockham such as the one discussed above. In this comparison, Ockham's is the purer and more insistent of the two versions of voluntarism.

On this account, which is clearly intended to accord to human-kind a capacity for initiation—for making genuine beginnings—analogous to God's mysterious powers of creation, Ockham's view was that God had provided humankind with "natural properties that can be followed by a meritorious act." Moreover, by Her antecedent disposing will "God is prepared to coact with everyone towards a meritorious act" and to give "precepts and counsels in order that . . . [they] should follow through with . . . meritorious act[s]." But God's antecedent disposing will does not determine everything that human beings do with these divine gifts. "Nevertheless, not everyone chooses a meritorious act; many, indeed, choose demeritorious acts. The latter, therefore, act contrary to the antecedent divine will" (Ockham, *Predestination*, p. 15, quoted by Adams from Ockham's *Commentary on the Sentences*). After these human acts have occurred, and hence contingent on their characteristics, God forms and acts on Her consequent disposing and fully determinative will (for example, concerning Peter's salvation or damnation). Because God neither knows nor determines what acts humans will choose, She can neither form nor know Her consequent disposing will (certainly She cannot form and hence cannot know Her intentions) until after they have made their choices.

By logical or otherwise-rational criteria, of course, these intricate maneuverings are no more successful than those of Duns Scotus, of Augustine, or of any of the numerous others who have wrestled with these conundrums. Indeed, if judged by such criteria, Ockham's discussion commits what he himself must regard as apostasy by making both the power and knowledge of God dependent on "perfection" by the contingencies—the mysteries—of human will and action.

Unlike his predecessors, however, Ockham not only admits but welcomes his "failure." Having repeatedly insisted that God's will cannot be obstructed, he acknowledges that human beings frequently and successfully act contrary to it and "explains" this inexplicable phenomenon simply by saying that it is their will to do so. Will marks the commencement of action but equally the terminus of explanation and understanding of its having commenced. And having reiterated, in the face of the discussions summarized just above, his conviction that "God knows all future contingents certainly and evidently," he says, "But to explain this clearly and to describe the way in which He knows all future contingents is impossible for any intellect in this . . . [human] condition" (p. 90).

Adams declares that Ockham's doctrine "leaves the intentionality of divine judgment utterly mysterious" (p. 20). If "utterly" commits an exaggeration (ultimately?), (and if Adams's use of "intentionality" betrays more than she may have intended about her own theory of action) Ockham himself might well object that her assessment confines too narrowly his conception of the domain of the mysterious; certainly he thinks that there is also much that is and can be expected to remain mysterious concerning "the intentionality of *human* judgment."[19] God's exercise of Her creative powers established conditions (faculties, capacities, objects on which to act, etc.) necessary to human action, but for some important classes of actions God has not provided—in Ockham's view could not have provided—the necessary and sufficient conditions of human action. And Ockham's doctrine of the freedom of the will is clearly intended to deny that those conditions are supplied by anything apart from or additional to God's will. Thus, for some important cases, the mystery of the commencement of human action is abated primarily in the weak sense effected by saying that action proceeds from the will, only by *naming* the source of the acting.

Perhaps more important for present purposes, it is doubtful that Ockham would regard Adams's comment as identifying a defect in, as opposed to an inescapable limitation on, his thinking. We do what we can with the intellects and the other faculties and powers that God gave us, but for whatever reasons, or for none, God has left Herself and us largely opaque to us.

Are these limitations to be regretted? Are they a source of difficulties in our relations with God? With one another? Ockham's answer to the second, and hence to part of the first and third, of these questions echoes Augustine. Our own best reckonings concerning God and God's determinate will for us "cannot be proved *a priori* by means of the natural reason available to us," but those understandings that are fitting to our human estate are "proved by means of the authorities of the Bible and the Saints, which are sufficiently well known." (p. 90). In respect to our belief in God's omniscience and omnipotence, the limitations of reason are made

---

[19]The relationship between will and knowledge or belief and desire, for example, is left mysterious. Is the human will limited by the antecedently acquired knowledge and beliefs and the previously formed desires of the person whose will it is? Or can I form a will concerning matters in respect to which I have none of these? These questions recur below.

good—or made sufficiently good for the relevant divine and human purposes as Ockham conceives them—by divine revelation. On this score, then, and despite our awareness of Ockham's intense involvement in the incessant and acrimonious disputes concerning "the Bible and the Saints,"[20] it may be well to resist the temptation to find a thin slice of wry in Ockham's "sufficiently well known."

Nor should we think that Ockham regarded revelation as so indeterminate as to be useless concerning intrahuman affairs. Salvation and damnation are matters of God's will and cannot be assured by obedience to Her commands or any other human actions. There is, however, no doubt that God intends us to obey the laws of the Decalogue and to heed the teachings of Christ and the apostles. Ockham may well have believed, moreover, that faith and the fortitude that it (or something equally mysterious?) provides is necessary if we are to act in the face of the manifold of contingencies that confront us; certainly he thought that faith assisted many in finding challenge and perhaps relish in circumstances never more than partly intelligible.

(If *these*, as it were, surrounding (re)assurances are no longer available, are there functional substitutes or analogues to them? Truths of reason? Constructed principles of justice? Constitutions? Deep conventions? Are opacities and unintelligibilities such as Ockham is discussing in these passages interstitial to the illuminations and transparencies? Is this in some sense necessary? Or is it the other way around?)

In these respects, however, Ockham reads very differently from Augustine. The radical uncertainty with which the mystery of God and God's highest creatures confronts the latter is reason not for otherworldliness or disdain for the present but for active efforts to do as well as we can in our place and our time. The freedom of will that God has accorded humankind (and that She left Herself or found Herself left with?) does exonerate God from evil. In addition, however, it at once requires individuals to form and act on their own wills and warrants them in taking an active interest in themselves, in regarding themselves and what they desire, think, and do here and now as fully worthy of their concern and attention. We are

---

[20]We should not forget that Ockham was summoned by the pope to defend his works, that he fled to Bavaria following the hearings, and that he spent much of the remainder of his life as an antipapal polemicist.

to remain conscious of the peerless power and knowledge of God and we are to submit to God's will whenever it is known to us. There is such a thing as sinful pride and we must guard against it. But acknowledging and using our freedom of action manifests fidelity to, rather than rebellion against, God; celebrating and doing our best with our freedom is one of the ways that we honor the God in whose image we were created. Indeed, our gratitude to God should extend from that which She has done for us to that which She leaves to each of us to do for ourselves. If the ways in which She is inaccessible to us and we are inaccessible to one another sometimes leave us unsettled and anxious, they manifest Her decision to make us in Her own image, to bring us closer to Her—more like unto Her—than She permits Her other creatures to come.[21]

•

Stating the matter as I have just done underlines what we might call the "God-centric quality" that Ockham's thinking shares with Augustine's and with that of his Thomistic theological opponents. Certainly in his own self-understanding Ockham's thinking was governed by scripture in the sense that God's revealed words settle all questions to which they speak directly and unequivocally. This being the case, and liberalism being an insistently secular political ideology, many will think that the reflections of Ockham and other theological voluntarists, while they might contribute something to our understanding of the ideas out of which liberalism was formed, can be of no more than analogical value to present and future liberal thinking and practice. (Of course, liberals and all others are at liberty to think, as a matter of personal conviction, as it were, that their political views are undergirded by religious dogma. If so, however, on the view in question they must either devise public political argumentation that is logically independent of that convic-

[21]For the view that Ockhamistic voluntarism and nominalism gave a powerful impetus to science, see Oberman, "*Via Antiqua* and *Via Moderna*." For the legitimation of self and self-assertion effected or set in motion by Ockhamistic thinking, see Blumenberg, *Legitimacy of the Modern Age*, esp. pp. 197, 346, 349. Blumenberg notes Ockham's argument that it cannot be *proved* that human beings *cannot* be creators in the same sense—albeit on a vastly reduced scale—as God (p. 533). Cf. Hobbes's notorious view that human beings improve on God's creation in various ways, most notably by adding the leviathan to it. And see below for discussion of Nietzsche's and other secular voluntarist urgings that we remake our conceptions of ourselves on the model of conceptions we have formed of God and the gods.

tion and that dogma or their liberalism is discredited as a candidate public philosophy in our time.)

The response to this objection, finally, is that an individuality-promoting liberalism can appropriate—to its thinking about human beings and their affairs—images, conceptions, and assessments that were developed concerning or projected on God or the gods. We have seen that Ockham himself makes more than a small beginning toward such an appropriation, and we will shortly be examining the analogous but yet more insistent efforts of the nineteenth- and twentieth-century thinkers of the "Man-God."[22] But let us approach this response by small and hopefully surer steps.

It is by now widely agreed that the view according to which theological and political questions differ and should be kept apart requires, if not a theology, a "metatheology," that is, a characterization of the subject matters, methods, and so forth, of theology that informs and warrants such conclusions. Many proponents of a strict separation, moreover, advocate it on the partly metatheological ground that theological questions—and religious issues more generally—have proven to be and will all but certainly remain deeply and irremediably divisive. Not all those who have accepted this conclusion have done so on the ground that (in human terms) God is humanly comprehensible only insofar as She chooses to reveal Her will, but the conviction that human faculties and powers do not suffice to sustain agreement concerning God's characteristics and purposes—or even civility among those who disagree concerning them—has been prominent in the argumentation for it. Thus distinctions between theology and politics are less than categorial; there is theology and secular ideology on both sides of the lines they draw.

These conceptual points are fortified by much of what we have inherited from the period intervening between Ockham and the present, indeed by much in the tradition of liberalism itself. However the late-medieval theologians may have understood themselves, for many of us Hobbes, Hume, Kant, Feuerbach, Marx, Nietzsche, Freud, and Wittgenstein (among many others) have engendered a powerful inclination to "anthropologize" their reflec-

[22]The striking phrase (but let's make it "Wo/Man-God") is Brian O'Shaughnessy's (*The Will*, vol. 1, p. liv).

tions and their sources, to regard the scriptures themselves and the various uses to which they and other of the resources of theology have been put as attempts by human beings to understand, to assess, and to identify appropriate ways in which to act concerning themselves and their circumstances. We can and often do look on medieval and all other conceptions (constructions) of God as attempts to attain improved purchase on questions about ourselves and our affairs.[23]

In conjunction with the results of my brief venture onto the terrain of theological voluntarism, these views of religion and theology may encourage us to think of the formulations thus far considered as a resource available for and valuable to liberal reflection and practice. As a next step toward realizing this possibility, let us examine the strong voluntarisms propounded by thinkers who "reoccupied" earlier theological positions.

---

[23]The "anthropological" view of thinking about God, incidentally, while obviously in conflict with beliefs that many religious people have held and do now hold, is not necessarily antireligious, certainly not antispiritual. (One might even say that if there were a God or gods that deserved our respectful consideration, it would be their will that our thinking about them should be for the purpose of better understanding ourselves their creatures. Why else would gods worthy of the name have any interest in our understandings of them?) Nor does that view necessarily conflict with the conviction that the most specifically or distinctively religious views ought to be kept as much apart from politics as possible. As is clear from the above, however, taking this stance does complicate, at least by comparison with certain unrealistically formulaic views, the ongoing task of distinguishing religion and politics. On these matters see Sanford Levinson, *Constitutional Faith* (Princeton: Princeton University Press, 1988). But see also Harold Bloom's fascinating notion of "theomorphism," a deep radicalization of the notion of "anthropologization," in *The Book of J*, trans. David Rosenberg, interpreted by Harold Bloom (New York: Grove Weidenfeld, 1990).

Bloom's conception is anticipated by Hannah Arendt: "Attempts to define human nature almost invariably end with some construction of a deity, that is, with the god of the philosophers, who, since Plato, has revealed himself . . . to be a kind of Platonic idea of man. Of course, to demask such philosophic concepts of the divine as conceptualizations of human capabilities and qualities is not a demonstration of, not even an argument for, the non-existence of God; but the fact that attempts to define the nature of man lead so easily into an idea which definitely strikes us as 'superhuman' and therefore is identified with the divine may cast suspicion upon the very concept of 'human nature'" (*The Human Condition* [Chicago: University of Chicago Press, 1958], pp. 12–13). Arendt's concluding warning will be pertinent to a later stage of the present discussion.

B. Philosophical Voluntarism: Will as Individuality's Resource and Redoubt

> We have a prerogative which some would attribute only to God: each of us,
> when we act, is a prime mover unmoved.
>
> —Roderick Chisholm

1. The Epistemology and Metaphysics of the Will

The medieval voluntarists, keying on scripturally given and hence, to them, undeniable truths, never doubted the reality of either the divine or the human will. Genesis recounted the beginning of all beginnings, God's creation of the universe out of Herself or ex nihilo, and the mystery they attached to the notion of will was essential to allowing them to discuss the creation without diminishing its Creator. Job, the letters of Paul, and teachings of fathers of the church also established the human will and invoked it as a kind of explanation of much that would otherwise be utterly inexplicable. Nor did the antivoluntarist theologians of the *via antiqua* deny either the divine or the human will. They were affrighted by the latter (and perhaps the former as well) and hence sought to surround it with fear, guilt, and shame, but they never questioned its reality or its importance.

When or as these revelational/theological considerations lost their standing as guarantees, the question of the reality of the will forced itself on philosophy (a development that was no doubt given impetus by the theological emphasis on the fundamentally mysterious character of the will). Difficult as it is to find postmedieval philosophers who do not regularly employ the term *will* and its cognates in discussing human action, officially or programmatically many of them treat it as no more than a name for other (putatively?) more tangible things such as desires, intentions, or dispositions, or they seek to banish it altogether.[24] From, say, Hobbes and David Hume to Gilbert Ryle and Donald Davidson, the will plays no

---

[24]In her—as always inimitable—survey of the history of the will, Hannah Arendt claims that the Greek philosophers had no concept of the will and treats much of the postmedieval rejection of the notion as a reversion to classical thinking in this regard. See vol. 2 of *Life of the Mind*, passim.

independent or substantive role in much of Western philosophical and empirical psychology and philosophy of action.

It must also be noted that reductions, dismissals, and denials of the will occur in many thinkers who can readily be classified as strong voluntarists in respect to their moral and political thinking. Hobbes and Hume are clear examples and Michel de Montaigne a plausible one among early-modern voluntarists, while thinkers as central to later strong voluntarism as William James and Sartre are often indifferent to questions about the status or character of the will; Nietzsche himself, no less than the theorist of the "will to power," was sometimes dismissive, not infrequently antagonistic, toward claims concerning it.

Perhaps, then, the concept or category of the will is a specifically religious or theological residue that we are better off without. Perhaps there can be a "willful," a voluntaristic and individuality-affirming/promoting liberalism, including one that appropriates elements of medieval voluntarism, in which the term *will* operates not as a metaphysical, ontological, or empirical category but as a rhetorically emphatic abbreviation of or stand-in for a variety of more tangible characteristics and attributes of human beings and their actings. Perhaps what we need is a semiotic (a pragmatics?) rather than a metaphysic or ontology of the will.[25]

However we resolve the question of the standing of the will as a force, faculty, or other differentiated entity, we must recognize that inquiry concerning it has been a major site of reflections concerning issues that we can hardly avoid. As in the theologians I have been discussing, secular theorists of the will have been trying to explicate

---

[25]Cf. Gilbert Ryle: "I hope to refute the doctrine that there exists a Faculty, immaterial Organ, or Ministry, corresponding to what it describes as 'volitions'. I must however make it clear from the start that this refutation will not invalidate the distinctions which we all quite properly draw between voluntary and involuntary actions and between strong-willed and weak-willed persons. It will, on the contrary, make clearer what is meant by 'voluntary' and 'involuntary,' by 'strong-willed' and 'weak-willed,' by emancipating these ideas from bondage to an absurd hypothesis" (*The Concept of Mind* [New York: Barnes & Noble, 1949], p. 63).

And Nietzsche (from whom I have taken the notion of a semiotic of the will): "moral judgment is never to be taken literally: as such it never contains anything but nonsense. But as *semeotics* [sic] it remains of incalculable value: it reveals, to the informed man at least, the most precious realities of cultures and inner worlds which did not *know* enough to 'understand' themselves" (*Twilight of the Idols*, trans. R. J. Hollingdale [Harmondsworth: Penguin Books, 1968], sec. 8, par. 1, p. 55).

the distinction between voluntary actions and involuntary movements, behaviors, or processes; between events that permit of explanation in terms of causally efficient antecedents and those that do not. Perhaps the notion of the will as an unmoved mover now sounds quaintly or even dangerously religious/theological; but do we have a better way to conceptualize, and at least to that extent to understand, sometimes-prized notions such as initiation and origination, spontaneity and creativity, self-determination and autonomy? It will further our consideration of these matters to look at attempts to defend the reality and importance of the will that proceed without appeal to revelation. Among the most accessible of such efforts are those of Arthur Schopenhauer and his twentieth-century descendent and heir Brian O'Shaughnessy.

Schopenhauer (sometimes partly followed in this respect by Nietzsche) distinguished between the "will in itself" and (as regards human beings and the higher animals) its "phenomenal manifestations" in this or that perception, thought, action, and so forth, that is (as he seems to have seen it), in all of the occurrences in the lives of all persons. The phenomenal manifestations of the will are brought about, that is caused, by sensations, motives, intentions, purposes, and the like, and each of these latter has an object or end toward which it moves. Indeed, each person "has permanent aims and motives by which he guides his conduct, and he can always give an account of his particular actions" (Schopenhauer, *World as Will and Idea*, p. 179). Moreover, "since . . . necessity is throughout identical with following from given grounds, and . . . these are convertible conceptions, all that belongs to the phenomenon, *i.e.*, all that is object for the knowing subject as individual, is in one aspect reason, and in another aspect consequent; and in this last capacity is determined with absolute necessity" (p. 298). This necessity, however, this pattern of strict determination, rather than extending to the will in itself, presupposes not only that the latter *is* (in-itself) but that it is self-determining. Completing the two passages just quoted in part: "but if [an individual] . . . were asked why he wills at all, or why in general he wills to exist, he would have no answer, and the question would indeed seem to him meaningless; and this would be just the expression of his consciousness that he himself is nothing but will, whose willing stands by itself and requires more particular determination by motives only in its individual acts at each point in time" (p. 179). "In another aspect . . . the same world is . . . objectivity of

same world is . . . objectivity of will. And the will [in itself] . . . is not idea or object, but thing in itself, and is . . . not determined, knows no necessity, i.e., is *free*" (pp. 298–99).[26]

The will in itself, then, is a, or rather *the*, vital force, the in itself, that which is necessary to, presupposed by, all movement (or at least all of our conceptions and hence identifications of movement?). In manifesting itself in the phenomenal realm the will in itself "avails itself" of other faculties, but the latter "no more constitute the vital force than the hammer and anvil make a blacksmith" (p. 158). Knowledge, or awareness, or consciousness of the will in itself, accordingly, is not on the basis of reason and does not consist of the patterns of necessity with which reason is exclusively concerned. The will in itself, then, is an epistemological necessity. Every demonstration of reason "requires an undemonstrated truth" (p. 80), "every explanation in natural science must ultimately end with . . . a *qualitas occulta,* and thus with complete obscurity" (pp. 97–98).

---

[26]Cf. Nietzsche: "*Two kinds of causes that are often confounded.*—This seems to me to be one of my most essential steps and advances: I have learned to distinguish the cause of acting from the cause of acting in a particular way, in a particular direction, with a particular goal. The first kind of cause is a quantum of dammed-up energy that is waiting to be used up somehow, for something, while the second kind is, compared to this energy, something quite insignificant, for the most part a little accident in accordance with which this quantum 'discharges' itself in one particular way—a match versus a ton of powder. Among these little accidents and 'matches' I include so-called 'purposes' as well as the even much more so-called 'vocations': They are relatively random, arbitrary, almost indifferent in relation to the tremendous quantum of energy that presses . . . to be used up somehow. The usual view is different: People are accustomed to consider the goal (purposes, vocations, etc.) as the *driving force,* in keeping with a very ancient error; but it is merely the *directing force*—one has mistaken the helmsman for the steam. And not even always the helmsman, the directing force.

"Is the 'goal,' the 'purpose' not often enough a beautifying pretext, a self-deception of vanity after the event that does not want to acknowledge that the ship is *following* the current into which it has entered accidentally? that it 'wills' to go that way *because it—must*? that it has a direction, to be sure, but—no helmsman at all?" (*The Gay Science,* trans. Walter Kaufmann [New York: Vintage Books, 1974], bk. 5, par. 360, pp. 315–16). Nietzsche's first kind of cause is strongly reminiscent of Schopenhauer's will in itself. And if we think of the rational necessity that Schopenhauer attributes to the phenomenal will a posteriori, as discovered by reason after the phenomenal will has manifested itself, then there is no great distance between Nietzsche and Schopenhauer as regards Nietzsche's second kind of cause. The difference, of course, is that Nietzsche wanted to get the "will" of his second paragraph out of scare quotes, to free it from its determinations, whereas Schopenhauer wanted to still the will in itself and thereby put an end to its phenomenal manifestations as well.

The will in itself is the undemonstrated and undemonstrable truth, the *qualitas occulta* at which all explanation terminates. It is and can only be "immediately comprehended" (p. 127). Knowledge or consciousness of it is and must be "the most direct knowledge," knowledge that "if we do not apprehend it and stick to it as such, we shall expect in vain to receive it again in some indirect way as derivative knowledge" (p. 118).

The will in itself is the thing-in-itself rescued from the philosophical oblivion to which Schopenhauer's teacher Kant had relegated it. It is the "inevitable condition and presupposition of every action" (p. 123). Without it there would be neither human action nor any other life or movement. Our unmediated, intuitive, but entirely certain consciousness of it is the foundation of all of our perceiving, thinking, and comprises "*kat' exochen*" or "*philosophical truth*" (p. 119) (truth as it would be known by God if there were one, as it is known by the Wo/Man-Gods that we are). Its phenomenal manifestations are shaped and directed by beliefs, desires, and intentions that are fully comprehended by reason, and reason's comprehension of them comprises scientific truth.

At the same time, in respect to "the human species," these shaping and directing forces distinguish every individual from all others so that each among them "has to be studied and fathomed for himself, which, if we wish to forecast his action with some degree of certainty, is . . . a matter of the greatest difficulty" (p. 147). More particularly, each person's conception of her good is given, that is determined, by her will, "good" signifying "*the conformity of an object to any definite effort of the will.*" Thus Schopenhauer proceeds to advance a metaethics that directly echoes that of Hobbes: "We call everything good that is just as we wish it to be; and therefore that may be good in the eyes of one man which is just the reverse in those of another" (p. 370).[27]

Thus the will in itself constitutes us and our world. To deny the will is to deny ourselves and our world. "No will: no idea, no

[27]Cf. the passage quoted from Hobbes in n. 60 below. Schopenhauer occasionally mentions Hobbes, and the large areas in which Schopenhauer's thinking, wittingly or otherwise, agrees with the latter's extend to his somewhat rudimentary contractarian political theory. See pp. 342ff. of *World as Will and Idea* where, inter alia, he favorably cites Hobbes's *De Cive* and argues that the state exists exclusively to maintain peace sufficient to allow individuals to pursue their particular ends. I discuss these of his views in Section IV below.

world" (p. 420). Individuation, however—that is, the delineations we effect among ourselves and our worlds—is the work of the phenomenal manifestations of the will.

Of course, in a sense of *denial* other than the one I have been using, Schopenhauer is perhaps the most unremitting of the deniers of the will. As he saw it, the phenomenal manifestations of the will are inveterately at odds with one another, and the will in itself is incessantly in conflict with "physical and chemical forces" that it can never subdue for long. Accordingly, the "ceaseless striving" (the characteristic that Schopenhauer most often affirmatively predicates of the will in itself) of the will, rather than yielding success or satisfactions, pleasure or happiness, all but inevitably results in a misery that ends for the individual only in her death and that will end for humankind only with the disappearance of the species. "The in itself of life, the will, existence itself, is . . . a constant sorrow, partly miserable, partly terrible" (p. 278).[28]

Schopenhauer's will in itself is intended to encompass the initiation of movement, the fact that animate creatures and things move *of their own accord*. The will in itself no more *explains* movement than the divine will of the theological voluntarists explains the doings of God,[29] but a philosophy that has no place for it fails to accommodate, to acknowledge, as we might say,[30] the single most

---

[28]Schopenhauer allows that the artist, above all the musical artist, by ascending to the contemplation of pure beauty, can achieve moments of respite from this suffering, as can the saint who by practicing a rigorous asceticism reaches a state of complete resignation. But these are palliatives and in any case are available to no more than a few. Rejecting suicide on the ground that it itself is an act and hence an expression of will, Schopenhauer counsels the letting happen of death by a starvation gradual enough to require little engagement or exercise of the will! (*World as Will and Idea*, p. 392.) Here as with Augustine we see that foregrounding the will is far from a certain means of promoting individuality.

[29]Schopenhauer's frequent use of vitalistic language only appears to belie this claim. As a *qualitas occulta* to which reason has no access, the will in itself cannot figure in explanations.

[30]I have in mind Stanley Cavell's notion of acknowledgment as developed in chap. 9 of *Must We Mean What We Say?* (New York: Scribners, 1969) and deployed in *The Claim of Reason* (New York: Oxford University Press, 1979), in *In Quest of the Ordinary* (Chicago: University of Chicago Press, 1988), and elsewhere. Neither Ockham's invocations of the divine and the human will nor Schopenhauer's invocations of the will in itself are fully parallel with Cavell's notion of acknowledging (for example) one's pains, but there is a suggestive analogy between them. In the ordinary sense of "know," Ockham can no more claim to know God's will or Schopenhauer to know the will in itself than on Cavell's Wittgensteinian view I can

important characteristic of human and more generally animate existence. On Schopenhauer's account of it, we can't do a whole lot with the notion of the will in itself, but nor can we get along without it.

It is nevertheless understandable that later thinkers have been dismissive of or antagonistic toward Schopenhauer's will in itself. As he himself insists, *no* instance of believing or thinking, hoping or fearing, doing or foregoing, perceiving, feeling, or judging can be so much as identified in terms of the will in itself. All of these states and events, occurrences and processes, and all of our delineations and understandings, explanations and assessments of them, all of our actions and reactions in response to them, are in terms of the phenomenal manifestations of the will, are in the differentiating terms of desires, intentions, purposes, motives, habits, dispositions, reasons, and the like. Since it is allowed that the concept of the will in itself can do none of this work, parsimony itself would seem to counsel that we banish it from metaphysics and ontology, dismiss it from philosophical and empirical psychology.[31]

Yet more pointedly in the present context, concern for individuality might itself seem to demand that we forswear or insistently subordinate anything like Schopenhauer's notion of the will. If the will in itself is a something common not only to all persons but to all of animate nature, does not insistence on it homogenize, subsume and subordinate, does it not contravene the very purposes of an individuating liberalism? Are not all affirmations of the will in itself likely to become what Nietzsche thought the Christian conception of the human will had always (save in Christ himself?) been, that is,

---

claim to know that I am in pain. Yet it is at least (!) as important to Ockham to acknowledge God's will, and to Schopenhauer to acknowledge the will in itself, as on Cavell's view it is to us to acknowledge our pains to ourselves and to one another. None of these acknowledgings explains the phenomena they acknowledge, but they play a salient role in our self-understandings and in many of our performances. Of course, "acknowledging the will" need not involve endorsing anything like Schopenhauer's epistemology and metaphysics.

(For a closely related use of the concept of acknowledging, see Hobbes, *Elements of Law*, I, chap. 11.)

[31]Cf. Nietzsche: "Schopenhauer's 'Will' is nothing else but the most general phenomenal form of a Something otherwise absolutely indecipherable" ("On Music and Words," vol. 2, in *The Complete Works of Friedrich Nietzsche*, ed. Oscar Levy [London: T. N. Foulis, 1911], p. 31. (This fragment was written in 1871, i.e., before Nietzsche had begun, at least officially, to distance himself from Schopenhauer.)

bases for doctrines of responsibility the demands of which can never be satisfied and that therefore generate self-consuming guilt and shame, unremitting blame and punishment? "One has deprived becoming of its innocence if being in this or that state is traced back to will. . . . The doctrine of will has been invented essentially for the purpose of punishment, that is of *finding guilty*. The whole of the . . . psychology of will, has as its precondition the desire of its authors, the priests at the head of the ancient communities, to create for themselves a *right* to ordain punishments—or their desire to create for God a right to do so. . . . [ellipses Nietzsche's] Men were thought of as 'free' so that they could become *guilty*: consequently, every action *had* to be thought of as willed" (*Twilight of the Idols*, sec. 7, par. 7, p. 53).[32]

Despite the passages I have thus far quoted from him, Nietzsche himself did not jettison the will in itself. In order to combat the uses Christianity made of the notion, he followed Schopenhauer in denying it any explanatory role[33] but rejected the latter's pessimism and appropriated the will to an understanding and an ideal at once life-affirming and (often) powerfully individuating. Before turning to these of his efforts let us examine the attempt of Brian O'Shaughnessy to give the will a more determinate and hence more respectable place in philosophical psychology and the theory of action.

Generically, O'Shaughnessy's theory of the will is strongly continuous with Schopenhauer's account of the will in itself. Will as life force, as movement, as striving; will as known to us directly and

[32]"The entire doctrine of the will, this most fateful *falsification* in psychology hitherto, was essentially invented for the sake of punishment. It was the social *utility* of punishment that guaranteed this concept its dignity, its power, its truth. The originators of this psychology—the psychology of will—are to be sought in the classes that administered the penal law, above all among the priests at the head of the oldest communality: they wanted to create for themselves a right to take revenge—they wanted to create a right for *God* to take revenge. To this end, man was conceived of as 'free'; to this end, every action had to be conceived of as willed, the origin of every action as conscious" (Friedrich Nietzsche, *The Will to Power*, trans. Walter Kaufmann and R. J. Hollingdale, ed. Walter Kaufmann [New York: Vintage Books, 1967], par. 765, pp. 401–2). Thus it became Nietzsche's project to divest the will and us of these burdens, to refashion the "free will" in a manner appropriate to "free spirits."

[33]In this respect he in effect also followed Ockham. So far as I have been able to discover, however, he never mentions Ockham, Duns Scotus, or any other late-medieval voluntarist. Insofar as he was aware of the *via moderna* theologians, they are represented for him by the repugnant Augustinian views of Martin Luther.

undeniably; will as a something without the acknowledgment of which there is a lacuna in our articulate conceptions of ourselves and of other animate creatures.[34] But O'Shaughnessy offers a more differentiated treatment of the will. Apparently eschewing Schopenhauer's distinction between the will in itself and its phenomenal manifestations, he attempts to delineate the differences between and the relationships among the will on the one hand and desires, intentions, beliefs, and other psychological components of and influences on bodily action on the other. In broad terms, his analysis and defense of the reality of the will falls into three interwoven and complementary categories: (1) attempts to show that the leading alternative accounts of bodily action, i.e., materialist or physicalist, behaviorist and neobehavioralist, and belief-desire-intention theories, such as Davidson's "intensionalist extroversionism" (as O'Shaughnessy styles it), presuppose but fail to encompass elements necessary to action—specifically the will; (2) analyses of the limits of the will, of processes in which the will plays no part (e.g., the workings of bodily organs such as the liver and kidneys) and events in which it has no or a narrowly circumscribed role (e.g., dreaming and laughing, belief formation); (3) affirmative characterizations of the will and its operations which, among other things, discredit theories of volitionism according to which the will is "private," is divorced from the body, is ineffable, magical, and so forth. The intricate, indeed rococo, detail of his treatment of (2) and (3) is for the most part beyond our present needs, but for reasons already indicated we must attend to his attempt to establish the will as an entity that is conceptually and empirically distinct as well as necessitated by the requirements of certain theories.

Traditional volitionisms, intensionalist extroversion, and O'Shaughnessy's revised volitionism reject physicalism and behaviorism because, very roughly, they fail to recognize self-consciousness, thereby losing the distinction between movements or behaviors and voluntary physical actions. Intensionalist extroversion analyzes voluntary physical actions into four elements and the relationships among them, namely, the occurrence, at a particular moment in time, of intending, desiring, knowing, and an event that

---

[34]It is important to recognize that O'Shaughnessy's theory is primarily concerned with will as an element in bodily action as distinct from its role in mental events and processes such as imaging, belief formation, and the like.

O'Shaughnessy dubs "the seeming" to the agent that she is attempting a particular bodily action (*The Will*, vol. 2, p. 262).[35] On this account, all "that is supposedly phenomenally special to voluntary action is the intention state's mutating to the point of having a here-and-now indexically given object," that is, a particular bodily action to take place at *this* time and place (ibid.).

This "tough-minded, extrovert, meager picture," he insists, "is strongly counter-intuitive." The items to which it restricts itself "fail to 'stitch together' as parts of one anything, be it event, process, state." More important than these factors, "and far more centrally significant than them all put together, is the occurrence of a single distinctive event of the type of *willing*" (ibid.).

To establish the reality of the distinct event-type of willing or striving, O'Shaughnessy argues from agential failures and agential illusions, that is, from cases in which the agent tries but fails to perform a bodily action and cases in which she tries, fails, but is under the illusion of having succeeded.

The argument from failure is presented through an example noted earlier: "A photographer asks an actor to lift his arm at t_{I} precisely (when the bell rings), and the 'take' is vital. At t_{I} the actor hears the bell; at t_{I} + .001 sec. an impulse starts down the arm; by t_{I} + .01 it has almost reached the muscles; at t_{I} +.01001 a special apparatus that is being worked at a distance by a gang of anti-social scientists destroys that neural impulse. Accordingly, the muscle fails to contract, the arm fails to move, the photographer swears at the 'star'! The empirical but vitally important question is: did the 'star' try to move his arm?" (p. 265).

Confronted with the anger of the photographer, O'Shaughnessy argues, the star must say more in his own defense than merely that he intended to raise his arm and was surprised (because in his experience his intentions almost always "mutate to a particular action") by its failure to rise. "*Must he not also say: 'I tried'?* Thus, how does he know that 'if I had tried at t_{I} I would have failed'?—except through knowing that he did try and fail at t_{I}? And what escape-type explanatory facts can he indicate to say how it is that he did not . . . [raise his arm]? Hardly: 'I forgot'. Hardly: 'I was

[35]As we see below, formulaically it cannot be treated as more than a seeming (although existentially it is almost always a reality, a knowing) because all of the elements may be present and yet the act be prevented. I leave aside numerous details of his account that are irrelevant here.

prevented'. And if he says: 'My arm would not work', how does he *know* it did not work? Simply through knowing that he knew he intended . . . [arm-raising] at t_1 and . . . [arm-raising] failed to occur? . . . Is there any conceivable way in which we would *not* say of this man: 'He tried and he failed'? No" (pp. 265–66).

In first knowing and then remembering that he tried to raise his arm, the star does not merely know (i.e., knows more than) the "thing in itself." The star knows and remembers a quite particular thing, namely, that he tried, strove, willed, to raise his arm. O'Shaughnessy's account is nevertheless reminiscent of Schopenhauer's in that this knowledge, and the memory of the initial and known event, is given "both immediately and *experientially*." The star does not infer his trying from his intention plus his failure; he "knows of his trying as we know of our sensations: that is, with absolute and non-inferential immediacy."[36] And while the failure brings the trying to the star's attention, trying also occurs "on normal occasions of success. That is, when we normally engage in voluntary physical action, a striving or willing event that is a psychological phenomenon also occurs. . . . In short, the situation of failure has uncovered both an awareness-of-willing *and* a willing that are normally present but masked by circumstances. A consciousness-of-striving *and* a striving as well. Awareness *and* will" (p. 266).[37]

O'Shaughnessy claims, then, that the distinct, irreducible, and experientially substantial event-type of willing is a component of all bodily action. Theories that deny or omit this event-type give an impoverished, a "tragically 'distant' and 'depersonalised'" account

---

[36]In reading this passage it should be borne in mind that for O'Shaughnessy there is an intimate, indeed a necessary, connection between willing and the sensations of perception. See *The Will*, vol. 1, p. xlviii and esp. vol. 2, chap. 8.

[37]In making the argument from illusion, O'Shaughnessy modifies the above example in two ways: the star is prevented from seeing that his arms do not move but is made to think that they do so by artificially generated kinaesthetic sensations. Thus "he intended to . . . [raise his arms] at t_1, and he both tried (which is a *will-event* rather than a consciousness-of), and also [trying to arm rise]-seemed-to-happen and [arm-rising]-seemed-to-happen (which are *consciousnesses-of* rather than willings). Thus since all these [psychic (see ibid., vol. 2, p. 73)] items can obtain independently of the occurrence of [the act of arm-raising], and the internal situation was indistinguishable from that which normally obtains, these must be further psychological ingredients of the normal successful voluntary act situation" (vol. 2, p. 267).

of bodily action. They effect no less than a "distancing of the self from the self" (pp. 265, 266).

On O'Shaughnessy's account of it, the will is potent, in one sense is irresistible, within its domain. Willing just is striving, to will *is* to strive. Thus there can be no such thing as a failed attempt to will (albeit, as we see below, there are conditions that must be satisfied in order for willing to occur). Moreover, will "is a psychic force in the psychic domain" (vol. 1, p. lii), a *force* that is sometimes impeded or counteracted but that always (efficiently) causes some effect or effects. Unlike some depictions of the divine will, however, on O'Shaughnessy's account of it the human will is anything but omnipotent. There is no such thing as efficacious extrabodily willing (so-called psychokinesis) (chaps. 2–3); the will cannot affect internal organs such as the liver;[38] in respect to all but the most primitive of actions[39] it operates or co-acts with perceptions, intentions, reasonings, and the like; it can prepare the way for, but not install, beliefs,[40] and since we can try to perform an act only if we believe it to be possible for us, to this extent willing presupposes "cognitive attitudes" that willing itself cannot produce;[41] the will cannot will itself: "logically necessarily, no trying or striving is ever immediately or non-instrumentally willingly produced. Necessarily, each movement of the will is a fresh and completely novel movement of the will. Inevitably, a new beginning" (p. 36).[42]

[38]"The functioning of most of our internal organs and musculature is in all probability not willed" (ibid., vol. 1, p. 29).

[39]See the discussion of subintentional actions, ibid., vol. 2, chap., 10. Of course, even in subintentional acts such as the aimless leg kickings of infants and the unconscious tongue movements of all of us the efficacy of the will requires the appropriate functioning of various bodily parts.

[40]"Necessarily *believings* are not actions, and also . . . necessarily there is no act that *is* the bringing about of belief; and the necessity has the strength of the entailment bond. We seem to have here a phenomenon that logically falls outside the domain of willable phenomena" (ibid., vol. 1, p. 28).

[41]"While we can choose to try to perform some acts, we cannot choose to try to perform acts we are convinced cannot occur; so that while trying . . . lies within the scope of the will, it simultaneously necessitates the obtaining of certain cognitive attitudes which clearly do *not*" (ibid., vol. 2, p. 46). Cf. the earlier discussion of Duns Scotus and Ockham. Because O'Shaughnessy thinks that cognitive attitudes are also our own in a strong sense (partly because our wills play a role in our acquiring them), there is no reason for him to think that this limitation on our wills constitutes an "imperfection."

[42]The above is only a part of O'Shaughnessy's list of the limitations on the will. The impression of its finitude created by his account is substantially heightened by the further details of his analysis of its workings.

As indicated by this severely selective synopsis,[43] O'Shaughnessy seeks to enhance the credibility of the will and of willing as a discrete psychological entity and process while at the same time embracing the traditional understanding that it is (in itself, as we are drawn to say) inexplicable, mysterious. He delineates the will by locating it in the body and by showing how its "movements" are interwoven with and dependent on other psychological phenomena such as perceptions and beliefs, desires and intentions, thereby attempting to disqualify skepticism concerning its reality; he insists that neither his nor any other such analysis can reduce its movements to or fully explain their occurrence by anything apart from itself, to that extent reiterating the view not only of Schopenhauer but of the theological voluntarists.

If the details of O'Shaughnessy's analytic of bodily action remain contestable (they are certainly contested),[44] the importance of his

---

[43]It is perhaps worth mentioning for readers unfamiliar with O'Shaughnessy's book that it runs to 696 anything-but-short pages.

[44]For an extended exegesis and critique, see Timothy Cleveland, "Acting, Willing, and Trying," Ph.D. diss., The Johns Hopkins University, 1986. Simply assuming the accuracy of O'Shaughnessy's characterizations of intensional extroversion, the disagreements between him and theorists such as Davidson seem to me to turn on three issues. (1) Whether to use the concept "action" to mark events such as tongue movements that are intentional under *no* description. (2) Whether the word "mutate" in the phrase "the intention state's mutating to the point of having a here-and-now indexically given object" does, or can be made to do, all the work done by O'Shaughnessy's "will" in conceptualizing bodily actions. (3) Whether a trying/striving/willing occurs in the many contexts in which as a matter of ordinary linguistic behavior agents do not in fact use the words "trying," "striving," or "willing" in describing, explaining, and defending their actions. Detailed treatment of these issues would take us very far afield, but the following remarks, intended to complement (and to that limited extent, to support) positions taken in the remainder of the discussion, may not be irrelevant.

Taking these issues in reverse order: (3) As regards actions that are intentional under some description, I see no very urgent reason to object to O'Shaughnessy's view that all actions involve a trying. (See *The Will*, vol. 2, chap. 9. But compare Cleveland, "Acting, Willing, and Trying," and George Wilson, *The Intentionality of Human Action* rev. and enl. ed. [Stanford: Stanford University Press, 1989], pp. 151ff.) As to (2), and again with respect to intentional actions, *if* the alternative is to talk of one set of intentional states "mutating" to another, O'Shaughnessy's invocation of the will, that is, of trying or striving, seems to me the less obscurantist of the two. (Later we will see that Nietzsche in effect rejects these choices, offers alternative means of incorporating the will in our accounts of our thinking and acting.) On the other hand, (1) the notion of a subintentional action, and more generally O'Shaughnessy's admittedly "very generous and artificial sense for 'voluntary'" (p. 255), has all of the earmarks of having been adopted precisely for the purpose of defending the reality of the will against intensional extroversion. (He allows that subinten-

theory lies in his attempt to couple a detailed theory of action to a notion that he claims is in important part unsusceptible to analytic disaggregation, in his notion of will as beginning, as initiation, in his insistence that for all of the limitations on it "every movement of the will is a fresh and completely novel movement of"—itself. In part because his analytic of action lessens our perplexities concerning ourselves,[45] with this notion he gives us reason to join his strong voluntarist predecessors in acknowledging, cheerfully as we might put it, the ultimately mysterious character of our actions.[46]

2. A Semiotic of the Will

From the standpoint of the present project, O'Shaughnessy's theory diminishes but does not fully dispose of the difficulties posed by

---

tional actions "are in themselves the very scrapings of the barrel of action" but insists that "they are theoretically of the first importance to any theory of action" [p. 62].) However this may be, a) the "actions" that he identifies as subintentional are of little interest for present purposes, and (*b*) his insistence on classifying them as voluntary is largely responsible for his rejection of a variety of plausible if partial accounts of that notion (esp. chap. 16) and his not especially illuminating conclusion that there is one but only one "psychological phenomenon common to all cases of voluntary action. Namely: the volition" (p. 250). Why should a thinker otherwise so heavily indebted to Wittgenstein think that *either* we find a single feature common to all uses of "voluntary" *or* "the concept of voluntary action is inchoate"? (p. 249).

[45]As compared with Schopenhauer, a major advantage of O'Shaughnessy's theory of action is signaled by my use of the word "lessen" in respect to the perplexities that attend those parts of our acting that both of them think are susceptible of analysis. In abandoning Schopenhauer's bizarre rational necessitarianism in respect to particular actions, he preserves the sense of complexity and unpredictability as regards even those dimensions of our conduct that we understand—or can hope to understand—best.

[46]"The astonishing thing about action is that it is possible at all. . . . Action seems like a leak from another realm or world into this world, a leak or intervention—an intervention such as God would effect were He able to engender change in the world without transgressing the Laws of Nature. . . . By action we irreducibly alter the state of the universe: a form or pattern appears that was not there before, the existence of which does not seem to follow in any way from the physical state of the universe beforehand. This is *creation*" (O'Shaughnessy, *The Will*, vol. 2, pp. 1–2). This conception of human action as wonder-ful cannot stand alone, must be located among numerous other conceptions and understandings that may be wonderful but are not, or not to the same extent, objects of wonderment. It is nevertheless the single most important idea in strong voluntarism, the idea—and ideal—in strong voluntarism that is most valuable to a liberalism with a heightened sense of and commitment to individuality.

the conception of will as initiator or unmoved but moving force. The notion of the will is undeniably attractive to, and is in some form unavoidable for, strong theories of individuality. Yet thinking of *the* will, conceiving of *it* as a single entity or force that plays a decisive role in all human actions, appears to deindividuate actions, to render them common or homogeneous rather than differentiated, distinct, unique. And, further, when the undeniable differences among human actions are put down to disparities among somatic constitutions, desires, beliefs, intentions, and the like, that is, to factors that are insisted to be subject not only to investigation, understanding, and assessment but to causal analysis (hence causally efficacious interventions by others?), the sense of individuality and novelty—certainly the sense of mystery and any protections it might afford—threatens to disappear. The introduction of the concept of the will into the theory of action does not by itself effect a sufficiently sharp distinction between strong and weak voluntarism. As O'Shaughnessy and to a lesser extent Schopenhauer deploy it, will operates to enable mutual understanding and access, that is, in much the same way as do rationality and reasonableness in the weaker forms of voluntarism discussed at the outset of Part Two.

It is not open to us entirely to resist or even to regret this tendency. Just as rest or quiet is a presupposition of the concept of movement, so sameness is a supposition of difference, familiarity of novelty, commonality or generality of individuality, the meaningful of the meaningless, understanding or comprehension of mystery. Indeed the latter of all but the first of these pairs must almost certainly be interstitial and at least in that sense subordinate to the former. For these and other reasons that will appear in due course, O'Shaughnessy's and related efforts to identify and to locate the will are contributive, not opposed to, present purposes.

We should consider, then, the possibility of a conception of will and its role in action that preserves the notion of initiation so deservedly prominent in the accounts given by O'Shaughnessy[47]

[47]O'Shaughnessy claims that the will is the very locus, the constitutive element of, individuation in the basic sense of having a sense of self as distinct from other. "Striving . . . never happens *to* one. Hence its voluntariness looks to be *intrinsic and derivative from nothing else.*" "Striving" meets the "absolutely vital need of providing an event that is *so* special that, howsoever compelled or mindless or automatic, its happening *in* one is necessarily never its happening *to* one. . . . For striving is willing. Necessarily, willing never happens to one. This . . . is precisely the distinctive

and Schopenhauer but that is less reductive, univocal, and mono-lithic than theirs.

One of the recurring themes in Nietzsche's protracted and often-ambivalent engagement with Schopenhauer consists in his claim that, as a matter both of intention and of logic, Schopenhauer made individuality an impossibility. As Nietzsche saw it, Schopenhauer's desire to repress or even to eradicate the will was simply another expression of the Christianity-generated hatred for everything hu-man and indeed worldly, everything less than the still eternality of God.[48] Consistent with this objective, and despite (or perhaps due

---

character of willing. This is its essence" (ibid., p. 260). Thus willing, along with the bodily action to which it is essential, is *"par excellence* an ego phenomenon. More, it is pre-eminently that through which the individuality of man finds objectifica-tion. . . . Indeed, it is uniquely through bodily action that men have an opportunity to alter the world in ways which affirm and actually consolidate their individuality" (vol. 1, p. liv). Nevertheless, on his own account of it willing is only a necessary, never a sufficient, condition of bodily action. Thus (with the partial exception of "subintentional" actions) the actions one actually takes, the actions that manifest or "objectify" one's individuality, cannot occur or be identified apart from the beliefs, desires, intentions, and so forth, that are also necessary to them. More serious, O'Shaughnessy insists on "the utter simplicity of trying." "Trying . . . [is] nothing but the . . . will moving in a certain direction. That, and no more" (vol. 2, p. 115). Will provides the *force* that no other agency can supply. "Thus [for example], while intention is a causal agency in the production of some actions, it is efficacious in those transactions pretty much as is the turning of a key in the opening of a door, *i.e.,* in removing the impediment to the efficacy of a thrust that acts *in a different way altogether.* Just as no key turning has without force ever caused a door to swing ajar, so no intention in the absence of will has ever caused a limb . . . to move. Action must . . . retain its fundamental character as force-laden and energetic expression of psychic thrust, and it would be to endorse a dictatorship of the intellect to permit the facts of control and significance to erase this primaeval element from one's theory" (vol. 1, p. lxii).

Once again, if the alternative were to endorse a "dictatorship of the intellect," I would be attracted to O'Shaughnessy's view. But the utter simplicity of will, its reduction to "force," "psychic thrust," "energy" necessarily deprive *it* of all indi-viduating effects, with the possible exception of the sense of self, of happening in rather than to. And, taken alone, even the latter seems to lack any account of a something rather than an anything or nothing that happens in the self. Fortunately, the alternatives are not those to which O'Shaughnessy would reduce us.

[48]"Against the theory that an 'in-itself of things' must necessarily be good, blessed, true, and one, Schopenhauer's interpretation of the 'in-itself' as will was an essential step; but he . . . remained entangled in the moral-Christian ideal . . . was so much subject to the dominion of Christian values that, as soon as the thing-in-itself was no longer 'God' for him, he had to see it as bad, stupid, and absolutely reprehensible" (Nietzsche, *Will to Power,* par. 1005, p. 521). The passage concludes in a manner relevant to the continuation of the discussion above: "He failed to grasp

to the character of) Schopenhauer's gestures toward *principium individuationis* such as particular objectives and purposes, Nietzsche found Schopenhauer's " 'individuum' meaningless, necessitating an origin in the 'in-itself' (and an explanation of his [i.e., the individual's?] existence as an 'aberration,' " and he accused him of comprising "the entirety of life hitherto in one development" (*Will to Power*, par. 379, p. 204).[49]

As we have seen, however, despite these and many other animadversions against Schopenhauer and other theorists of the will, Nietzsche was very far from abandoning the notion. Enlisting in the company that sees will as initiator, as a kind of locus of beginnings, he adopted it as a necessary supposition and then proceeded to disaggregate it in ways intended to avoid the evils wreaked by the Christian doctrine of free will and the mischiefs worked by Schopenhauer's reifications.

"I require the starting point of 'will to power' as the origin of motion. Hence motion may not be conditioned from the outside—not caused——I require beginnings and centers of motion from which the will spreads—" (p. 295).[50] But the possibility of satisfy-

---

that there can be an infinite variety of ways of being different, even of being god" (ibid.). Cf. *Human, All Too Human*: "Even the word 'will', which Schopenhauer remoulded as a common designation for many different human states . . . has . . . through the philosopher's rage for generalization [been] . . . pressed into the service of all kinds of mystical mischief [and] . . . misemployed towards a false reification [such] . . . that all things possess *one* will and, indeed, *are* this one will (which from the description they give of [it] . . . is as good as wanting to make God out to be the *stupid Devil*)" (Friedrich Nietzsche, trans. R. J. Hollingdale. 2 vols. [Cambridge: Cambridge University Press, 1966], vol. 2, pt. 1, par. 5, pp. 215–16).

[49]For reasons partly discussed above, one suspects that Nietzsche would find that O'Shaughnessy's treatment of the relation between will on the one hand and intentions, purposes, and so forth on the other makes matters worse rather than better in this regard. See, for example, *Gay Science*, bk. 5, par. 360, pp. 315–16, and the numerous other derogatory references to "purposes" and related notions that are scattered liberally through his works.

[50]This passage appears in a footnote added to par. 551 by Walter Kaufmann. He identifies its source as vol. 16, p. 507, of the Grossoktav edition of Nietzsche's *Werke*.

In *Beyond Good and Evil* Nietzsche expresses a very similar thought in the form of an "hypothesis": "we *must* experiment with taking will-causality as our only hypothesis. . . . Enough said: we must risk the hypothesis that everywhere we recognize 'effects' there is an effect of will upon will" (trans. Marianne Cowan [Chicago: Henry Regenry, 1955], par. 36, pp. 44–45). This passage ends with one of the many articulations of what often appears to be a Nietzschean reduction every

ing this requirement[51] is forfeited if we treat the will, *à la* Schopenhauer or O'Shaughnessy, as a single and internally simple or monolithic entity, faculty, or force. The will that Nietzsche "supposes" or hypothesizes, rather, is "a resultant, a kind of individual reaction which necessarily follows a host of partly contradictory, partly congruous stimuli—the will no longer 'effects' anything, no longer

bit as severely deindividuating as Schopenhauer's will in itself. If the above "hypothesis" is made credible, "we should be justified in defining *all* effective energy unequivocally as *will to power*. The world seen from within, the world designated and defined according to its 'intelligible character'—this would be *will to power* and nothing else" (ibid.). Taken as descriptive-explanatory, of course, this "causal hypothesis" must be understood in the light of Nietzsche's well-known "perspectivalist" views concerning causality and science, not in some empiricist or positivist fashion. More important, this and Nietzsche's innumerable other discussions of the "will to power" must be understood as articulations of an ideal. I discuss the notion from this perspective below.

[51]From a Schopenhauerian standpoint, the "requirement" would be viewed as epistemological. The will is that *qualitas occulta* that is presupposed by all knowing. I take it that for Nietzsche it is at once conceptual (or perhaps ontological?) and axiological. The concepts of action and movement, concepts that are at the very center of Nietzsche's thinking, presuppose notions such as initiation and origination, of a starting point and a beginning. He requires the notion of beginnings in the sense that without it he could not formulate other thoughts that are of immense importance to him.

But Nietzsche does not want merely to "formulate thoughts" about action and movement, he wants to liberate those notions from the constraints of Christian and other moralities, to celebrate them as giving exhilaration and gaiety to life. If we did not posit will to power, if we hypothesized causes of action external to those who act, then the joy and delight, the torment and anguish attendant on them, would either disappear or transfer to some site other than the person doing the acting.

Nietzsche's often acerbic attacks on "playacting" and especially on the excessive "theatricality" of the Greek life that he otherwise admired are relevant here. (See, for example, *Gay Science*, bk. 5, par. 356, pp. 302–4.) Theatricality in the sense of acting with at least one eye to the reactions of the "audience," while it does not shift the efficient cause of action outside of the person who acts, diminishes the "actor" by according to the audience determination of the "meaning" (the "final" cause?) of the action. Much of Nietzsche's own counterideal is expressed by his frequent and always strongly valorized use of notions such as self-containment and solitude, cleanliness and fastidiousness.

These features of Nietzsche's thinking are importantly problematic and will have to be given more detailed consideration below. My own appreciation for these among his views, however, has been enhanced by considering them in connection with Hannah Arendt's—in other respects recognizably Nietzschean—insistently theatrical conception of political action. For a subtle exploration of this theme in another but hardly irrelevant context, see Michael Fried, *Absorption and Theatricality* (Berkeley: University of California Press, 1980).

'moves' anything."[52] Here, with no apologies for the length of the quotation, is Nietzsche's most detailed characterization/ appreciation of "the" will:

Philosophers are in the habit of speaking of "will" as though it were the best-known thing in the world. Schopenhauer in fact gave us to understand that will alone is really known to us, completely known, known without deduction or addition. But it seems to me once again that Schopenhauer . . . did only what philosophers are always doing: he took over and exaggerated a *popular judgment*. Willing seems to me to be, above all, something *complicated*, something that is a unity in word only.[53] The popular judgment lies just in this word "only", and it has become master of the forever incautious philosophers. Let us be more cautious, then; let us be 'unphilosophical'; let us say: in every willing there is first of all a multiplicity of feelings: the feeling of a condition to get *away* from, the feeling of a condition to get *to*; . . . furthermore, an accompanying muscular feeling which, from a sort of habit, begins a game of its own as soon as we "will"—even without our moving our "arms and legs". In the first place, then, feeling— many different kinds of feeling—is to be recognized as an ingredient in willing. Secondly, there is thinking: in every act of the will there is a thought which gives commands—and we must not imagine that we can separate this thought out of "willing" and still have something like the will left![54] Thirdly, the will is not merely a complex of feeling

[52]Friedrich Nietzsche, *The Anti-Christ*, trans., R. J. Hollingdale (Harmondsworth: Penguin Books, 1968), par. 14, p. 124. The appearance that the last clauses of this passage *formally* contradict statements previously quoted from Nietzsche is dissolved in what follows, but as is clear from the passage as a whole Nietzsche (like Ockham) rejects the very possibility of a fully coherent account of the will. It is not to be thought, however, that he (any more than Ockham) laments the unavailability of such an account.

[53]Here, as through much of his work, Nietzsche quietly aligns himself with a form of nominalism strongly reminiscent of Ockham. The next sentences indicate that, as with Ockham, his use of phrases like "a unity in word only" are dismissive of misguided philosophical views but not of the bringing together and subsuming effected by the "popular" uses of the word. Indeed for both Ockham and Nietzsche (as for Hobbes) the act of naming, especially when it involves bringing manifestly disparate phenomena together under a single name, is among the most creative of divine and human powers.

[54]This last clause, and its vital role in the whole notion that the will is a complex, a manifold of mutually interdependent elements that meld into and out of one another, marks the most important difference between Nietzsche and O'Shaughnessy. Of course, O'Shaughnessy agrees that the will functions, can only function effectively, in company with the other elements that Nietzsche summons, but his analytic

and thinking but above all it is a passion—the passion of commanding. What is called "freedom of the will" is essentially a passionate
superiority toward a someone who must obey. "I am free; 'he' must
obey"—the consciousness of this is the very willing; likewise the
tension of alertness, that straightforward look which fixes on one
thing exclusively, that absolute valuation which means "just now this,
and nothing else, is necessary", that inner certainty that there will be
obedience—all this and whatever else is part of the condition of one
who is in command. A man who *wills* is giving a command to something in himself that obeys, or which he believes will obey.[55] But now
let us note the oddest thing about the will, this manifold something for
which people have only one word: because we, in a given case, are
simultaneously the commanders *and* the obeyers, and, as obeyers,
know the feelings of forcing, crowding, pressing, resisting, and moving which begin immediately after the act of the will: because, on the
other hand, we are in the habit of glossing over this duality with the
help of the synthetic concept "I"—for these reasons a whole chain of
erroneous conclusions, and consequently false valuations of the will,
has weighted down our notion of willing, so much so that the willer
believes in good faith that willing *suffices* to produce action.[56] Because in the majority of cases there was a willing only where the effect
of the command, the obedience, i.e. the action, was an *expected* one,
the *appearance* translated itself into the feeling that there had been a
necessary effect. In short, the willer believes, with a considerable
degree of certainty, that will and action are somehow one. He credits
the success, the execution of the willing, to the will itself, therewith
luxuriating in an increase of the feeling of power which all success
produces. "Freedom of the will" [when disencumbered of Christian
and other moralistic albatrosses] is the word for that manifold pleasurable condition of the willer who is in command and at the same
time considers himself as one with the executor of the command—as

---

of the will purports to factor "it" out of the complex, to make it identifiable and
intelligible in "its" own right. Could we identify an event as a "striving" apart from
the other elements? No.

[55]The many places in which Nietzsche appears to equate willing with commanding, to reduce it to commanding, must be read with this passage in mind. "Commanding" is used as an abbreviation, a stand-in, for the whole complex of interwoven elements here described.

[56]And hence feels responsibility, all too often guilt or shame, for the action.
Nietzsche's hope, of course, that is, a major element in his ideal, is a situation in
which, liberated from the life- and individuality-destroying constraints of morality
(that is, with those constraints replaced by self-containment and self-discipline), the
complex of elements that he calls will to power do suffice to bring about action.

such enjoying the triumph over the resistance, but possessed of the judgment that it is his will itself that is overcoming the resistance.[57] In this fashion the will adds the pleasurable feelings of the executing, successful instruments, the subservient "lower wills" or 'lower souls' (for our body is nothing but a social structure of many souls) to his pleasurable feeling as Commander. *L'effet c'est moi*—the same thing happens here that happens in any well constructed community [yuk!]. In all willing, then, there is commanding and obeying on the basis . . . of a social structure of many "souls". This is why a philosopher should consider himself justified in including willing within the general sphere of morality—morality understood as the doctrine of the rank-relations that produce the phenomenon we call "life".— (*Beyond Good and Evil*, par. 19, pp. 20–22)[58]

Nietzsche's concluding claim seems to me to be convincing. His intricate semiotic (descriptive ontology?) of the will captures much of that to which it is explicitly responsive, that is "its" many-faceted place in "popular judgment," in our speaking, thinking, and act-ing.[59] Importantly, it does so in a manner that creates the expecta-

[57]This is Nietzsche's rendering of what O'Shaughnessy calls happening in, rather than to, of identifying with the act, of identifying the act with the self and vice versa. (On this point see also George Wilson's helpful discussion of "sentient direc-tionality" and "sentient control" [*Intentionality of Human Action*, pp. 88–89, 146–48]. Wilson is agnostic concerning the will and volitionism, but his highly detailed refutation of Davidson's version of causalism is valuably complementary to Nietzsche's rather more casual treatment of the matter.) Nietzsche makes clear that the self, the "I," is itself a shifting, fluctuating complex, not a single, simple, or unchanging entity, but it is also evident that he wants not only to endorse but to promote to new intensities one's sense of one's self and the pleasures of its "com-manding."

[58]Let it be underlined immediately that the overwhelmingly predominant ten-dency of this discussion is to treat will and willing as occurring within individual persons, not in relations between or among persons, and certainly not in relations between a collectivity such as a church, nation, state, or government and the individuals who make it up or who are ruled by it. For reasons that will appear in greater detail below, on Nietzsche's understanding of the will, notions such as "general will," "collective will," "national will," and "class will" are oxymoronic. But this is by no means the worst that he had to say about these repugnancies. (For reasons that will become evident later, it is particularly important to emphasize Nietzsche's use of the language of "rank relations" to speak of a hierarchy of elements within, rather than among, individuals.)

[59]Compare Wittgenstein: "Ask yourself how you draw a line parallel to a given one 'with deliberation'—and another time, with deliberation, one at an angle to it. What is the experience of deliberation? Here a particular look, a gesture, at once

tion of, and that vigorously champions, initiative, individuality, plurality, and the like. If we follow some of the many intriguing leads that he and other major secular voluntarists give us, we can readily view it as an elaboration on the "anthropologized" theological voluntarism considered earlier. As such, it speaks directly, albeit in a sharply controversial manner, to the concerns of this essay. A liberalism that appropriated something like Nietzsche's affirmation of "the will" would be less avid for commonality, transparency, and cooperation; it would be more appreciative and celebratory of diversity, disagreement, and mutual indifference. Perhaps it would even diminish somewhat liberalism's notorious ambivalence concerning politics, the state, and the rule of some over others that politics and the state invariably involve.

III   *Liberalism and Strong Voluntarism*

The desirability of such an appropriation cannot be assessed without attention to features of Nietzschean and other strong voluntarisms, including a number that are undeniably offensive, that I have thus far left aside. We will, however, be better positioned to evaluate these if we first note respects in which robust forms of voluntarism are already present in liberalism, sometimes quite prominently so.

Consider the array of views, now often called by the generic name of "antiperfectionism" but salient in liberal thinking and practice since the time of Constant and Kant, according to which our conceptions, convictions, and dispositions, our preferences, predilections, and patterns of action are, and can be expected to remain, diverse and even incommensurable. For all of their differences, the

---

occur to you—and then you would like to say: 'And it just is a *particular* inner experience'. (And that is, of course, to add nothing).

"(This is connected with the problem of the nature of intention, of willing.) . . .

"When I look back on the experience I have the feeling that what is essential about it is an 'experience of being influenced', of a connexion—as opposed to any mere simultaneity of phenomena: but at the same time I should not be willing to call any experienced phenomenon the 'experience of being influenced'. (This contains the germ of the idea that the will is not a *phenomenon*.)" (*Philosophical Investigations*, I, 174, 176).

various formulations of views of this sort tend to converge on the conclusion that there are quite definite but not necessarily regrettable limits on our capacities to assess, to influence, and even to understand one another's thinking and acting.

Now-familiar doctrinal expressions of this kind of view include the following: the argument of Rawls and numerous others that there is an ineliminable plurality or diversity of conceptions of the human good; the more far-reaching idea associated with Isaiah Berlin and by him with Constant and Mill that there is no possibility of melding our various values and principles into one harmonious (or lexically ordered) conception and no rational basis on which to demonstrate the superiority of any one of the partial conceptions that have been or might yet be conceived; and the yet more radical notion that there are deep misunderstandings in the whole idea of interpersonal criteria for assessing the merits or even the meaningfulness of normative conceptions.[60]

These formulations at the theoretical level are influenced by and may have influenced a variety of ideas and practices characteristic of liberal ideology and liberal societies. The following may be regarded as plausible examples: insistence upon notions of privacy both in the sense of a realm of activity properly immune from control or even scrutiny by government and in the yet stronger meaning of tastes, preferences, and the like that are "nobody else's business" or the "business" of others only by my explicit invitation or encouragement; suspicion of all forms of paternalism and endorsement of the frequently associated idea that governments should be neutral among ends and purposes, concerning themselves instead with conditions conducive to the achievement of whatever objectives individuals and groups—for whatever reasons or for none—set for themselves; enthusiasm for a variety of constitutional and other rights that are exercised or not at the discretion of those whose rights they are; generalized skepticism concerning authority and support for

---

[60]In philosophical form this last view is usually associated with Hume, with emotivists such as Ayer, Carnap, and Schlick, and sometimes with deconstructionism. It is stated with his usual elegance in a famous passage by Hobbes that is worth reciting yet again: "But whatsoever is the object of any man's appetite or desire, that is it which he for his part calleth *good*: and the object of his hate and aversion *evil*; and of his contempt, *vile* and *inconsiderable*. For these words of good, evil, and contemptible, are ever used with relation to the person that useth them: there being nothing simply and absolutely so; nor any common rule of good and evil, to be taken from the nature of the objects themselves" (*Leviathan*, chap. 6, pp. 48–49).

dissent, civil disobedience, and conscientious refusals to discharge various obligations created by the exercise of authority; preference for "market" or "mixed" as opposed to "command" economies on grounds such as that preferences, utility schedules, and the like are entirely or in important respects mutually incommensurable.

Let us tarry a bit with these several clusters of ideas.

Several elements in Rawls's theory align him—and us to the extent to which his increasing (if largely unsubstantiated!) tendency to speak in "our" name is warranted—with the more robust forms of voluntarism. An example is the emphasis he gives to our tendency simply to take as givens, to make little or no attempt to alter, assess, or even to understand, one another's conceptions of the good. Rawls treats this remarkable (albeit less than uniform) characteristic of liberal democratic societies as an extension to much of moral and especially political life of attitudes concerning religious beliefs and practices that gradually won acceptance in the aftermath of the religious wars of the sixteenth and seventeenth centuries. In doing so he leaves open (but can be construed as endorsing) the doctrine advanced by some defenders of a quite radical religious pluralism, namely, that for important purposes conceptions of the good are personal or even private in a deep sense, that we *are able to* understand and assess them only, or primarily, to the extent that others choose to reveal themselves to us. Yet more striking, he promotes a considerable mutual diffidence in this regard on the ground that it serves objectives such as autonomy and success in achieving our ends and purposes as each of us conceives of them. On this reading, Rawls is—and we are—strong voluntarists both in recognizing definite limitations on our access to one another and in welcoming and promoting, rather than regretting and seeking to reduce, those limitations.

Of course this is hardly the whole or even the most prominent part of the Rawlsian theory (or the Rawlsian story concerning liberal democratic societies). The formation and pursuit of conceptions of good (what Rawls and many others call—oddly, or indiscriminately, from a strong voluntarist point of view—the "rational" component in human activities) can and should be informed, disciplined, and controlled by mutually agreed and strictly enforced conceptions of right or justice (the "reasonable"). Justice has "absolute weight" against all other considerations, and conceptions of the good that are contrary to justice are to be accorded no weight whatsoever in deciding on and acting within the "basic structure" of institutional arrangements and the distribution of rights and duties, freedoms and opportunities, that those arrangements effect. In addition to warranting an array of authoritatively established and enforced requirements and prohibitions, Rawls encourages use of a variety of noncompulsory means to bring about overlap and convergence among the large array of conceptions of the good that are permitted by the principles of justice. In all of these respects his theory claims that we often can understand one another, that we should try to do so, and that we should use our understandings to influence and in important respects to control one another's conceptions and pursuit of the good. When we focus on these features of his argument, Rawls presents himself and us as subscribers to the weaker form of voluntarism.[61]

[61]It should be added that there are reasons for thinking that for Rawls even this subscription is effective only outside the "basic structure" and only qualifiedly so in that otherwise-diversified domain. First, within the bounds of the culture to which it is specific, the substantial restrictions and requirements of the "reasonable" are to be imposed despite, or rather because of, conflicts between them and the actual beliefs, desires, objectives, and so forth, of this or that member of society. Second, the authority of the legislature and other governmental agencies that operate after completion of the first and second of the "four-stage sequence" is formally limited only in that their decisions must respect the conclusions reached in the "original position" and at the "constitutional" stage. Within those limits, governments and the majorities or pluralities that elect them *may* regulate conduct as those who compose them see fit. Third and most important, it is arguable that for Rawls the agent-neutral "reasonable" and the "full" as opposed to merely "rational autonomy" enabled by the institutionalization of the former are the governing objectives. On this as opposed to the reading given above, agent-relative and merely "rational" conceptions of the good are necessary but subsidiary components in what at bottom is a strongly perfectionist and not even a weakly voluntarist theory.

Rawls's response to the first two points is the view, familiar in weaker forms of voluntarism, that "voluntary conduct" properly encompasses actions that are required by authority but on behalf of which there are considerations that, in reason, ought to be convincing to the agents to whom the restrictions legitimately apply. As to the third point, I have argued elsewhere for the perfectionist interpretation (Richard E. Flathman, *The Philosophy and Politics of Freedom* [Chicago: University of Chicago Press, 1987], chap. 9), but I am now inclined to the view that in this respect Rawls's theory manifests a deep ambivalence, one that is widespread in the culture about which he is reflecting.

As a last caveat, we should note that Rawls is now presenting all of these views, but especially the more strongly voluntarist among them, as based on observation and as contingent conclusions, not philosophically established truths. Describing his theory as "political not metaphysical," he advances the claim that there is an ineliminable plurality of conceptions of the good and the closely associated argument that in government, politics, and political philosophy we should largely eschew concern with such conceptions, as arising out of a specific cultural experience, not philosophical analysis or reflection. Whatever may be the explanations,

The Berlinian formulation and its analogues in general belief and practice give strong voluntarism a larger and more emphatic expression. The notion that there is an ineliminable plurality of conceptions of the good is extended to include conceptions of right, of justice, of political community, and so forth, without apparent limit, and with this extension goes rejection of the idea that justice (or anything else) has absolute weight against all other considerations. And in arguing for these conclusions Berlin and the thinkers on whom he draws elaborate on and frequently celebrate the diverse, unstable, and often-conflicting character of beliefs and ideals, thoughts and actions.[62]

Here too, however, these robustly voluntarist ideas are cheek by jowl with elements that are closer—in some respects yet closer than Rawls's—to the first than to the second of the versions of voluntarism examined above. We cannot refute or discredit one another's objectives and ideals, but in addition to being able to understand them, we can give one another comprehensible, pertinent, and cogent reasons in defense of our own. Although convinced that they cannot *demonstrate* the superiority of their moral and political commitments, Berlin and Berlin's Mill, Constant, Hampshire, Bernard Williams, and others of this persuasion not only hold resolutely to them[63] (a characteristic they share with, say, Augustine,

---

our experience has taught us both that members of liberal democratic societies form and pursue a diversity of ends and purposes and that attempts to still this tendency by the use of political power or governmental authority do great harm while failing of their purposes. See esp., John Rawls, "Justice as Fairness: Political Not Metaphysical," *Philosophy and Public Affairs*, 14 (Summer 1985), 223–51; "The Idea of an Overlapping Consensus," *Oxford Journal of Legal Studies*, 7, no. 1 (1987), 1–25; "The Priority of Right and Ideas of the Good," *Philosophy and Public Affairs*, 17 (Summer 1988), 251–76. The stronger form of voluntarism, then, would presumably be regarded as unwarranted in cultures more homogenous or more effectively disciplined than those of the modern, liberal, constitutionalist, and democratic West. I see no reason to quarrel with this understanding, but it certainly provides grounds for hesitation before the thought of a more homogeneous and disciplined political culture.

[62]An elegant formulation of this type of view is available in Stuart Hampshire, *Innocence and Experience* (Cambridge: Harvard University Press, 1989). Hampshire does insist, however, that a quite thin and primarily procedural conception of justice must constrain all other activities.

[63]" 'To realise the relative validity of one's convictions', said an admirable writer of our time, 'and yet stand for them unflinchingly, is what distinguishes a civilized man from a barbarian' " (Berlin, *Four Essays on Liberty*, p. 172).

Ockham, Luther, James, and Nietzsche) but believe that they often can, and for the most part should, articulate to others the considerations that convinced them of their merits (a view that they share with, say, Anselm, Duns Scotus, Aquinas, Kant, Hegel, and Mill). Moral and political discourse cannot achieve and should not pursue (including in respect to justice, right, or rights) the kind of unanimity that would be mandated by rationally necessary (or hermeneutically unequivocal?) conclusions, but it can and should strive for mutual understanding and the respect and appreciation that such understanding engenders. Moral and political principles and institutions cannot be invested with the certainty or stability of a system of mathematics, but with perseverance and a bit of moral luck, participants in them can develop and sustain arrangements that diminish compulsion and coercion among them and otherwise enhance their opportunities for voluntary conduct.

The third and most radical of the formulations that I mentioned above has seldom if ever been explicitly embraced by soi-disant liberal thinkers. Certainly there are few liberals who would endorse the passage I earlier quoted from Hobbes, Hume's reason-disparaging "emotionalist" moral psychology, the early Ayer's meta-ethical insistence that utterances of "good" and "evil," "right" and "wrong," are "evincings" devoid of meaning, or the claim of post-modernist deconstructionists that every presumption of more or less definite mutual or even self-understanding can and should be exposed as illusory. Liberals have (1) acknowledged a diversity of beliefs and values and have promoted extensive freedoms to act on them. They have (2) sometimes been prepared to recognize and even to welcome certain limitations on mutual intelligibility and other modes of access. But they have also insisted (3) that these very features of human affairs can be sustained only where there is an ample stock of widely shared understandings, a considerable and quite stable body of norms and rules sustained and enforced by mutual discipline, substantial cooperation, and rationality and/or reasonableness sufficient to enable all of these. Interpreting the thinkers I have now put before us as undermining or actively seeking to destroy the possibility of satisfying the requirements of (3), and hence also putting (1) and the *limited* character of (2) into jeopardy, liberals have for the most part been suspicious of or antagonistic toward them.

But one could take most of what is said in the previous paragraph as reasons why liberals should give sympathetic consideration to the views of the strong voluntarists. If liberals are committed to, attracted by, or have genuinely experienced the appeal of (1) and (2), if they have done so in respect to conceptions of the good and the right, of duty and obligation, of virtue and vice, as well as the gustatorial, sartorial, and recreational, then the strong voluntarists will help them to replace a set of highly contestable diachronic and synchronic observations, a faute de mieux, or a set of prejudices with an elaborately articulated and closely textured array of explicatory and affirmational considerations. And whether they are without doubt that (3) is possible and that (1) and (2) are dependent on it, in some perplexity about these matters, or—as in my own case—tantalized by the prospect of diminishing somewhat the burden of (3) on (1), on (2), and hence on themselves, the strong voluntarists will give them a good read and a good think.[64]

IV *The Morality and Politics of Strong Voluntarism*

Discursive as they admittedly are, the foregoing remarks display disagreements and dissonances that will be familiar to anyone knowledgeable concerning the history of liberal theory and practice. The bearing that strong voluntarist views have on these oppositions will be easier to assess if we restate the issues in terms of the obstinately reiterated distinction—which forms something of a leitmotiv in the foregoing remarks about liberalism—between the "private" and the "public" realms.

[64]These remarks are not meant to insinuate that John Duns Scotus or William of Ockham, Montaigne or Hobbes, were liberals *avant de lettre*, or that Schopenhauer or Nietzsche deserve posthumous canonization as such. Having noncoincidentally adverted to this possibility, however, I indulge myself to the extent of the following further albeit admittedly rhetorical observation: communitarian critics of liberalism from Bradley, Bosanquet, and Figgis (if not Burke and Hegel) to Leo Strauss, Alasdair MacIntyre, and Charles Taylor have argued that Hobbes's radical agent-relativity and atomism (strongly reminiscent of, and possibly indebted to, Ockham) is what liberalism came from and finally amounts to and that a fragmented, anomic, emotivist, and would-that-it-could-be-Nietzschean culture is what it has of course produced. Even if we reject their accounts of liberalism, attention to what these critics argue for gives liberals reason to be receptive to the positions these critics argue most vehemently against.

Much in the history of liberalism encourages us to regard this distinction as liberalism's attempt to combine elements of strong voluntarism with qualities and characteristics that the leading proponents of such a voluntarism treat as in conflict with their views. Under the rubric of the properly private domains of life, liberals have insisted that numerous activities and practices be insulated against demands for accountability and responsibility, protected against regulation by government, and exempted from the requirements of all but the most narrowly personal aspects of our moral and other ideals. At the same time, however, some liberals have promoted public values such as justice, community, the common good, and civic or republican virtue, and numerous others have insisted on public provision of conditions such as peace and defense, security of property, or a minimal welfare that they hold to be essential to any and all private satisfactions ("public goods" if not publicly established or authoritative values). Claims on behalf of the private realm typically valorize will and spontaneity, independence and autonomy, individuality and diversity, and are accompanied by skepticism concerning the reach of rationality, reasoning, and the principles and rules, duties, and responsibilities that those human abilities sometimes allow us to delineate and to justify to one another. In contrast, argumentation concerning the public domain stresses already-established commonalities as well as the possibilities for extending them through knowing, judging, mutually convincing justification, and the like.

Liberals have from time to time held the belief or held out the hope that, despite—or rather because of—the differences between them, these two domains can be not only compatible but complementary; that the institutions and arrangements of the public realm can provide conditions that protect and otherwise enhance private activities while at the same time preventing the latter from becoming mutually destructive or self-defeating; that private life will allow outlets for impulses and energies that would be disruptive of the public realm and permit of a range of personal gratifications that public affairs cannot provide, will unsettle monotonous uniformities, and in these ways will enliven society as a whole and contribute indirectly to the quality of public affairs.[65]

Strong voluntarists have shown little enthusiasm for the public-

---

[65]For a recent, albeit qualified, articulation of this aspiration, see Richard Rorty, *Contingency, Irony, and Solidarity* (Cambridge: Cambridge University Press, 1989).

private dichotomy as such, and insofar as they have employed analogous distinctions they have drawn their lines at rather different places from those where liberals have typically drawn theirs. Some among them, however, can be read as endorsing and even enhancing optimism regarding the aspiration to achieve and maintain a mutually advantaging (which is almost certainly not to say harmonious) relationship among dimensions of human activity that, though hardly different in kind, can—and for some purposes should—be distinguished. Nietzsche in particular can be read in this way.[66]

From a strong voluntarist perspective, the most objectionable formulations of the public-private distinction are those that dissociate public values and arrangements from private desires and activities and insistently, or even systematically, subordinate the latter to the former. Much as the theological moralities of Augustine and the thinkers of the *via antiqua* subjected individual desires and purposes to the higher requirements of religion and its vision of eternal life, these political moralities seek to impose "an order of rank of human impulses and actions. These valuations and orders of rank are always expressions of the needs of a community and herd:

[66]I say "can" be read this way. In trying to make this claim good in the following pages, I quote extensively from Nietzsche's works. I believe that the "evidence" I present shows that the themes and valuations that I attribute to him are indeed features of his thinking, are more than attributions to him of views that I would like him to hold because his doing so would make him more appropriable for my purposes. But first, anyone who is appreciative of Nietzsche's thinking will take it as a given that all readings of his (or just about anyone else's) thinking will be conditioned, however knowingly, by the purposes for which they are constructed and given. Second, I do not claim to be a Nietzsche specialist. I have consulted his works only in English translation, I have read very selectively in the secondary literature concerning him, and I have rummaged indiscriminately through his major texts, largely ignoring questions of time and circumstance of composition, changes in purpose and outlook, and the like. I have not tried to make his thinking appear systematic or harmonious, but I have licensed myself to treat it as continuous in the sense of returning repeatedly to themes and problematics that were of concern to him throughout his brief but incredibly intense life as a thinker and writer. The "Nietzsche" (perhaps he should be "nietzsche") of the following pages is *mine*; I am more than happy to share him with anyone who finds his thoughts engaging, but the question that matters to me is whether his ideas, as I have construed and appropriated them, speak pertinently and provocatively to the concerns that inform and motivate this work.

(I issue this apologia at this juncture because I have felt my own limitations most sharply in writing in response to these aspects of Nietzsche's thinking. Most if not all of what I have just said could as well be said about the discussions of Augustine, of Ockham, of James, etc.)

whatever benefits it most—and second most, and third most—that is also considered the first standard for the value of all individuals. Morality trains the individual to be a function of the herd and to ascribe value to himself only as a function." The content of such moralities, the particular demands they make of individuals, has varied importantly; given the likelihood of "essential changes in the forms of future herds and communities, states and societies, we can prophesy that there will yet be very divergent moralities" (*Gay Science*, bk. 3, par. 116, pp. 174–75). What has been and will remain constant among them is that they "teach virtue as an ideal *for everyone*; they take from virtue the charm of rareness, inimitableness, exceptionalness and unaverageness—" *Will to Power*, par. 317, p. 175.[67]

For reasons we have partly considered, one could regard these voluntarist objections to political idealism and moralism as supportive of liberalism. For at least two centuries classical republicanism, political communitarianism, radical participationism, Arendtian conceptions of political action, and other views to which the strong voluntarist critiques most obviously apply have typically been presented as critiques of liberalism and as alternatives to liberal arrangements and practices. If liberalism is guilty of a form of idealism, it has idealized the private, not the public, the individual or group, not the state or collectivity; if it has promoted a morality for everyone, it is at most the morality of enlightened self- or group interest, hardly one of republican or civic virtue, of my station and its duties, of the common good or public interest. If we emphasize these features of liberalism, the abhorrence of Nietzschean or other strong voluntarisms for individuality- and plurality-diminishing idealisms might well translate into support for liberal thinking and practice.

If this rejoinder were entirely without merit, if liberalism as we have known it were entirely unreceptive to strong voluntarism, the

---

[67]Schopenhauer's formulation of a closely related objection is more specifically political. He castigates the "extraordinary error that the state is an institution for furthering morality; that it arises from the endeavour after this, and is, consequently, directed against egoism. As if the inward disposition, to which alone morality or immorality belongs, the externally free will, would [should!] allow itself to be modified from without and changed by influences exerted upon it! Still more perverse is the theory that the state is the condition of freedom in the moral sense, and in this way the condition of morality" (*World as Will and Idea*, p. 355).

thought experiment conducted in this essay would have to be regarded as an exercise in perversity. But, also counterfactually, if the
rejoinder were fully persuasive there would be no need to conduct
the experiment. More than a few liberal thinkers and publicists
(particularly those who put their emphasis on "democracy" in the
highly equivocal expression "liberal democracy") have been attracted to republican and related orderings of the public and the
private;[68]; more telling, all liberal democratic societies socialize and
educate to "civic virtues" that dispose and "duties of citizenship"
that require citizens to subordinate personal and group interests to
a more encompassing—and at least in that sense, a higher and
nobler—purpose or good. In short, the rejoinder under consideration poses rather than settles a major issue that must be addressed.
Let us provisionally treat it as the question whether liberalism can
sustain its commitment to both sides of the public-private distinction without thereby endorsing ideals and practices that are deeply
objectionable from a strong voluntarist point of view. And let us
inquire whether the strong voluntarists, despite their antipathy to
liberalism, can help us toward an affirmative answer.

It should be emphasized at the outset that strong voluntarism is
not opposed to ideals as such, indeed that it *is* an idealism, even a
form of what is now commonly called perfectionism. In this regard,
its insistence, in Nietzsche's words, is that "whatever kind of bizarre
ideal one may follow . . . one should not demand that it be *the* ideal:
for one therewith takes from it its privileged character. One should
have it in order to distinguish oneself, not in order to level oneself"
(*Gay Science*, bk. 5, par. 382, pp. 346–47). Nietzsche deepens this
point in respect to the "strange, tempting, dangerous ideal" that all
of his works explore, the ideal "of a spirit who plays naively—that
is, not deliberately but from overflowing power and abundance—
with all that was hitherto called holy, good, untouchable, divine."
Identifying himself as an "argonaut," not an evangelist of "this"
ideal, he maintains that he "should not wish to persuade anybody"
of it or to it because he would not "readily concede *the right to it* to
anyone" (*Will to Power*, par. 349, pp. 191–92, emphasis added).

---

[68]For a recent example, see Bruce Ackerman, "Constitutional Politics/ Constitutional Law," 99 *Yale Law Journal* (December 1989), 453–547, and (in more muted
form) *Social Justice in the Liberal State* (New Haven: Yale University Press, 1980).
My own badly confused attempt to incorporate elements of classical republicanism
into liberalism is on display in *The Practice of Rights* (New York and London:
Cambridge University Press, 1976). Cf. my *Toward a Liberalism*, esp. chap. 3.

The Morality and Politics of Strong Voluntarism

My ideal is *mine*: " 'This is what *I* am; this is what *I* want:—*you* can go to hell!' " (ibid.).[69]

Nor is strong voluntarism unqualifiedly hostile to the state, to politics, or to arrangements and practices that are public in the less specifically political sense of being supported by beliefs and values, conventions and norms, that are widely shared and against which dissent and deviance are little tolerated. We will have to attend to the fact that the concerns of the nineteenth-century voluntarists focused on public life in the latter, not the former, sense, but we will begin by looking at the views of Schopenhauer and Nietzsche concerning the state.

For Schopenhauer the state is a device contractually created for the exclusive purpose of diminishing somewhat the wrongs that individuals would otherwise suffer at one another's hands. It has no affirmative concern with right conduct, and it attempts to deter, through punishments but in no other way, wrong conduct only insofar as identifiable individuals are harmed by it.[70] Schopenhauer entertains no very high hopes for the efficacy of the state and law,[71]

---

[69]Cf. Zarathustra: "May your virtue be too exalted for the familiarity of names: and if you must speak of her, then do not be ashamed to stammer of her. Then speak and stammer, 'This is *my* good; this I love; it pleases me wholly; thus alone do *I* want the good. I do not want it as a divine law; I do not want it as human statute and need: it shall not be a signpost for me to overearths and paradises' " (Friedrich Nietzsche, *Thus Spoke Zarathustra*, trans. Walter Kaufmann [New York: Penguin Books, 1966], pt. 1, sec. 5, p. 36).

These considerations "notwithstanding, . . . most idealists at once propagandize for their ideal as if *they* could have no right to the ideal if *everyone* did not recognize it" (*Will to Power*, par. 349, p. 192). Nietzsche regards such propagandizing and the attempts at imposition that are its usual companions as expressions of fear, weakness, and ressentiment. In his view, which I find highly persuasive, insofar as idealists make their ideals into principles, rules, and other imperatives for everyone, they thereby betray themselves and discredit their ideals.

[70]"If it were possible to conceive an infliction of wrong with which no suffering of wrong on the part of another was connected, the state would, consistently, by no means prohibit it." Equally, "will and disposition, merely as such, do not concern the state at all, but only the *deed* . . . on account of its correlative, the *suffering* on the part of another" (*World as Will and Idea*, p. 354). These passages should not be read as enunciating a Schopenhauerian version of the public-private distinction. It is true that he makes the will private in a deep sense and excludes it from the concern of the state. But it should not be thought that all of its "phenomenal manifestations," all deeds, are properly subject to state regulation. The state concerns itself with conduct exclusively to the extent that it imposes identifiable and substantial harms on others.

[71]"But as yet the state has always remained very far from this goal. And even if it attained to it, innumerable evils essential to all life would still keep it in suffering;

---

but he is convinced that we would be worse off without it (albeit equally convinced that matters rapidly become *yet* worse when the state exceeds the limits he assigns to its purposes and activities).

Although the state and politics are clearly not at the center of Nietzsche's concerns, quite disdainful remarks concerning them appear with increasing regularity in his later works.[72] As with the least qualified of his condemnations of ideals, however, his most vituperative remarks—including those concerning public life in the wider sense—seem to be directed against corrupted and corrupting misconceptions rather than the institutions and activities themselves. The difficult question whether he entertained the possibility of a future that would be beyond the state and politics leads into both the most engaging and the least welcome possibilities broached by his thinking,[73] but he clearly thought that states had been and in

---

and finally, if they were all removed, ennui would at once occupy every place they left" (ibid., p. 360). See the continuation of this passage for some of the more baleful of Schopenhauer's pronouncements.

[72]The vitriol is at its most concentrated in the section entitled "On the New Idol" of *Thus Spoke Zarathustra* pt. 1, sec. 11, pp. 48–51. Here are two small samples: "The state tells lies in all the tongues of good and evil; and whatever it says it lies— and whatever it has it has stolen. Everything about it is false; it bites with stolen teeth, and bites easily. Even its entrails are false. Confusion of tongues of good and evil: this sign I give you as the sign of the state. Verily, this sign signifies the will to death. Verily, it beckons to the preachers of death" (p. 49). As to politicians and rulers: "Watch them clamber, these swift monkeys! They clamber over one another and thus drag one another into the mud and the depth. They all want to get to the throne: that is their madness—as if happiness sat on the throne. Often mud sits on the throne—and often the throne on mud. Mad they all appear to me, clambering monkeys and overardent. Foul smells their idol, the cold monster: foul they smell to me altogether, these idolators" (p. 50). Not bad!

[73]It is beyond question that he abhorred nationalism and state socialism and looked forward to something like European union. See, for example, *Human, All Too Human*, vol. 1, sec. 8, par. 475, pp. 174–75. But he also had great contempt for anarchism (his comments suggest that he was familiar with it primarily in its communitarian variants) and for "libertinage, the principle of '*laisser-aller*'" which he regarded as the "counterprinciple" of will to power (*Will to Power*, par. 122, p. 75), that is, for the two most pronouncedly antistate ideologies of his time. The engaging possibility to which I allude is of an individuality-oriented rather than a communitarian anarchism. The unwelcome one is that his notions of "free-spirited-ness" and the "overman" promote not self-mastering individuality sought by anyone who finds it appealing but posits and is intended to justify the political, social, and cultural dominance of a narrow and arrogant elite. The undeniably numerous passages that suggest the latter view (see for example, *Anti-Christ*, par. 57, pp. 176–79) make it clear that the members of such an elite would regard the tasks of

his time would remain instrumentally necessary to "free-spirited-ness" as he understood and treasured it.

There are several respects in which Nietzsche's views about the state and politics differ little from Schopenhauer's. In the comparatively lengthy discussion in *Human, All Too Human*, he characterizes the state as "a prudent institution for the protection of individuals against one another" (vol. 1; sec. 5, par. 235, p. 113). These protections are afforded primarily through law and the punishments it assigns to the actions it forbids. But law "does *not* forbid the disposition that produces these actions—for it needs these actions for other ends" (*Will to Power*, par. 204, p. 119). The most that "punishment is able to achieve . . . is increase of fear, circumspection, control over the instincts. Thus man is *tamed* by punishment, but by no means *improved*; rather the opposite."[74] Even in ordinary criminality "some qualities also find expression which ought not to be lacking in a man" (*Will to Power*, par. 740, p. 392). To the extent that systems of criminal law succeed in inducing guilt and shame[75] they disable those with whom they deal from or for everything that is worthwhile.

More generally, "legal conditions are necessarily exceptional conditions, since they limit the radical life-will bent on power and must finally subserve, as means, life's collective purpose, which is to create greater power constellations. To accept any legal system as sovereign . . . to accept it, not merely as an instrument in the struggle of power complexes, but as a *weapon against struggle* . . . is an anti-

---

political rule as distasteful and would perform them only if they were unable to find reliable functionaries to do so on their behalf. On this reading, however, the state is to be sustained not as a support for individuality in virtually any of its innumerable possible manifestations but as an instrument of class or "rank" control.

[74]Friedrich Nietzsche, *The Genealogy of Morals*, Second Essay, trans. Francis Golffing (Garden City: Doubleday, 1956), sec. 15, p. 216.

[75]The more usual results of such attempts, as Nietzsche sees them, are as follows: in the criminal, "punishment hardens and freezes; it concentrates; it sharpens the sense of alienation; it strengthens resistance." And these tendencies are reinforced because the same objectives generate "spying, setting traps, outsmarting, bribing, the whole tricky, cunning system which chiefs of police, prosecutors, and informers have developed among themselves; not to mention the cold-blooded legal practices of despoiling, insulting, torturing, murdering the victim" (ibid., sec. 14, pp. 214–15; see generally secs. 14–15, pp. 214–18). Law and punishment, then, ought to be thought of in deterrent terms, not at all as rehabilitative, and as retributive exclusively in the sense that only those who have broken the law should be punished.

vital principle which can only bring about man's utter demoraliza-
tion and, indirectly, a reign of nothingness" (*Genealogy of Morals*,
Second Essay, sec. 11, p. 208). Or in terms that avoid the dubious
biologizing while manifesting the antinomian tendencies always
implicit in his thinking, "all rules have the effect of drawing us away
from the purpose behind them and making us more frivolous."[76]

These and related views colored Nietzsche's thinking about liberalism, socialism, and other political ideologies, about the democratic movement of his time, and about politics and political participation generally. As an historical matter, the "human polity" had
its origin not in contract or agreement but in violence and imposition, indeed in "a pack of savages, a race of conquerors . . . fiercely
dominating a population perhaps vastly superior in numbers" (sec.
17, 219). Appropriately enough, therefore, the "old conception
of government" distinguished "two distinct spheres of power, a
stronger and higher and a weaker and lower" and hoped for little
more than a not-too-brutal relationship between them (*Human, All
Too Human*, vol. 1, sec. 8, par. 450, p. 165). Liberalism effectively
contested the rapidly growing dominance of government and helped
to establish institutions which, "as long as they are still being fought
for . . . promote freedom mightily" (*Twilight of the Idols*, sec. 10,
par. 38, p. 92). Unfortunately, liberalism's successes and the democratic movement that it—perhaps unwittingly—helped to spawn
engendered a "new" conception according to which government "is
nothing but an organ of the people" (*Human, All Too Human*, vol.
1, sec. 8, par. 450, p. 165), an organ through which the people can be
"liberal" with themselves, can provide themselves with any number
of "benefits." As a consequence, "there is [now] nothing more
thoroughly harmful to freedom than liberal institutions. One
knows, indeed, *what* they bring about: they undermine the will to
power, they are the levelling of mountain and valley exalted to a
moral principle, they make small, cowardly and smug—it is the herd
animal which triumphs with them every time."[77]

[76]Friedrich Nietzsche, *Daybreak*, trans. R. J. Hollingdale (New York: Cambridge
University Press), 1982, bk. 4, par. 322, p. 159.

[77]These discussions can be usefully compared with the influential historiography
of the state and liberalism presented by John Stuart Mill in the first chapter of *On
Liberty*. Nietzsche betrays little or none of Mill's ambivalence concerning the events
they both chart.

I had not attended to these and related passages in Nietzsche when I began to

The Morality and Politics of Strong Voluntarism

As bad as liberalism soon became, socialism—"the logical conclusion of the *tyranny* of the least and the dumbest" (*Will to Power*, par. 125, p. 77)—took over the "new conception" of government engendered by liberalism and attempted to use it to create a despotism far worse than those that liberalism had contested. "Socialism is the fanciful younger brother of the almost expired despotism whose heir it wants to be; its endeavours are thus in the profoundest sense reactionary. For it desires an abundance of state power such as only despotism has ever had; indeed it outbids all the despotisms of the past inasmuch as it expressly aspires to the annihilation of the individual, who appears to it like an unauthorized luxury of nature destined to be improved into a useful *organ of the community*" (*Human, All Too Human*, vol. 1, sec. 8, par. 473, p. 173). Having deprived itself of the support that religious pieties had provided to earlier despotisms, socialism attempts to secure the unquestioning submission that it craves by "driving the word 'justice' into the heads of the half-educated masses like a nail so as to rob them of their reason." But this and other forms of deception and manipulation will never suffice to sustain its power, and it can rule "only through the exercise of the extremest terrorism."[78]

---

work in and around liberal theory. Having noticed them, I do not want to associate myself with his cavalier remarks concerning the herd, cowardice, and so forth. In other—and I think separable—respects, however, the passage just quoted crystallizes resistances that I have come to have concerning liberalism as it has evolved in the approximately one hundred years since Nietzsche wrote these words.

Compare in these regards the observations of Michael Oakeshott concerning liberalism: " 'Liberalism' was concerned with what I have called the menace of 'sovereign' authority and with constitutional devices to reduce it. If it had any theoretical understanding of a state it was that of an association in terms of assured 'natural rights' recognized as civil conditions to be subscribed to in conduct, and the menace was identified as the propensity of rulers to inhibit the enjoyment of these rights by the exercise of lordship. But these 'natural rights' came to include the enjoyment of certain substantive conditions of things capable of being assured only in the exercise of lordship (e.g. employment, medical attention, education) and consequently what was menacing became, not a lordly managerial government, but a government which failed in its lordly office of assuring to subjects the enjoyment of these conditions or one which imposed other similar but deprecated conditions, like religious uniformity" (*On Human Conduct*, p. 245, n. 2).

[78]Nietzsche regularly paired socialism and anarchism and evidently thought that the anarchists intended a communal despotism every bit as destructive of individuality as the state despotism promised by socialism.

It would be entirely absurd to associate Nietzsche with the crudely self-congratulatory "capitalism" that has been trumpeting its triumph as the "socialisms" of the

Nietzsche's sole good word for socialism is that it teaches "in a truly brutal and impressive fashion, what danger there lies in all accumulations of state power, and to that extent to implant mistrust of the state itself. When its harsh voice takes up the watchword '*as much state as possible*' . . . soon the opposite cry comes through with all the greater force: '*as little state as possible*'" (ibid.). And if prized off the passion for mediocrity that has taken over liberalism,[79], the democratic institutions that some liberals sought to establish—or rather the institutions of "the democracy to come"—can help to make the latter cry effective.

Properly understood, "democratic institutions are quarantine arrangements to combat that ancient pestilence, lust for tyranny." The purpose of adopting them should be "to create and guarantee as much *independence* as possible: independence of opinion, of mode of life, and of employment" (vol. 2, pt. 2, par. 293, p. 384). Following out this line of thought, Nietzsche could imagine a future democracy in which the state, rather than merely being constrained within narrow limits, would decay and perhaps even disappear. "Disregard for and the decline and *death of the state*, the liberation of the private person . . . is the consequence of the democratic conception of the state; it is in this that its mission lies" (vol. 1, sec. 8, par. 472, p. 172).[80]

The democracy we actually have, however, has rather different tendencies. Aside from the ominous fact that much of the democratic movement has adopted that dangerous "new" conception of the state that we have already encountered, that which "now calls

---

Soviet bloc have been collapsing before our eyes. It can hardly be denied, however, that Nietzsche was remarkably prescient concerning what those "socialisms" would and did become.

[79]"The honorable term for *mediocre* is, of course, the word '*liberal*'" (*Will to Power*, par. 864, p. 462). This passage was an exaggeration when Nietzsche penned it, and those who repeat similar sentiments today are guilty of the same kind of excess. But we should not confuse exaggerations and falsehoods.

[80]Strictly, of course, a democratic movement that led to the death of the state would be self-annihilating, would be the end of demo-*cracy*.

The material I have omitted in this quotation reads: "(I take care not to say: of the individual)"; because the distinction between "person" and "individual" is not usual in Nietzsche's work, this parenthetical insertion is difficult to construe; but given his conception of individuality, a plausible interpretation would be that no merely political or otherwise social development would *suffice* to bring about genuine individuality. Most political and social arrangements obstruct and suffocate individuality, but to the extent that they "liberate persons" they conduce to it.

itself democracy differs from the older forms of government solely in that it drives with *new horses*: the streets are still the same old streets, and the wheels are likewise the same old wheels.—Have things really got less perilous because the wellbeing of the nations now rides in *this* vehicle?" (vol. 2, pt. 2, par. 293, p. 384).

Nietzsche makes a number of quite specific, even institutional, proposals for making things less perilous. Some of these are reminiscent of the recommendations of other nineteenth-century thinkers who saw merit as well as inevitability in democracy but were anxious to preserve its "liberal" character when that meant fear of and desire to control it. From a class or political-sociological as distinct from an ideological perspective, "the three great enemies of independence . . . are the indigent, the rich and the [political] parties." Thus if democracy is to guarantee as much independence as possible, it "needs to deprive of the right to vote both those who possess no property and the genuinely rich" and it must "likewise prevent everything that seems to have for its objective the organization of parties" (ibid.).

Nietzsche's better considered response to the "perils" he discerned was to cultivate a certain stance, at once acceptant and distancing, toward the state and politics. The continuing utility of the democratic state requires "general obedience" to its laws. But this obedience has to be "proud"; has to be "conditional," not submissive; has to proceed from the strength and self-command of those who sometimes accord it, sometimes refuse it. And even at their most "useful," the democratic state and its politics will be "very boring" to those of insight and spirit, will be viewed by them as a burden they must carry because of the as yet inadequate self-discipline of those around them (par. 289, p. 383).[81]

In respect, then, to the conception of the state as the organ of the people and of participation in politics as the means of giving health

---

[81]As to the undiscerning, the enthusiasts for the delights of the political hurly burly: "O you poor devils in the great cities of world politics, you gifted young men tormented by ambition who consider it your duty to pass some comment on everything that happens—and there is always something happening! Who when they raise the dust in this way think they are the chariot of history! Who because they are always on the alert, always on the lookout for the moment when they put their word in, lose all genuine productivity! . . . The event of the day drives them before it like chaff, while they think they are driving the event—poor devils!" (*Daybreak*, bk. 3, sec. 177, p. 107). Cf. the discussion of Hobbes's aversion to political activity, supra, Chapter 1.

and vitality to that organ, "nothing is *more* desirable than caution and slow evolution" (vol. 1, sec. 8, par. 450, p. 165). But Nietzsche's wariness concerning the state and public life generally (strongly reminiscent, as we have seen, of elements recurrent, if often recessive, in liberalism) did not lead him to reverse his judgment that they had made vital contributions to realization of the best of human possibilities or to think that we could now dispense with them. His abundant and trenchant hyperbole against the state, politics, and what we might call public culture coexists—that is, stands in what he clearly regards as unresolvable tension with—repeated and insistent avowals of their importance and indeed their indispensability.

In company with the other voluntarists we have considered, Nietzsche rejected the view that human beings are "by nature" or "by God's creation" well suited to one another or to their world. He acknowledged that we are "provided" with energies and abilities essential to a rich and "felicitous" (to appropriate Hobbes's quite pertinent criterion) life and he relentlessly combated those forms of asceticism and self-abnegation that lead to passivity and gloom.[82] Echoing (albeit unwittingly and perhaps inadvertently) one of the great themes of Hobbes's political thought, however, Nietzsche was a theorist of making and becoming not of discovery and attunement, of acting to bring about our selves and circumstances appropriate to the kinds of selves we have dimly envisaged.

This "making" is neither quick nor easy and it certainly does not proceed in a uniform or a linear fashion. Notoriously, Nietzsche thought that much of the "construction" that had gone on over the centuries of human experience had in fact effected an "unmaking," a reduction of human beings to "herd animals." And he put much of this deformation to the charge of the state, politics, and "public" institutions and practices such as religion, morality, and education. But his genealogies of organized (of more rather than less) collective and mutually disciplining activities tell another story as well, a story of "preparations" necessary to (though never sufficient for) human beings at least some of whom can resonate with and perhaps be inspired by an ideal such as "free-spiritedness." His elaboration of this theme of preparation testifies eloquently to his appreciation of the value of public life in both its narrower and its more extended meanings.

---

[82]Whatever else the famous *amor fati* is or isn't, may or may not be, it is an affirmation, not a denial.

The most condensed articulations of this theme are in his discussions of promising and of related but more general notions such as remembering and fidelity, responsibility and self-command. "To breed an animal with the right to make promises—is not this the paradoxical problem . . . and is it not man's true problem?" (*Genealogy of Morals*, Second Essay, par. 1, p. 189). It is humankind's "true problem" because in the absence of the capacities necessary to making and keeping promises human activity would be aimless and random, would be beyond the agent's control. As Duns Scotus, Ockham, Montaigne, and Hobbes had all insisted before Nietzsche, "willful" conduct, while made impossible by externally imposed controls, also presupposes considerable command over the agents own deliberations,[83] decisions, and choices.

So far from being naturally given, however, the capacity to establish and maintain such self-command is continuously in conflict with tendencies rooted deeply in human beings—indeed with powers that are themselves necessary to self-command. These include ignoring, selecting among, and forgetting or repressing many of the elements of our experience, capacities without which human beings "can't be done with anything" (ibid.).[84] But if the other powers, the other elements of the will, require spaces in which to function, they

[83]As with Hobbes before him, Nietzsche was attentive to and insistent on the point that deliberation is a form de-liberating, a process of taking away liberties that were available to the agent prior to her deliberations. Also as with Hobbes, for Nietzsche deliberation is done exclusively by individual persons: it can be done "collectedly" but not collectively. If there is a disagreement between him and Hobbes, it lies in his conviction that, a certain preparation having been accomplished, the free spirit will often act without deliberation.

[84]In the picturesque passage from which this phrase is drawn, Nietzsche brings these powers together as the "faculty of oblivion" and identifies its role as "that of a concierge: to shut temporarily the doors and windows of consciousness; to protect us from the noise and agitation with which our lower organs work for or against one another; to introduce a little quiet into our consciousness so as to make room for the nobler functions and functionaries of our organism which do the governing and planning. The concierge maintains order and etiquette in the household of the psyche; which immediately suggests that there can be no happiness, no serenity, no hope, no pride, no *present*, without oblivion." It is clear that the activities of the faculty of oblivion are primary elements in that concatenation of diverse elements that Nietzsche calls the will. Suppressing, ignoring, and even what we might call active as opposed to passive forgetting are willful operations or processes. As primary elements in his notions of solitude, moderation, and magnanimity—hence of individuality—his powerful emphasis on these elements is directly relevant to anxieties that drive conservative and communitarian objections to liberalism and that have sometimes overtaken liberals as well.

also need "materials" on which or with which to operate, materials that the "naturally forgetful" character of human beings tends to eliminate or to render inaccessible. Therefore the human animal "has created for itself an opposite power, that of remembering, by whose aid . . . oblivion may be suspended." The workings of this "opposite power" are most manifest "where it is a question of promises. By this I do not mean a purely passive succumbing to past impressions, the indigestion of being unable to be done with a pledge once made, but rather an active not wishing to be done with it, a continuing to will what has once been willed, a veritable 'memory of the will'; so that, between the original determination and the actual performance . . . a whole world of new things, conditions, even volitional acts, can be interposed without snapping the long chain of the will" (p. 190).

Developing this power, "breeding an animal" in whom it is strong enough sometimes to overcome both the internal and the external forces that conflict with it, involves "the preparatory task of rendering man up to a certain point regular, uniform, equal among equals, calculable." Promising, responsibility, "standing security" for oneself, or "disposing" of one's future in this manner "presuppose" this preparation. Such actions and qualities of character are possible only for those who have "learned to separate necessary from accidental acts; to think causally; to see distant things as though they were near at hand; to distinguish means from ends." And where this preparation has taken place, it has occurred primarily by means of "the custom character of morals," through that "labor man accomplished upon himself over a vast period of time," often with "brutality, tyranny, and stupidity." Without "custom and the social strait-jacket" human beings would never have become calculable, reliable, or efficacious (sec. 2, pp. 190–91).[85]

Nietzsche extends versions of this view over the entire realm of meaning and mutual understanding. Because *nothing* is given by, simply appropriable from, extrahuman sources, all meaning, all belief, all interpersonal understanding must be created and maintained by agreement among some and imposition on many others. Anticipating views that were developed with much greater philosophical subtlety by Wittgenstein (cf. the discussions in *supra*,

---

[85]Here again it is fruitful to compare Nietzsche's discussion with Mill's treatment of the movement from barbarism to civilization in *On Liberty*.

Chapters 2 and 3), Nietzsche insisted that "not truth and certainty are the opposite of the world of the madman, but the universality and the universal binding force of a faith; in sum, the non-arbitrary character of judgments. And man's greatest labor so far has been to reach agreement about very many things and to submit to a *law of agreement*—regardless of whether these things are true or false" (*Gay Science*, bk. 2, par. 76, p. 130). In the yet more general terms of a rudimentary theory of meaning:

> "What, ultimately, is commonness?—Words are sound-symbols for concepts; concepts, however, are more or less definite image-symbols for frequently returning and concurring sensations, for sensation-groups. To use the same words is not a sufficient guarantee of under-standing; . . . ultimately one must have one's experiences in *common*. That is why the people of one nation understand each other better than members of several nations even when they share a language; or rather, when people have lived with each other for a long time under similar conditions (of climate, soil, danger, needs, work), then there *arises* something from them that can 'come to an understanding', i.e. a nation [language-games and a form of life in the Wittgensteinian lingo]. A similar number of frequently returning experiences has gained the upper hand in everyone's psyche over those that occur more rarely; regarding them one comes to a more and more rapid understanding (the history of a language is the history of an abbrevia-tion process); upon this rapid understanding one feels more and more closely allied (*Beyond Good and Evil*, par. 268, pp. 217–18).[86]

Important for present purposes, Nietzsche deploys these views to distinguish himself from the proponents of *laisser-aller*, of "liber-tinage," and from others who "think they are clever" and "who imagine they are 'free', in fact freethinkers" (*Beyond Good and Evil*, par. 188, p. 93). Every morality, every public culture, is a "tyranny" in the sense that it constrains and compels those who live under or in it. However, so far from this being "an objection to it . . . everything of freedom, subtlety, boldness, dance, and craftsmanlike certainty that one can find on earth, whether it applies to thinking, or ruling, or speaking, or persuading—in the arts as well as in codes of conduct—would never have developed save through the 'tyranny of such arbitrary laws' " (ibid.).

[86]The most sustained and philosophically technical development of these views is in *Will to Power*, esp. parts. 466–67, pp. 261–331.

It is clear from these remarks that for Nietzsche the disciplines worked by public life and culture are of continuing, not merely preparatory, importance. He seeks changes in temperament and character, wants the cultivation of something akin to what Aristotle called dispositions.[87] The last passages quoted are particularly important for their indication that dispositions are necessary, distinctively so, for "free-spirits" and "free-spiritedness." As we see in greater detail below, it is precisely in his "elitist" moments, in the most objectionably "aristocratic" dimensions of his thinking, that Nietzsche insists most strongly on control, restraint, and even a kind of responsibility.

How are we to reconcile these themes with Nietzsche's blistering assaults on the actual religions and moralities, states and politics, about which he wrote? Whether mutually compatible or otherwise, what bearing does the combination of the two have on liberal theory and practice? A distinction between form and content, or perhaps between form and motive or purpose, will take us a part of the way toward answering these questions.

As we have seen, in Nietzsche's view the public cultures and political arrangements that were hegemonic in his time had taken their origins in the desires of an "elite" to impose its dominance on a "mass." As they passed through the various permutations I have partly discussed, they diminished disorder and conflict, instituted regularities and commonalities. In these respects they did and are doing "preparatory" work in Nietzsche's sense. Moreover, to the extent that "solitary personalities" have survived their leveling demands, "In a certain sense, *the latter can maintain and develop himself most easily in a democratic society*: namely, when the coarser means of defense are no longer necessary and habits of order, honesty, justice and trust are part of the usual conditions" (*Will to Power*, par. 887, p. 473).[88]

---

[87]As Bonnie Honig has pointed out to me, however, for Nietzsche, as distinct from Aristotle, there is no sense in which we are pre-disposed, by nature as it were, to these dispositions.

[88]Nietzsche sometimes allows more than this: "In contemporary society a great deal of consideration, of tact and forbearance, of good-natured respect for the rights of others, even for the claims of others, is quite widespread; even more, a certain benevolent instinctive estimation of human value in general, which finds expression in trustfulness and credit of all kinds. Respect for man—and not merely for virtuous men—is perhaps what divides us most sharply from a Christian evaluation. . . . This moral liberality is one of the best signs of our age. . . . If anything can reconcile us to our age, it is the great amount of immorality it permits itself without thinking any

As Nietzsche sees them, however, the purpose of almost all of these formations (pre-Socratic Greece and Renaissance Italy are partial, short-lived, but illuminating and even inspiring exceptions) has been to eliminate, not to enhance, individuality and diversity. Predictably, therefore, their regularities are monotonous and repressive, their commonalities those of a "herd" pervaded by that most destructive form of hatred of self and other that Nietzsche calls ressentiment.[89] Accordingly, discipline, responsibility, calculability, and the like have to be "transvaluated," have to be preserved in form but converted in content and purpose from engines of social control, commonality, and conformism into wellsprings of self-control, diversity, and individuality.

This transformation, if it can occur at all except in and for a solitary few, cannot be effected collectively, cannot be brought about by a "society" or "culture," cannot be the work of the state and politics, armies, political parties, churches, universities, or any other organized entities. As necessary as they have been and in all likelihood will remain, these entities and agencies are suffused by, are the bearers and sustainers of ressentiment, of fear and hatred of the uncertain and the unknown, the novel and the distinctive. Whenever they undertake more than the protective and the narrowly preparatory, they consolidate and solidify the worst features of the existing understandings and arrangements.

Transvaluations, rather, are the work of individuals, of persons who show that they have benefited *the most* from the "tyranny of arbitrary laws" by achieving a *self*-discipline, a *self*-containment and fastidiousness far beyond that which the "laws" require of them. Nietzsche's characterizations of these "men of the future" exhibit both the severity and the grandeur of his "ideal":

---

the worse of itself." Yet more generally: "Let us not think meanly of that which two thousand years of morality have bred in our spirit!" (*Will to Power*, par. 267, p. 153).

These statements parallel the more celebratory claims of liberal apologists. In Nietzsche's view, however, it is either too early or too late for smug complacency. This "liberality," this "permitted" immorality that we have been bred to accept, is but a poor thing by comparison with the Renaissance, which was distinguished by "the great amount of *admitted* immorality" (par. 747, p. 395), and certainly with that state of affairs "beyond good and evil" of Nietzsche's fond imaginings.

[89]Compare the discussions of James's "Chautaukua society" and especially of Tocqueville's treatment of the "monotonous" character of life in the American civil society, supra, Chapter 2.

"We now need many preparatory courageous human beings who cannot very well leap out of nothing, any more than out of the sand and slime of present-day civilization . . .—human beings who know how to be silent, lonely, resolute, and content and constant in invisible activities; human beings who are bent on seeking in all things for what in them must be *overcome*; human beings distinguished as much by cheerfulness, patience, unpretentiousness, and contempt for all great vanities as by magnanimity in victory and forbearance regarding the small vanities of the vanquished; human beings whose judgment concerning all victors and the share of chance in every victory and fame is sharp and free; human beings with their own festivals, their own working days, and their own periods of mourning, accustomed to command with assurance but instantly ready to obey when that is called for—equally proud, equally serving their own cause in both cases; more endangered human beings, more fruitful human beings, happier beings! (*Gay Science*, bk. 4, sec. 283, p. 228)[90]

If we parse these remarks into the categories of public and private, much in this and the very large number of similar passages in Nietzsche's works suggests that the activities for which he hopes will be primarily "private" rather than "public." Indeed the activities will be "privatized" in senses that many liberals both fear and disdain. This impression is strengthened both by Nietzsche's combination of disdain and caution for the state and publicly established morality and by the many remarks (e.g., "serving their own cause in both cases" in the passage just quoted) that are not only elitist but radically egoistic in manifesting an all but exclusive concern for the individual's own well-being, a purely instrumental attitude toward all others. (Recall: "This is what *I* am; this is what *I* want:—you can go to hell!") Having "transvaluated" the values of public life, the "overcoming" human being must radically distance herself from them and it. Because she recognizes her deep indebtedness to public life (in both the narrower and wider senses of "public"), this distancing necessarily involves not only an ambivalence but a "pathos," a never-to-be-ended struggle not only with others but with those dimensions of herself that are what they are because public life has been and is what it is. But if she relents in this struggle, indeed if she fails to conduct it ferociously and even ruthlessly, she betrays her ideal and thereby betrays herself.

[90]Note the continuities between this passage and the general theme of "breeding" and "preparation."

The Morality and Politics of Strong Voluntarism

In one strain of his thinking, manifest in some of the remarkably diverse characteristics praised and promoted in the passage from *The Gay Science* quoted just above, this concern for distance leads to Nietzsche's immense regard for self-containment, "cleanliness," "solitude," and "silence." The free-spirited human being protects and enhances herself by "withdrawing" (we will see that this rarely means physical isolation) from the company of all but those few whom she recognizes as of her own disposition or "rank." She assiduously avoids not only ruling and politics but social intercourse in all but its most intimate and selective forms. She may acknowledge (albeit "conditionally") certain obligations to government and law, but she asks as little as possible of public life, makes few if any affirmative efforts to contribute to it.

But withdrawal is but one of the strategies that Nietzsche proposes to the "overman." Decidedly less palatable is his not infrequent suggestion that the overman, and sometimes the class or "rank" of the overwo/men, regard the "herd" as a resource at her or their disposal. On this view, it is not only likely but better that those who make up "the herd" remain as they have now become, that is trained, predictable, calculable. Those who have "self-overcome" are not merely relieved of the need to protect themselves through "the coarser means of defense," they are provided with easily exploitable human resources. "I have as yet found *no* reason for discouragement. Whoever has preserved, and bred in himself, a strong will, together with an ample spirit, has more favorable opportunities than ever. For the trainability of men has become very great in this democratic Europe; men who learn easily and adapt themselves easily are the rule: the herd animal, even highly intelligent, has been prepared. Whoever can command finds those who *must* obey: I am thinking, e.g., of Napoleon and Bismarck. The rivalry with strong and *un*intelligent wills, which is the greatest obstacle, is small."[91] "In itself, there is nothing sick about the herd

[91]The remark about "strong and *un*intelligent wills" might be read as making a comparison with the unremitting and therefore unproductively agonal character of life in pre-Socratic Greece. There is no doubt that Nietzsche admired the spirited self-assertion that he thought he had encountered in the heroic age, and it is clear that he thought the continual conflict prevented many of the evils that developed after its decline. But there are suggestions, especially in the early essay "Homer's Contest," that the very pervasiveness of struggle, the absence of "troops" that could be commanded, made great achievements impossible. Through ostracism, "the all-excelling individual was to be removed in order that the contest of forces might re-

animal, it is even invaluable; but, incapable of leading itself, it needs a 'shepherd'" (*Will to Power*, par. 282, p. 160). So far from withdrawing from the herd, on this view the overwo/man or overwo/men take and insistently maintain command over it. And she or they do so to serve "their own causes."

The motif of domination and exploitation of the herd yields one rendering of Nietzsche's remark that "we" now need human beings of a superior kind. On this construal, the "we" of this passage consists of the overwo/men themselves; they need an enlargement of their company sufficient to permit them to dominate the herd. And this interpretation, certainly the prevailing one through much of this century, takes plausibility from Nietzschean remarks such as: "My philosophy aims at an ordering of rank: not at an individualistic morality. The ideas of the herd should rule in the herd—but not reach out beyond it: the leaders of the herd require a fundamentally different valuation for their own actions, as do the independent, or the 'beasts of prey', etc." (par. 287, p. 162).[92]

If we were interested in making a judgment about the man Friedrich Nietzsche, the prominence of views such as these in Nietzsche's writings would be adequate grounds for accepting his own judgment that he was an opponent, even an enemy, of individuality-affirming liberalism. Again, if our purpose were to systematize or harmonize, perhaps even to estimate the predominant tendencies of the ideas presented in his works, we might have to conclude that his views are antagonistic to such a liberalism. It is not contrary to such a liberalism to reject on one's own behalf, even to disdain in one's own name, much or even all of what other persons think and do. Nor is it contrary to such a liberalism to contest and to seek by

---

awaken, a thought which is hostile to the 'exclusiveness' of genius in the modern sense but which assumes that in the natural order of things there are always *several* geniuses which incite one another to action, as much also as they hold one another within the bounds of moderation. That is the kernel of the Hellenic contest-conception; it abominates autocracy, and fears its dangers; it desires as a *preventive* against the genius—a second genius" (*The Complete Works of Friedrich Nietzsche*, ed. Oscar Levy [London: T. N. Foulis, 1911], vol. 2, pp. 57–58). As we see below, however, this passage and the whole theme of "the higher man," is subject to quite different interpretations. Properly understood, "moderation" is a quality that is not only compatible with but necessary to the kinds of lives Nietzsche most admires.

[92]Remarks of this sort occur at intervals through most of Nietzsche's writings, but they are particularly prevalent in the section of *Will to Power* from which the above quotation is taken, that is, pars. 274–87, pp. 156–62.

argument, influence, and example to alter beliefs, activities, and practices that one finds obnoxious or merely objectionable. The illiberal and antiliberal character of those of Nietzsche's views that we have just been considering resides instead in the crude, rampantly de-individuating categories on which they depend and in his readiness to treat his personal repugnance for that multitude of persons subsumed by his categories as sufficient reason for putting them at the disposal of himself or those of his rank. The "respect for persons" that has been so much discussed in recent liberal theorizing, the privileging of freedom, independence, autonomy, and the like that is salient in virtually all liberalism, do not and cannot require either agreement with others or subordination of oneself or one's ilk to others. For reasons that we have begun to see, they cannot *require* so much as understanding the beliefs, hopes, and fears of others. But any even minimally defensible understanding of these notions forbids the cavalier presumption vis-à-vis others that Nietzsche frequently arrogates to himself.

Our purposes being other than those just envisioned, we can continue to pursue the questions that have been before us throughout, to ask whether, *quand même*, strong voluntarism *à la* Nietzsche contains elements that would advantage liberalism as we have known it.

Underlining a clause in (this formulation of) Nietzsche's otherwise-repugnant declaration of a philosophy of rank (but recall note 58 above) will help us to regain our earlier momentum toward a strongly affirmative answer: "The ideas of the herd should rule in the herd—but not reach out beyond it." The "herd" is as it is; those who make "it" up believe what they believe, fear and hate what they fear and hate, hope what they hope. For *many* purposes, their ideas should be accepted, should "rule" their activities and arrangements. In the sense—to my mind, quintessentially liberal—of the Declaration of Independence's "decent respect for the opinions of mankind" they should be respected. In this sense of respect, respecting their ideas does not entail agreeing with them, obviously does not require or even recommend abandoning one's own ideas or objectives in favor of theirs ("—but not reach out beyond it"). Thus differences will remain, conflicts will occur, revolutionary wars may well be fought. (Respect in this sense is not "neutralism.") But those above, below, or otherwise apart from "the herd" are no more justified in compelling, coercing, or otherwise engineering changes in those ideas *on the ground that* their ideas are superior than "the herd" is justified in imposing its ideas on others.

If these remarks seem more a rejection of than a gloss upon Nietzsche's "the ideas of the herd should . . . ," consider the manner in which he opens his single most extended discussion of the state and politics. Asking "permission to speak" in the face of the demagogic clamor and "great *al fresco* stupidities" of the political parties of the democracies, he first says that, as with natural disasters, "one has no choice" but to adjust as best one can to the political changes that have taken place. But this is not his last thought on the matter. "Moreover, if the purpose of politics really is to make life endurable for as many as possible, then these as-many-as-possible are entitled to determine what they understand by an endurable life; if they trust to their intellect also to discover the right means of attaining this goal, what good is there in doubting it? They *want* for once to forge for themselves their own fortunes and misfortunes; and if this feeling of self-determination, pride in the five or six ideas their head contains and brings forth, in fact renders their life so pleasant to them that they are happy to bear the calamitous consequences of their narrow-mindedness, there is little to be objected to. . . ." (*Human, All Too Human*, vol. 1, sec. 8, par. 438, p. 161). Disdainful, yes; unpretty, no doubt; but should we deny him permission to speak? And in Nietzsche's diction "want," "entitled," "for once," and especially "self-determination" and "pride" express more than mere tolerance, more than resignation to a regrettable fate.

The appropriate caveat immediately follows and leads us to some of the most engaging and indeed estimable of Nietzsche's thoughts. If there is little to be objected to, that is "always presupposing that this narrow-mindedness does not go so far as to demand that *everything* should become politics in this sense, that *everyone* should live and work according to such a standard" (ibid.). If this condition were satisfied, the state, politics, and public life could be more than merely necessary as preparation and sources of control and protection, could provide opportunities valuable to a certain (perhaps large) number of persons. And at least a part of Nietzsche's response to this possibility, rather than "que sera sera," would be: "Good!" "Enjoy!" "Go for it!"

A closely connected part of his response speaks both to the question of domination/exploitation by those of a higher "rank" and to the notions of solitude, cleanliness, and the deeply individuating character of the Nietzschean ideal properly understood. "For a few must first of all be allowed, now more than ever, to refrain from politics and to step a little aside: they too are prompted to this by pleasure in self-determination; and there may also be a degree of pride attached to staying silent when too many, or even just many, are speaking. Then these few must be forgiven if they fail to take the happiness of the many, whether by the many one understands nations or social classes, so very seriously and are now and then guilty of an ironic posture; for their seriousness is located elsewhere, their happiness is something quite different, their goal is not to be encompassed by any clumsy hand that has only five fingers" (ibid.).

Manifesting Nietzsche's hatred of the "lust for tyranny" with which we are already familiar, these remarks go further and suggest that the necessity—and in that sense the justification—of elite domination and indeed of elite involvement may have passed. The "herd" has now been well enough "prepared" to allow the free spirits to "step aside" from public affairs, to devote themselves to "dancing even near abysses."[93] This reading, moreover, is true to Nietzsche's pronounced tendency to think that his ideal of free-spiritedness could be so much as understood and pursued (there is no such thing as achieving "it," once and for all as it were) only in "solitude," that is, in no more than occasional converse except (and quite possibly *even*) with those few who the would-be free spirit deems genuine friends or worthy enemies.

Nietzsche's articulations of the connected themes of solitude and cleanliness are frequently in language that expresses a disdain for others that many have found as destructive as it is arrogant. But even his disdain (and he is sometimes quite complimentary) is as much for that in himself which he despises and seeks to overcome, and his response to it consists in large part in efforts to enhance his

---

[93]"One could conceive of such a pleasure and power of self-determination, such a *freedom* of the will that the spirit would take leave of all faith and every wish for certainty, being practiced in maintaining himself on insubstantial ropes and possibilities and dancing even near abysses. Such a spirit would be the *free spirit* par excellence" (*Gay Science*, bk. 5, par. 347, pp. 289–90).

In another idiom, "the city" has become—or might some day become—sufficiently safe to permit those who are *in* and therefore unavoidably affected *by* but who cannot be fully *of* it to leave its affairs to others. The difference, of course, is that the city is or would now be safe not only for platonic "philosophers" but for all "free spirits," not only "safe for" but conducive to individuality and plurality.

self-discipline rather than his control over others. Thus for those who can quell their hurts and resentments, his disdain is as likely to protect them against him as vice versa and will be viewed by them as a threat to their well-being only if they have let their self-esteem become hostage to his judgments of them. Yet more affirmatively, since solitude is not to be confused with loneliness or isolation, there can be such a thing as mutual solitude and it is not impossible that by a kind of force of example it will sometimes yield an unsought but nevertheless reciprocal enhancement.

> Flee, my friend, into your solitude: I see you stung all over by poisonous flies. Flee where the air is raw and strong.
> Flee into your solitude! You have lived too close to the small and the miserable. Flee their invisible revenge.
> No longer raise up your arm against them. Numberless are they, and it is not your lot to shoo flies. (*Thus Spoke Zarathustra*, pt. 1, sec. 12, pp. 52–53)

Would Zarathustra's advice differ if the numberless others had been "prepared" to the point that they were less "poisonous," if the free spirit could dispense with "the coarser means of defense" against them? The answer is "not much different." "If we live together with another person too closely, what happens is similar to when we repeatedly handle a good engraving with our bare hands: one day all we have left is a piece of dirty paper. The soul of a human being too can finally become tattered by being handled continually" (*Human, All Too Human*, vol. 1, sec. 7, par. 428, p. 158). Would matters change if relationships became yet more refined, if we "handled" one another with soft clean gloves or delicate instruments? "What? Never to be allowed to be alone with oneself? Never again to be unobserved, unprotected, free of leading-reins and gifts? If we are always surrounded by another, the best of courage and goodness in this world is rendered impossible" (*Daybreak*, bk. 5, par. 464, p. 194).

Some involvements and relationships are manifestly more contaminating, more destructive of free-spiritedness than others, but solitude, quiet, and repose are not merely means to individuality, they are components of it. "Active men are generally wanting in the higher activity; I mean that of the individual. They are active as officials, businessmen, scholars, that is to say as generic creatures, but not as distinct individual and unique human beings. . . . As at all times, so now too, men are divided into the slaves and the free; for he who does not have two-thirds of his day to himself is a slave, let him be what he may otherwise: statesman, businessman, official, scholar" (*Human, All Too Human*, vol. I, sec. 5, par. 283, p. 132).

In one of his many transvaluations, Nietzsche holds that those who are conventionally regarded as vigorous and active are in fact characterized by "stupid obedience" to the "laws of mechanics" of social life, of a passive going with the flow of opinions and events that surround them. "The laziness that lies in the depths of the soul of the man of action prevents man from drawing the water up from his own well" (pars. 283, 286, pp. 132–33). Worse, a person of this sort *"waits* for an opinion of himself" from others "and then instinctively subordinates himself to it—by no means always a 'good' opinion, however; just as likely a bad or an unfair one" (*Beyond Good and Evil*, par. 261, p. 209).[94] By contrast, the "repose" of those who have achieved genuine solitude is alive with the play of the powerful forces internal to them, vibrant with "some sort of ardor and thirst that constantly drives the soul out of the night into the morning and out of the gloom, the 'gloominess', into the light, the glowing, the deep, the delicate" (par. 271, p. 224).[95]

Solitude, then, is first and foremost self-overcoming, it is that self-discipline and command of self which Nietzsche regards as the essence of willing and willfulness.[96] The solitary overcomes her

[94]Cf. the following remark in *The Gay Science*: "A thinker needs no applause and clapping of hands, if only he is assured of his own hand-clapping; without that he cannot do. Are there people who can dispense with that also and altogether with every kind of applause? I doubt it" (bk. 4, par. 330, p. 260).
This passage may well express the core insight in Hobbes's distinction between "worthiness" and "worth" or "value." See *Leviathan*, chap. 10, and supra, chap. 1.
[95]*From the land of the cannibals.*—In solitude the solitary man consumes himself, in the crowd the crowd consumes him. Now choose" (*Human, All Too Human*, vol. 2, pt. 1, par. 348, p. 291).
[96]The passions, desires, ideas, dispositions, and so forth, contend with one another, but self-overcoming involves neither extirpating them nor simply maintaining a Humean—or Madisonian—arena or theater in which they somehow balance one another and hence keep one another under some degree of control. The strong-willed person, whom we now see to be the person of solitude, *commands* the outcomes of the struggles that take place within her. (This is one ground on which Nietzsche thought he had gone beyond the heroic Greek notion of contest. Contrary to what might be suggested if we projected from that notion, however, his "commanding" occurs within individuals, is not and could not be a "collective" willing or commanding on the model of such repugnant notions as "general will," "national will," and their ilk.)

impulse to let herself be determined by others—whether to toady to their wishes or to act reflexively against them;[97] she takes command of the passions that well up in her and submits her ideas to critical scrutiny.[98]

Accordingly, solitude is not isolation, not renunciation;[99] it promotes privacy in a sense deeper than is usual in even the most privatizing versions of liberalism, but it has little to do with the

[97]In a passage that is important for assessing his most disdainful remarks about the herd, the poisonous flies, and so forth, Nietzsche describes his own "retreat into solitude" as "a self-defense against a contempt for men that had become pathologically clairvoyant—this determined self-limitation to what was bitter, harsh and hurtful to know" (*Gay Science*, Preface for the Second Edition, par. 1, p. 33). This passage expresses one of the main senses in which "distancing" always involves a "pathos," an engagement with, as well as a separation from, the self as it has been and the others through relations with whom the self has, in part, become what it is and formed an ideal of what it might be. I am indebted to William Connolly and Bonnie Honig for discussions of this and related points concerning "solitude" and its always intricate relation to individuality.

[98]Nietzsche reviled the "English psychologists" who insistently and perversely located "the effective motive forces" of human action "in the blind and fortuitous association of ideas; always in something that is purely passive, automatic, reflexive, molecular, and, moreover, profoundly stupid" (*Genealogy of Morals*, First Essay, par. 1, p. 158). My entire discussion of him can be viewed as an interpretation of his rejection of determinism and behaviorism, of his theory of voluntary action. Although not cast in the idioms that have become characteristic of the philosophy of action in our time, his works are an extended and highly detailed contribution to that subject matter.

[99]"*Do not renounce*:—To forego the world without knowing it, like a *nun*—that leads to a fruitless, perhaps melancholy solitude. It has nothing in common with the solitude of the *vita contemplativa* of the thinker: when he chooses *that* he is renouncing nothing; on the contrary, it would be renunciation, melancholy, destruction of himself if he were obliged to persist in the *vita practica*: he forgoes this because he knows it, because he knows himself. Thus he leaps into *his* element, thus he gains *his* cheerfulness" (*Daybreak*, bk. 5, par. 440, p. 187). The thoughts here expressed are essential to understanding a central Nietzschean thematic, that I am largely avoiding, that is, nihilism. The passage quoted is an articulation of what he sometimes calls "active" or "practical" as opposed to "passive" and "destructive" nihilism.

If we associate the "vita practica" with political life, the passage also signals the great distance between Nietzsche and Arendt in particular, and between Nietzsche and civic republicanism and democratic participationism more generally. It puts him in company with "knowing" political withdrawalists such as Montaigne and Hobbes, with thinkers who "engaged" with politics and much else in large part by "distancing" themselves from them. In societies such as theirs, Nietzsche's, and our own—that is, societies that are pervaded with a morally charged and therefore onerous politicality this stance can never be more than partly achieved or maintained, and the attempt to sustain it must be full of "pathos."

notional self-subsistence of Cartesian epistemology and nothing whatever to do with that (largely imaginary) social and political "atomism" which critics of liberalism claim to find in the latter (would that there were more to it!). The forces and tendencies that the individual must overcome have for the most part been implanted ("bred") in her by the culture and society in which she is a participant, and even those that are native or congenital to her are what they are only in and by virtue of the languages that she shares with others. Much more affirmatively, Nietzsche often writes as if solitude as he understands and treasures it is as an existential matter impossible without that most delicate but delectable mode of association that he calls friendship.

It is certainly true that Nietzschean solitude demands the refusal of numerous commitments and interactions, requires narrow selectivity as regards associations and engagements. Much of the solitary's involvement with her society will be vicarious, indirect, as an ironic observer who maintains distance (but, again, a "pathos of distance") rather than as an "active" participant. But this "standing aside" is only one part of the configuration that is solitude, and many of the positive and negative counsels through which Nietzsche delineates the ideal protect and otherwise work to the advantage of those from whom the solitary distances herself.

The most obvious point in this regard is one on which we have already touched, that is, the matter of ruling and domination. One of the rhymes that form a prelude to *The Gay Science* is entitled "The Solitary." It runs as follows:

> I hate to follow and I hate to lead.
> Obey? Oh no! And govern? No indeed!
> Only who dreads himself inspires dread.
> And only those inspiring dread can lead.
> Even to lead myself is not my speed.
> I love to lose myself for a good while,
> Like animals in forests and the sea,
> To sit and think on some abandoned isle,
> And lure myself back home from far away,
> Seducing myself to come back to me.
> (no. 33, pp. 53, 55)

In the prose of (antipolitical) political theory, this would translate into an ideal as far from rule and domination as it is possible to go,

beyond individualistic anarchism to a thoroughgoing antinomianism, even to the near mysticism that is intimated by Nietzsche at his
most resolutely Dionysian.[100]

If others have nothing to fear from such visionaries, Nietzsche
was keenly aware that this very fact often intensifies their resentment and hatred of them.[101] Perhaps for this reason, and because in
any case this is but one of many moments in his thinking, he has
further counsels for those who must achieve and sustain their solitude in politically organized societies and cultures suffused with
ressentiment. If followed, these counsels might help to calm "the
herd" (hence also to calm those who make a life—or at least a
career—of fearing the herd?) as well as furnish the solitaries with
insulation that, finally, only a certain kind of heroism can provide.

As to ruling in the sense of wielding the power and authority of
government, for the would-be solitary it is at best a lesser evil.
"Some rule out of a desire to rule; others so as not to be ruled;—to
the latter ruling is only the less of two evils" (*Daybreak*, bk. 3, par.
181, p. 108). The former, those who want to "acquire the feeling of
power" of *this* kind, will resort "to any means" and will disdain
"nothing that will nourish" that feeling. Those who undertake rule
in the latter spirit "become very fastidious and noble" in their tastes,
"find few things to satisfy" them (ibid., bk. 4, par. 348, p. 165).
Rulers of the first type enlarge and extend the state, use it to impose
a personal or class despotism; under rulers of the second kind, the
state is likely to diminish, to relax its control over society.[102]

---

[100]Whatever else we might think of Nietzsche's poetic effusion, it is not in conflict
with his claim that "*this world is the will to power—and nothing besides!* And you
yourselves are also this will to power—and nothing besides!" Addressed as it is to
"you best-concealed, strongest, most intrepid, most midnightly men," it is clear
from this famous concluding peroration that the will to power is above all a will to
self-overcoming. And this is precisely what the solitary of his rhyme must achieve
(*Will to Power*, par. 1067, p. 550).

[101]Those who have achieved self-control and independence thereby "become
insufferable for others" (*Gay Science*, bk. 4, par. 305, p. 245).

[102]Nietzsche may have this in mind when he imagines "a society flushed with such
a sense of power" that its "penal code becomes more lenient," even that it lets "its
offenders go unpunished" so that "justice ends by suspending itself" (*Genealogy of
Morals*, Second Essay, par. 10, pp. 204–5). Such a society would have evolved
beyond justice to moderation and magnanimity. In respect to the specifically political aspects of society, however, the connection between the two themes is mediate,
not direct. Nietzsche never urges solitaries to undertake governance in order to
bring about a relaxation of governmental control. But perhaps he hoped that their

The Morality and Politics of Strong Voluntarism

These remarks about political rule are not more than occasional applications of views that Nietzsche develops much more fully concerning matters that are public in the wider sense and especially concerning relationships that most liberals regard as private. Three of his great themes, all of them inseparable from the notions of *self*-command and *self*-overcoming, are moderation, a disposition to what I will call magnanimity (in part because Nietzsche himself sometimes uses this word of the qualities in question, in part because of the striking affinities between Nietzsche's descriptions and Aristotle's analysis of the virtue of magnanimity in book 4 of the *Nichomachean Ethics*), and a further set of qualities that bear a surprising resemblance to conventional conceptions of compassion, self-subordination, or even self-sacrifice.

As with other manifestations of what is at bottom the will to power, moderation has been deformed by Christian and Schopenhauerian asceticisms, by liberalism, and by other views propounding commonality, self-hatred, and self-abnegation. At once fearing and hating their passions and pleasures, they misconstrue moderation to mean dull, stultifying mediocrity. Moderation has been represented as "asceticism, as a fight with the devil, etc." The dismal but predictable effect of this centuries-long campaign is that "the best things have been slandered because the weak or the *immoderate* swine have cast a bad light on them" (*Will to Power*, par. 870, pp. 465–66, emphasis added).

True moderation requires strength, is a manifestation of willfulness or the strength of will in the face of a plethora of powerful and conflicting forces that one would not be without, would not want to still. "The faith in the pleasure of moderation—that pleasure of the rider on a fiery steed!—has been lacking hitherto. The mediocrity of weaker natures has been confused with the moderation of the strong!" (p. 466). As on its corrupted or deformed conception, true moderation involves control, a sense of "measure," of proportion, of taste. But the proportionality must be among the humanly admirable qualities and characteristics. "The natural delight of aesthetic natures in measure, the enjoyment of the beauty of measure, was overlooked or denied, because one desired an anti-eudamonistic

---

example, the example of the moderation and the magnanimity they practice in their personal conduct and relationships, would assist those disposed to rule in acquiring these characteristics, in becoming "fastidious" in their ruling.

morality" (ibid.). Driven by a debased and self-debasing conception of what is substantively worthy and unworthy in themselves, the weak and immoderate "let themselves go," go all the way (to fanaticism) with their asceticism. The truly moderate person, by contrast, attends to adverbial considerations, takes "pleasure in forms; taking under protection everything formal, the conviction that politeness is one of the greatest virtues; mistrust for letting oneself go in any way, including all freedom of press and thought, because under them the spirit grows comfortable and doltish and relaxes its limbs" (par. 943, p. 497).[103]

If we go by the most familiar distinctions between self-regarding or prudential qualities and the other-regarding characteristics that are called virtues, Nietzsche's account of moderation puts it—and magnanimity, compassion, and the other characteristics that he admired and promoted—squarely in the former category. Indeed, Nietzsche's works are full of expressions of disdain for altruism or other-regardingness in general and for most of the virtues as traditionally construed. It is evident from his remarks about politeness, however, that moderation has great import for, provides real protections and advantages to, any and all "others" with whom the Nietzschean moderate becomes involved. As we will shortly see, this is yet more obviously the case concerning magnanimity and compassion. For these reasons, and because the distinction between self- and other-regarding is of importance for the public-private dichotomy and the related issues in liberal theory that are my guiding concern, we have to consider this matter more closely.

According to Nietzsche's genealogy of morals, the notions of good and evil, the delineation of the virtues and vices, and the whole distinction between egoism and altruism, prudence and morality, took their beginnings from the class interests of various early ruling groups.

---

[103]Nietzsche's contempt for romanticism was due primarily to its "letting go," its disdain for the "classical" or classicist insistence on form, manner, and hence "good manners" such as politeness and cleanliness. He sometimes attempted to reshape his version of Dionysianism to include these latter elements, but the abiding tension in his thinking—from *The Birth of Tragedy* forward—between the Dionysian and the Apollonian, manifests this concern.

It is not to be thought, incidentally, that his remark about "freedom of press and thought" indicates any desire for censorship, for governmental or societal restriction of publication and other forms of expression. It is for the individual to "censor" herself.

The Morality and Politics of Strong Voluntarism

The origin of the opposites *good* and *bad* is to be found in the pathos of nobility and distance, representing the dominant temper of a higher, ruling class in relation to a lower, dependent one. . . . Such an origin would suggest that there is no *a priori* necessity for associating the word *good* with altruistic deeds, as . . . moral psychologists are fond of claiming. In fact, it is only after aristocratic values have begun to decline that the egotism- [egoism?-] altruism dichotomy takes possession of the human conscience; to use my own terms, it is the herd instinct that now asserts itself. Yet it takes quite a while for this instinct to assume such sway that it can reduce all moral valuations to that dichotomy—as is currently happening throughout Europe, where the prejudice equating the terms *moral, altruistic,* and *disinterested* has assumed the obsessive force of an *idée fixe. (Genealogy of Morals,* First Essay, par. 2, pp. 160–61)

(Again, compare James's discussion of "Chautaukua society" and Oakeshott's lamentations concerning "mass society" and its "individuals manqué" and "anti-individuals.")

Interpreted in the perspective provided by this passage, Nietzsche's treatment of moderation can be viewed as an attempt to revive an aristocratic value. As he frequently said of himself (especially in *The Will to Power*), he was a proponent of "moraline free" *virtu* on the pre-Socratic Greek, Roman, and Renaissance models, not of *virtue* as Christianity, Kantianism, and other perverting moralisms had deformed it. And if the reign of *virtu* also benefits the herd, that is an unintended consequence to which Nietzsche is indifferent. In this regard, Nietzsche's transvaluation of values is a straightforward reversal, a reversion from altruism back to the egoism that had been subverted.

Attractive as it may be to Nietzsche's critics, this construal neglects both empirical and conceptual aspects of Nietzsche's thinking. As to the former, the long history of herd moralism cannot simply be rescinded or transposed. Whether deservedly or not, the herd *is* the ruling class, does have the power to impose its wishes and its values. Worse, the highest and noblest members of modern societies are themselves heirs to the same history that eventuated in the hegemony of the herd, must overcome themselves as well as the herd. Conceptually, moderation is partly defined in terms of, is partly constituted by, relationships among persons. Some of the "forms" that the moderate person respects are forms of *inter*action (for example, one can be neither polite nor impolite to oneself);

maintaining "proportion," "measure," and "poise" is partly a matter of calibrating and stabilizing the relationships between my thoughts and actions and those of others. Nietzschean solitude, as we might put it, is not a spatial or territorial conception and condition, and it is no more than partially a physical one.

These matters are yet clearer in respect to magnanimity and "compassion." As would be true of a political society that had moved beyond justice, the magnanimous person is so "flushed with a sense of power" that she believes she can abide with indifference or with equanimity the worst harms that others can inflict on her. The "virtues that incur costs" belong "among non-equals," are devised and practiced by "the superior, the individual; they are the virtues of *rulers* bearing the sense: 'I am sufficiently powerful to put up with a palpable loss, this is a proof of my power'—and thus are virtues related to *pride*" (*Human, All Too Human*, vol. 2, pt. 2, par. 34, pp. 318–19).[104] Magnanimity, then, is deeply self-regarding, self-affirming. But it is also, intrinsically and necessarily, other-involving. I can secure this proof of my power only by relating to you, only by making myself vulnerable to you. Nor does the magnanimous person passively await and then elect to overlook or to disdain the harms others do to her. Zarathustra loves "him whose soul squanders itself, . . . who casts golden words before his deeds and always does even more than he promises" (*Thus Spoke Zarathustra*, Zarathustra's Prologue, par. 4, pp. 15–16). Indeed, the fully magnanimous person might deliberately make herself subordinate to others. A person who has "conquered" herself properly considers it *her* right to punish, pardon, pity, and judge herself. Having attained to this self-estimation, however, she "can freely relinquish it to another, to a friend for example—but [s]he knows that [s]he therewith confers a *right* and that one confers rights only out of the possession of *power*" (*Daybreak*, bk. 5, par. 437, p. 187).

This squandering, this surpassing of one's commitments, this knowing bestowal of rights, is likely to advantage others in ways that go well beyond "forgiving" their trespasses.

In the literal sense of making oneself "co-passionate" with the suffering of others, Nietzsche rejected—or all but rejected—the value of compassion. Compassion in this Christian and Rousseauis-

---

[104]"Rulers" means, for the foreseeable future, those who rule themselves, not those who rule others.

tic sense is diminishing, leveling. The higher man "is proud *not* to have been made for compassion. . . . Distinguished and courageous men . . . are at the opposite end from that morality which sees the characteristic function of morality in pity or in doing for others or *désintéressement*. Belief in oneself, pride in oneself, basic hostility and irony against 'selflessness' is as sure a part of distinguished morality as an easy disdain and cautious attitude toward the fellow-feelings and the 'warm heart' " (*Beyond Good and Evil*, par. 260, pp. 205–6).

Nevertheless, "Zarathustra is gentle with the sick. Verily, he is not angry with their kinds of comfort and ingratitude. May they become convalescents, men of overcoming, and create a higher body for themselves!" (*Thus Spoke Zarathustra*, pt. 1, sec. 3, p. 33). Nevertheless, the higher, "the distinguished man . . . helps the unhappy, . . . not—or at least not mainly—from compassion, but more from an internal pressure that has been built up by an excess of power" (*Beyond Good and Evil*, par. 260, p. 205).

In sum:

Where are your greatest dangers?—In pity.
What do you love in others?—My hopes.
Whom do you call bad?—Those who always want to put to shame.
What do you consider most humane?—To spare someone shame.
What is the seal of liberation?—No longer being ashamed in front of oneself. (*Gay Science*, bk. 3, pars. 271–75, p. 220)

V   *Toward A More Willful Liberalism*

It is worth observing at once that the views we have been considering draw much of the sting of even the most obnoxiously "elitist" elements in Nietzsche's thinking. If the overwo/men have the misfortune of being involved in ruling in the political sense, they will rule fastidiously and with a view to their earliest possible disengagement from this self-diminishing activity. On the more welcome assumption that they form a cultural, not a political, "aristocracy," they will for the most part go their own ways, will leave the "lower" ranks (and to a large extent one another) to their own political and other devices. If these distancings deprive the herd of the "benefits" promised to them by other philosophers of rank from Plato to Matthew Arnold and Vladimir Ilyich Lenin, they will insulate its members against offensively paternalistic ministrations. In short, to the extent that Nietzsche was an elitist, he at least had the good sense to shun noblesse oblige, to see the incongruity in the view that orders or strata that are irremediably "lower" can nevertheless appreciate the qualities of their betters sufficiently to be advantaged by the attentions of the latter. If Friedrich Nietzsche's personal sentiments were too often ungenerous, narrow, and ill-considered, I see nothing antagonistic to *liberalism* in the moral and political views that connect with those sentiments in Nietzsche's thinking.

Reserving further discussion of elitism for a bit later, I now draw together the threads of my discussion of the public and the private. The strong voluntarisms we have considered offer little support for, assemble substantial considerations against, those political moralisms that employ an insistent distinction between the public and the private realms as part of privileging the former at the expense of the latter. Theories of high citizenship, of republican virtue in the service of res publica or the commonweal, of Arendtian political action, even (or perhaps especially) those that fly the flag of virtu rather than Christian virtue, are anything but "moraline free." If proponents of these ideals have sometimes been as invidious as Nietzsche himself in their estimations of the likely incidence or distribution of the qualities of character and conduct that they esteem, they advance ideals that are "in common" or "for everyone," ideals that are to take precedence over all competing desires and interests, objectives and purposes. They posit and are all too often keen to impose a "good" or set of interwoven goods that, in reason or truth if not in general estimation, is "common."

But "how could there be a 'common good'! The expression contradicts itself: what can be common cannot have much value" (Nietzsche, *Beyond Good and Evil*, par. 43, p. 50).[105] Or, if this is overstated in its seeming dismissal of the possibility of a genuine convergence on "forms" that everyone has reason to respect, that

---

[105]Cf. Wittgenstein: "What is good is also divine. Queer as it sounds, that sums up my ethics. Only something supernatural can express the Supernatural.

"You cannot lead people to what is good; you can only lead them to some place or other. The good is outside the space of facts" (*Culture and Value*, ed. G. H. von Wright in collaboration with Heikki Nyman, trans. Peter Winch [Chicago: University of Chicago Press, 1980], p. 3e).

which is "common" cannot have much value if it is an end that is inflicted on individuals who regard it as alien or unworthy. As manifested in the thought and action of, say, a Machiavelli, these conceptions may have contributed to the "preparatory" work that has needed and may again need doing. As ideals, a more willful liberalism will reject them.

There is a further point, at once difficult and instructive, that requires consideration here. It is arguable that a liberalism such as we are contemplating should be open to the possibility of individuals and even entire societies for whom Arendtian political action and republican virtue are as appealing, even as essential, as are solitude, the pathos of distance, and free-spiritedness to the Nietzschean. Perhaps there are some for whom these ideals, these ways of life, *constitute* free-spiritedness, are the very embodiment of self-overcoming.

There is one respect in which a voluntarist liberalism should adopt this view. We sometimes think of politics as occurring on sites and in venues other than the state, in associations that are voluntary in ways that the state as we know it is not and cannot be. There is no reason for liberalism to oppose, in these settings, "political" ideals such as Arendtian "self-disclosure" and "glory" or the virtuous commitment to "public" life and its shared values that is demanded by classical or civic republicanism. No one who is attracted by a Nietzschean conception of individuality will herself embrace or even admire ideals that make the individual so deeply and incessantly dependent on the responses of others (albeit, just possibly, she could do so if the "others" were "worthy" friends or enemies), but fidelity to the view that each person should construct and pursue her own ideal—however bizarre—would seem to require accommodation to those whose ideals they are.

The difficulty is that these and related ideals such as democratic participationism do not readily abide restriction to particular societal domains. They are advanced "for everyone," are resolutely promoted to standing as properly authoritative for—or over—all those who make up a society that is politically organized in the more definite sense of having a government that claims authority over all of its members and a politics that takes its foci and most of its life from the actions of that government. It is true that some, many— perhaps all but a few—of the members of a political society may be excluded or excused from many or all forms of political participation. These restrictions and concessions, however, are effected in order to serve the ideal; conflicts between it and the activities and purposes of nonparticipants are to be resolved in favor of the ideal.

With the qualification expressed, therefore, a strongly voluntaristic liberalism must contest these political ideals, must expose their anti-individuating proclivities and oppose efforts to institutionalize their understandings and requirements. Nor is doing so "illiberal." A strongly voluntarist liberalism would be the most open and accommodating, the least censorious and restrictive, of any theory or ideology that is political in the sense of countenancing—however ruefully—notions such as the state, authority, and rule.[106] But such a liberalism is and must be more than "a series of denials."[107]. As with Nietzsche, it is a form of idealism in that it affirms and promotes values such as individuality and plurality. These values can be manifested in and realized by a great diversity of ends and purposes, dispositions and styles, manners and modes of life. But they are somethings, not anythings or nothings. There are arrangements and understandings that are conducive to and supportive of them, others that hinder and thwart them. If liberalism stands for these values, it cannot be antiliberal to stand against thoughts and actions that are antagonistic to them or otherwise incompatible with them.

If we remain within our earlier outline of the public-private distinction, a kind of algebraic transposition of the foregoing remarks would suggest that a voluntaristic liberalism would favor public arrangements and institutions exclusively to the extent that they serve private values. This was certainly Schopenhauer's view of the state, and the passages in Nietzsche that are most approving of liberalism and of democratic institutions and cultures are compatible with something like this understanding of the public-private relationship.[108] If unburdened of the "new" conception of govern-

---

[106]On this usage, theories such as anarchism and antinomianism, which refuse these inherently objectionable notions, should be described as antipolitical. Because these antipolitical theories are yet more open to possibilities, yet more averse to imposition and restriction, they haunt all forms of liberalism and particularly its strongly voluntarist formulations.

[107]The phrase is Alasdair MacIntyre's in *Against the Self-Images of the Age* (New York: Schocken Books, 1971), p. 283. All forms of liberalism stand for, as well as against, numerous ideas and ideals. If this had not been true, MacIntyre and other opponents of liberalism could hardly have devoted themselves to attacking the political and social understandings and arrangements that they blame liberalism for.

[108]If only because the early theological voluntarists were not dealing with a "state" in the modern sense, it is at best a matter of speculation what Ockham, Duns Scotus, Nicholas of Autrecourt, and others would think about these matters. But if we indulge the thought that the Roman church was the predominant "public"

ment, and if willing to let the free spirits stand aside from public life in all its forms, Nietzsche would have neither much personal enthusiasm for nor any very deep objection to a society that was liberal and democratic in these ways. Although not a likely recruit to the liberal or the democratic cause, his critique of liberalism and of liberal or representative democracy was far less severe than those of the radicals of the Left and the Right of our time. Certainly he would have nothing to do with the regimentations and disciplined mobilizations that the latter assiduously promote.

This account nevertheless misleads in ways that deflect us from some of the most attractive features of strong voluntarism and of a liberalism that incorporates them. The willful, free-spirited, self-overcoming individual is a "private" person in that she holds herself apart from much that transpires in her human environment. But first, the craving for "cleanliness" that keeps her "remote" from government and politics is also reason to "stand aside" from the affairs of family and business, church, school, and club. In its Schopenhauerian, Nietzschean, and Jamesian variants, strong voluntarism accepts the sometimes-liberal view that the state and politics pose distinctive dangers to individuality and plurality, require a special wariness. Particularly as Nietzsche sees the matter, however, the state and the politics that the state's existence generates would not be what they are apart from the traditions and cultures that encompass them, characteristics that pervade private as well as public relations as liberals have drawn that distinction. Second, the free spirit recognizes that these same influences have worked their way deeply into her own beliefs and values so that her distancing and struggle must be from and with herself as well as those around her. In short, the free spirit is both a public and a private person— and hence neither—by criteria that have commonly informed liberal versions of this distinction.[109]

---

institution of their time, it is perhaps not implausible to treat their attempts to contest its domination while accepting its religious "legitimacy" as akin to Nietzsche's stance toward the states and the politics of his time.

[109]If pressed to an alternative terminology, a strongly voluntarist liberalism might shift from "public versus private" to language such as "public versus personal," or better, to a distinction between that which is general, shared, or common and that which is individual. If valuable as a means of dramatizing commitment to the values of individuality and plurality, such alternative contrasts would also obscure more than they would illuminate. In these regards, our need is for more refined and particularized characterizations of individuals and their activities, not encompassing categories.

If we persist in thinking of the free spirits or overwo/men as constituting a class or caste, these understandings should further diminish anxieties concerning elite domination. The struggles of the members of the elite are first and foremost with themselves; the domination they seek is first and foremost over themselves. Related but more important points materialize if we follow the numerous strong voluntarist suggestions that free-spiritedness and self-overcoming, if not conceptions that can be grasped and appreciated by everyone, are for *anyone*, not for a distinct political, social, or cultural stratum. Understood in this way, strong voluntarism articulates understandings, and particularly an aspiration, that are absolutely vital to liberalism.

Let us begin with an essential but minimal point. Any conception worthy of the name of liberalism must credit the great preponderance of human beings with considerable capacity for self-command or self-control, with the ability to—for the most part—discipline themselves against activities that are grossly destructive of self and others. No doubt in part engendered and maintained by public life, if these do not become and remain capacities of most individuals, society can maintain a modicum of order only by taking on the character of quintessentially illiberal institutions such as prisons and military camps, hospitals and asylums. Understood as for anyone, and construed in the light of Nietzschean notions such as moderation and magnanimity, willfulness in the sense of this kind of self-command is both more and less than an ideal, does more than counter despotism and other forms of depravity. On this understanding, willfulness is a presupposition of liberalism and of the possibility of a liberal society.

In the main modern versions of strong voluntarism, self-command is impossible without public life, but public life at its best cannot itself create or sustain individuality, too often diminishes or even destroys it. The first part of this formulation distinguishes strong voluntarism from what Nietzsche calls "libertinage" and from much of what has since come to be called "libertarianism." Strong voluntarism doesn't attempt to provide, in advance and on the basis of (say) a theory of political economy, a recipe for determining what the state or other aspects of public life can and cannot, should and should not do. Nietzsche's "as little state as possible" expresses a generalized caution that is rooted in the view that state action is itself diminishing of individuality and plurality. But because there are other threats to these values, some of which may be most effectively countered by law and punishment, it would be foolish to restrict the state to the enforcement of contracts, to maintaining a legal tender, to preventing economic monopoly, or to providing protections against force, fraud, or violations of other notional natural rights. There may be circumstances in which the state should do more than these things, others in which it should do less.[110]

The second aspect of the formulation (public life at its best cannot create or sustain individuality) is complementary to the first but is more forceful in directing our attention to the more affirmative—and hence also to the more inspiriting—dimensions of the ideal of willful individuality. In ideological terms this part of the formulation argues the futility of the attempt to *achieve* individuality by the methods of, say, state socialism or welfare state liberalism. To adapt a familiar formula, public policies and arrangements can "hinder" the coarsest of the "hindrances" to free-spiritedness. Accordingly, there may be circumstances under which the measures characteristic of socialist and welfare states will be appropriate. But it is a blatant misunderstanding and betrayal of that ideal to equate it with the benefits that public life in such polities sometimes provide.

Self-control, moderation, magnanimity, respect for "forms" and adverbial considerations, and conditions of life conducive to these, are elements in all strong voluntarist conceptions of individuality. Without them individuality disappears into herd behavior or deteriorates into self-indulgence and "letting go." But neither these nor any other elements comprise or constitute individuality or free-spiritedness. Phrases such as the following (weak echoes of the much more vibrant and evocative language that Nietzsche often manages) bring us a bit closer to the conception: the free spirit goes beyond the self-discipline that prevents harmful or destructive conduct and forms and acts upon images and objectives that complicate and endanger, amplify, heighten, and intensify her life. At once "prepared" and enabled, impaired and disabled, by the culture in which she imagines, thinks, and acts, she enacts[111] and reenacts

---

[110]More generally, Nietzsche would have nothing but disdain for the preoccupation with truck and barter that has become characteristic of much libertarianism. His concern is with the making and living of lives, not with "making a living."

[111]I again take the terminology of "self-enactment" from Michael Oakeshott whose articulations of it and the companion notion of "self-disclosure" are splendid evocations of a strong voluntarist conception of individuality. See *On Human Conduct*, pp. 36–45, 62–64, 70–79, 234–42, 274–79, and passim.

herself in part by availing herself of its accumulated capital, in part by contesting its prejudices and presuppositions,[112] above all by descending into the dark waters of her impulses and inclinations, ascending into the opaque mists of her visions and fantasies.

But language of this sort can do no more than outline strong voluntarist conceptions of individuality. Willful individuality cannot be captured, certainly cannot be explained, in or by any formula. We encounter and sometimes recognize and acknowledge "it" in the thinking and acting, the loves and hates, the joys and despairs, of ourselves and other persons. "It" may take place dramatically before, and with great consequences for, innumerable others—Joseph Welch at the Army-McCarthy hearings, Andrei Sakharov vis-à-vis the Soviet regime; it may be inconspicuous and entirely or primarily self-affecting—my cultured aunt listening to rock rather than Mozart in the privacy of her apartment, my elderly uncle putting his savings in the bank and later into stocks rather than beneath his mattress. "For it needs many nobles and many different kinds of nobles *to make nobility*. Or—as I once said in a parable—'Isn't the most divine thing of all that there are gods but no god'" (*Thus Spoke Zarathustra*, pt. 3, sec. 11, p. 239).[113]

Nietzsche's parable returns us to themes that have recurred throughout our exploration of strong voluntarisms. From the rever-

---

[112]"The conditions which compose a moral practice are not theorems or precepts about human conduct, nor do they constitute anything so specific as a 'shared system of values'; they compose a vernacular language of colloquial intercourse. This language is not a vocabulary of abstract nouns denoting recognized *bona* of human conduct in terms of which actions and utterances may be judged, approved or disapproved. Nor is it a language spoken on some occasions (e.g. when explicit moral 'valuations' are being discussed) and not on others; it is spoken, well or ill, on every occasion of human intercourse. Like any other language, it is an instrument of self-disclosure used by agents in diagnosing their situations and in choosing their responses; and it is a language of self-enactment which permits those who can use it to understand themselves and one another, to disclose to one another their complex individualities, and *to explore relationships far more varied and interesting than those it has a name for* or those which a commonplace acceptance of so-called 'moral values' would allow" (ibid., p. 63, emphasis added).

[113]I quote here from Marianne Cowan's translation (Chicago: Gateway Editions, 1957). Walter Kaufmann, whose edition of *Zarathustra* I have otherwise used, translates the same passage as follows: "For many who are noble are needed, and noble men of many kinds, that there may be a nobility. Or as I once said in a parable: 'Precisely this is godlike that there are gods, but no God'" (p. 203). Without attempting to adjudicate between the translations as such, Cowan's language says better what I want the passage to say.

ent Ockham through the skeptical Hobbes to Schopenhauer the atheist and Nietzsche the self-styled "Anti-christ", the strong voluntarists have regularly turned to images of the divine (and of the extra- or superhuman more generally) to elicit, evoke, and give allure to their ideal for humankind. They have done so, we might say, because they have largely deprived themselves of the devices and stratagems on which such promotional activities ordinarily rely. The conceptions they promote circumscribe and in important respects exclude the use of standard modes of argumentation and persuasion such as subsumption and deduction, causal and other forms of explanation, and even honorific characterizations that are at once definite and general.[114]

This explanation, however, threatens to confuse one of the major effects of the phenomenon in question with its cause. The strong voluntarists were not opposed to encompassing but sharply delineated categorization, nomothetic explanation, or deductive and inductive inference as such.[115] Rather, they were radically discontent with the conceptions of God, the gods, and especially humankind that privilege or require these devices as the primary or even the exclusive means of understanding and evaluating human beings and their conduct. They appropriated and projected images of the divine

[114]As I have emphasized from the beginning of these reflections, the history of strong voluntarism represents an inherently problematic adventure in ideas and images. In order that the voluntarist position can be so much as entertained, those to whom it is recommended must have something approaching a definite conception of what counts as accepting or rejecting it. But every attempt to provide it with definiteness and stability sufficient for this purpose threatens the individuality and particularity, the idiosyncrasy and even mystery, that it aims to celebrate and promote. Again, definite descriptions, generalizations, classifications and inferences, explanations and predictions, are the devices to which we most often look for intelligibility and the equanimity that it sometimes provides. To the extent that strong voluntarism eschews these, it assures that it will be disturbing to many, guarantees resistance to itself. As it seeks to allay anxieties by analysis and explication, construal, comparison, and projection, it diminishes its distinctiveness and perhaps its appeal to those for whom it has the greatest attraction. My discussions in these pages trace the efforts, necessarily never more than partly successful, of the major proponents of the position to sustain a creative tension between these inveterately competing objectives.

[115]Certainly no one who has read Duns Scotus or Ockham, Hobbes, Schopenhauer, or O'Shaughnessy would accuse them of any aversion to these modalities. The accusation is sometimes made against Nietzsche, but anyone who is tempted by it should consult, in particular, his lengthy discussion of what can appropriately be called his philosophy of logic in book 3 of *The Will to Power*.

and the superhuman because—in some of their forms—they afford inspiriting and ennobling (or, as in Schopenhauer and sometimes Oakeshott, perhaps James and Arendt, consoling) conceptions of and ideals for humankind.

How can it come about for "an individual to posit his own ideal and to derive from it his own law, joys, and rights"? In much of the human experience doing so has "been considered . . . the most outrageous human aberration and as idolatry itself." Many of humankind's religious conceptions, moreover, have reinforced this self-denial and self-stultification. Monotheism in general and Christianity in particular insist upon a "doctrine of one normal human type," promote a "faith in one normal god beside whom there are only pseudo-gods." And this doctrine posed "the greatest danger that has yet confronted humanity. It threatened us with the premature stagnation that, as far as we can see, most other species have long reached; for all of them believe in one normal type and ideal for their species, and they have translated the morality of mores definitively into their own flesh and blood." But germinating in the religious impulse was a seed that could become the strange but beautiful growth that is the genuine individual. Those few who, unaccountably, first "dared" to seek and go their own way "felt the need to apologize to themselves, usually by saying: 'It wasn't I! Not I! But *a god* through me'." But the "through *me*" was the small beginning of something "wonderful."

> The wonderful art and gift of *creating* [emphasis added] gods—polytheism—was the medium through which this impulse could discharge, purify, perfect, and ennoble itself; for originally it was a very undistinguished impulse, related to stubbornness, disobedience, and envy. Hostility against this impulse to have an ideal of one's own was formerly the central law of all morality. There was only one norm, *man*; and every people thought that it possessed this one ultimate norm. But above and outside, in some distant overworld, one was permitted to behold a *plurality of norms*; one god was not considered a denial of another god, nor blasphemy against him. It was here that the luxury of individuals was first permitted; it was here that one first honored the rights of individuals. The invention of gods, heroes, and overmen of all kinds, as well as near-men and undermen, dwarfs, fairies, centaurs, satyrs, demons, and devils was the inestimable preliminary exercise for the justification of the egoism and sovereignty of the individual: the freedom that one conceded to a god in his relation

to other gods—one eventually also granted to oneself in relation to laws, customs, and neighbors. (*Gay Science*, bk. 3, par. 143, pp. 191–92)

One of Nietzsche's most splendid images: the free spirit "would be a centaur, half beast, half man, and with angel's wings attached to his head in addition" (*Human, All Too Human*, vol. 1, sec. 3, par. 241, p. 115).

This is history only in the sense that this passage is itself a major moment in the emergence of O'Shaughnessy's nineteenth-century Wo/Man-God. But Nietzsche's splendid mythologizing speaks for or in the spirit and idiom of all of the strong voluntarists.[116] These gods, devils, and other fabulous creatures are images of the spontaneous, the untrammeled, the singular. Literally construed, the process of projecting them involves human beings in looking above, below, or apart from themselves in search of creatures to worship, to admire, and to emulate, to love, to hate, and to fear. More plausibly construed, it involves human beings willfully fashioning and enacting images of and ideals for themselves out of their own hopes and fears, successes and failures, delights and disappointments. So construed (that is, as "theomorphism" *à la* Harold Bloom), these activities are much more than inestimable preliminary exercises; they are the adventures of human self-fashioning and self-enactment, the proud escapades of human individuality.

Talk of gods and demons, of imaging and imagining, of willful adventures of self-creation, is certain to revive and to intensify philosophical resistance and moral and political anxiety. There is no need to reiterate the particular respects in which the strong voluntarists locate these notions and activities in cultures and traditions, condition them upon agreements, conventions, and various other "preparations," and discipline them by and with requirements such as moderation, magnanimity, and compassion. Something further

---

[116]An expression of his hatred of Christianity, Nietzsche's tirade against monotheism reflects what appears to be his lack of familiarity with other than the Augustine-Lutheran tradition of theological voluntarism. Ockham's one God—to say nothing of the God of the author of the *Book of J* as so splendidly recreated by Harold Bloom—was a many-splendored and by no means predictable creature, a fecund not a circumscribing source of human ideals. In general, Nietzsche greatly exaggerated the uniformity of Christian doctrine and practice, underestimated its contributions to plurality and even individuality.

should be said, however, by way of coordinating (not harmonizing) these latter features of strong voluntarism with the notions of mystery, spontaneity and origination, singularity, and limited mutual accessibility that give this tendency of thought and sensibility its distinctive character. Remarks concerning this intrinsically difficult matter will bring us to a brief concluding discussion of strong voluntarism and liberalism.

Few would now entertain the notion of banishing or even narrowly confining indeterminacy, inexplicability, and limited mutual unintelligibility from human affairs. Doing so was long deemed a viable, even an essential, project (so that nineteenth-century voluntarists such as Kierkegaard, Nietzsche, and James still felt it necessary to contest it at the level of general theory), but twentieth-century developments in science, in philosophy, and in literature and the arts have pushed this aspiration to the intellectual periphery. At the same time, it is widely appreciated that all arguments to the effect that these features of thought and action are ineliminable, and all statements proffering instances of partial or entire meaninglessness (and other radical indeterminacies), necessarily supposit for (as Ockham would say) their own meaningfulness and hence for criteria thereof that, while liable to change, are operable over stretches of time that exceed their own articulation and over a domain larger than that which they themselves occupy.

In short, there is something of a convergence on the view that the apparently conflicting sets of desiderata that the strong voluntarists promote are in fact compossible and in that sense compatible. Yet more abstractly, meaninglessness and other forms of indeterminacy and partial mutual intelligibilities, and partial and more or less stable meaningfulnesses and mutual intelligibilities, are equally undeniable at the level of general theory. If so, the conceptual or philosophical objective is not to derive or otherwise subordinate one set from or to the other; it is to identify instances of each and to chart relationships between and among them. And the same philosophical circumstance permits us to pursue, as I have been doing in the foregoing pages, the related but more insistently practical objective of assembling reminders of the former in order to break down resistances grounded in residual rationalist and positivist suppositions[117] and, in this and other ways, to enhance receptivity to the

---

[117]Or in theories of "human nature" of the kind that Hannah Arendt seems to have in mind in the passage I quoted from *The Human Condition* in note 23 (Part

idea that quite radical diversities, incommensurabilities, and so forth, including those strongly protected by limited mutual intelligibility, are to be welcomed, not feared.

I will try to make these unfortunately abstract remarks somewhat more concrete by applying them to the strong voluntarist formulations we have been considering. Ockham conceives of God as mysterious will and of human beings as created by God in Her likeness; Nietzsche thinks of gods as created by human beings out of images they have of themselves; but the results are similar in that on both accounts human beings and their gods are, in part, creatures characterized by partly mysterious will. In these and other ways, both thinkers, and all of the strong voluntarists, place great emphasis on notions such as mystery, inexplicability, contingency, origination, singularity, and incommensurability.

But this is but one dimension of strong voluntarist thinking. We have seen that all of these writers, while insisting on the ultimately mysterious character of the will, endeavor to abate that mystery by locating the will in thought and action, distinguishing among its elements or its manifestations, identifying its limitations, and the like. More obviously, the propositions "God is mysterious will" and "Human beings are, in part, creatures of mysterious will" are not themselves intended to be mysterious. It is assumed that they will be understood as at once denying and affirming certain characteristics of God, the gods, and human beings. It is also intended that the statements will be taken to mean (their perlocutionary force will be understood as being) that human beings should honor those qualities in themselves that they honor in God and the gods, that they should cultivate in themselves and acknowledge and encourage in others the characteristics that make them like unto God and make their affairs like unto the affairs of the gods. And it is further assumed that their knowledge of or shared beliefs about the characteristics of God, the gods, and themselves will tell them, at least generically, how and how not to go about doing these things. Moreover, Ockham, Hobbes, James, and especially Nietzsche are at some pains to extend and enhance this "know-how" and "know-how-not-to." Their works, again especially the works of Nietz-

---

Two) supra. Although I find worse than unappealing Arendt's vision of positive freedom achieved exclusively through political action, she is without question one of our most acute critics of the conceptions, both within and without liberalism, that have been the great enemies of individuality.

sche—that son of a preacher and a preacher's daughter—abound
with what might as well be called sermonizing about how life
should and should not be lived. The mystery, the singularity, the
mutual inaccessibility that they esteem and promote reside within
and among, are inconceivable apart from, the manifest, the ordinary, the shared, even the common elements of human experience.[118]

These conceptions, and particularly the relationships among the
elements of which the conceptions consist, cannot be fully specified,
above all cannot be finally or permanently settled or fixed. But they
can and must be invested with continuity. No small part of the
conceptual- and psycho-dynamic of the strong voluntarist discourse
that I have been exploring is generated by attempts to maintain a
creative tension among the idiosyncratic and the generic, the predictable and the disturbing. In insisting, endlessly, that human beings cannot and should not try to understand God, the theological
voluntarists make evident their own powerful desire to do just that.
Nor is this mere weakness, failure, or self-betrayal on their part.
They call on themselves and are called on by others to act; whatever
else it involves, action requires beliefs and judgments, intentions
and purposes; these require considering; considering requires considerations that are more than episodic, more than transient. By
adopting the belief that they cannot understand God, that their
attempts to do so are futile and counterproductive, the theological
voluntarists create within themselves, as it were, beliefs and desires
countervailing to the desire to understand God and hence also
countervailing to the desires that make them unreceptive or unre-
sponsive to God's will. The insisting on what from one perspective
can be viewed as the metalevel questions (the question whether we
can understand, as distinct from the question whether this or that
understanding is plausible, cogent, warranted) can be viewed as a
way of sustaining these countervailing beliefs and desires and hence
of sustaining their responsiveness to God's will because it is God's
will.

"Secular" voluntarism has a similar logic and psychologic or
psychodynamic. If it is harder to sustain a fertile relationship among

[118]Stanley Cavell's sensitive and imaginative explorations of the relationships
among these elements of experience, in part captured in his notion of acknowledgment, are a rich source of insight into these very difficult matters.

its elements—albeit it is not obvious that the theological voluntarists have had continuous success in this task—this is because it is more difficult for human beings to accord to the wills of one another the privilege that, as a deep convention in our tradition, attaches to God's will. The view that God is a human construction diminishes this difference, and this must be a major reason why those who want the order and predictability that they think nothing but submission to God's will makes possible (a thought to which they are strictly not entitled because it presupposes their knowing that God's will is orderly and predictable so that the actions of those who submit to it will have the same characteristics) are so distressed by this view (and by analogous views concerning meaning, truth, logic, reason). That it is not always or even generally thought to be impossible to sustain such a productive relationship is evidenced by any number of doctrines about obedience—to parents, teachers, the law, authority generally—about respecting others, and so forth. All of these are attempts at partial, more or less lasting, stabilization of that which can never be settled or fixed.[119]

A major reason why these attempts can never be more than partially successful is rooted in one of the main arguments in their favor, that is the incomplete intelligibility of those wills to which we are urged to submit or that we are urged to respect. If I cannot understand what your will is, I cannot submit to it in the sense of knowingly and deliberately acting in accord with it or so as not to impede it. I can act on injunctions such as these only if I know not only that you have a will but what your will is in this or that respect. Because I cannot know, or can know only imperfectly, why you have formed the will that you have, if we accept the view that understanding *what* requires understanding *why*, the doctrine is incoherent.

These considerations help us to understand the role of divine revelation in theological voluntarism (and to understand why many have thought that secular voluntarism, deprived as it is of this fallback, is untenable) but also why various analogues to the given that is revelation can be discerned in secular voluntarisms. Through revelation God makes Her will sufficiently understandable to humankind to permit them to act in accord with it in certain minimal

---

[119]These remarks are influenced by Richard Rorty's discussion of "meta-stability" in chap. 4 of *Contingency, Irony, and Solidarity.*

but essential respects. Analogously, the commands of a Hobbesian sovereign or the prohibitions of a Schopenhaurian state, a Nietzschean "law of agreement" or the "intimations" of an Oakeshottian "tradition," are said to afford guidance adequate to the needs of lives that must in some measure be led in company with others.

On all of these views, then, we are talking not about understanding versus not understanding (or analogous modalities) but rather about various degrees and fluctuating combinations of mutual understandings, misunderstandings, and the absence—even the impossibility—of understanding. At their most lyrical, strong voluntarists sometimes write as if the quest for even minimal mutual intelligibility could and should be abandoned, that all mutual access engenders diminishing mutual dependence, and that each of us can and should make her own self and go her own way in some sense so radical that it can scarcely be made articulate.[120] But this is not the

---

[120]In one extended discussion Nietzsche takes this tendency to the extreme of attacking consciousness and self-consciousness and both insisting upon the reality and urging the cultivation of a kind of pre- or extralinguistic and pre- or unconscious thinking or communing with the self as an utterly private, utterly unique something. (He seems to associate his notion of "the incomparably personal, unique, and infinitely individual" self with Leibniz, presumably with the latter's "window-less monads," but he does not specifically mention this conception.) Consciousness and self-consciousness are products of the felt need—usually generated by fears and anxieties—to communicate with others, a need that leads to shared and hence necessarily flattening and homogenizing language and to a host of other demeaning and corrupting dependencies.

"Even now," that is, despite centuries of socialization into language and hence consciousness, "by far the greatest portion of our life actually takes place without this mirror effect; and this is true even of our thinking, feeling and willing life, however offensive this may sound to older philosophers. *For what purpose*, then, any consciousness at all when it is in the main *superfluous?*"

In answer to this question, Nietzsche offers the "extravagant surmise" that "*consciousness has developed only under the pressure of the need for communication*; that from the start it was needed and useful only between human beings (particularly between those who commanded and those who obeyed); . . . a solitary human being who lived like a beast of prey would not have needed it. . . . As the most endangered animal, [man] . . . *needed* help and protection . . . had to learn to express his distress and to make himself understood." Thus "the development of language and the development of consciousness . . . go hand in hand. Add to this that not only language serves as a bridge between human beings but also a mien, a pressure, a gesture. . . . Consequently, given the best will in the world to understand ourselves as individually as possible, 'to know ourselves,' each of us will always succeed in becoming conscious only of what is not individual but 'average.' Our thoughts themselves are continually governed . . . by the 'genius of the species' that commands it—and translated back into the perspective of the herd." Accordingly, "the world

position that predominates in their thinking. Rather, they place distinctive emphasis and value on will and individuality while exploring and doing their bit further to complicate the diverse and conflicted character of human thinking and acting.

•

Liberalism as we know and have known it is unthinkable without components that are integral to, but more vigorously propounded

---

of which we can become conscious is only a surface- and sign-world, a world that is made common and meaner; whatever becomes conscious *becomes* by the same token shallow, thin, relatively stupid, general, sign, herd signal, all becoming conscious involves a great and thorough corruption, falsification, reduction to superficialities, and generalization" (*Gay Science*, bk. 5, par. 354, pp. 297–300).

Nietzsche's view of language as necessarily concealing and distorting of a deeper reality aligns him with numerous thinkers from Plato forward. As I think is indicated by his sarcastic reference to "older philosophers," however, insofar as he actually endorses the notion, the "world" that figures, or rather the worlds that figure, in his "surmise" are radically plural and mutually opaque, not systematically and above all not *mutually* transparent.

This deeply ambivalent, if not ironic, discussion has to be read along with numerous passages that we have already considered, particularly those in which Nietzsche makes "laws of agreement," above all laws of agreement concerning language, a necessary condition of "everything of freedom, subtlety, boldness, dance, and craftsmanlike certainty that one can find on earth." Indeed, in the discussion in *The Gay Science* presently before us he says that humankind has "developed subtlety only insofar as this is required by social or herd utility" (p. 299). It seems clear that Nietzsche, along with all strong voluntarists, not only credited but insisted on the notion that individuals have a "well" or reservoir of psychic, spiritual, and other resources that are their own in some quite radical sense. But he was no romantic, primitivist, or transcendentalist, no friend to the notion that human beings could live a subtle, engaging, joyful life on the basis of those resources alone. In ways that I have tried to present, Nietzsche attempts to maintain not to resolve the tension between the notion of capacities and powers that are deeply individual and his understanding that culture, sociality, and even politics are necessary to and enabling as well as diminishing of the kinds of human lives he envisioned. Accordingly, there is no single passage or discussion that adequately summarizes or represents his views. Excellent complements to the passages just quoted from *The Gay Science*, however, are the following remarks from *The Will to Power*: "It is a measure of the degree of strength of will to what extent one can do without meaning in things, to what extent one can endure to live in a meaningless world *because one organizes a small portion of it oneself*" (par. 585, p. 318).

Because the theological voluntarists thought of humankind as created by, and for this and other reasons having an inescapable relationship with, God it was difficult and perhaps impossible for them to so much as conceive of an individuality as unqualified as that which Nietzsche surmises. (This, incidentally, was one of the deepest reasons for Nietzsche's abhorrence for monotheism and particularly Christianity.) "Is this importunity from heaven, this inescapable supernatural neighbor,

in, strong voluntarism. A fortified and intensified liberalism, one that better articulates, protects, and promotes liberalism's most distinctive and estimable understandings and values, will converge yet much more closely with strong voluntarism.

The first of these claims is at its least deniable in respect to the substantial, continuing, and quite widely distributed capacity for self-discipline and self-control discussed a few pages back. It is of course possible to achieve and sustain a degree of order and stability, to generate political and military power or economic efficiency and productivity, by disciplines and controls of quite other kinds. In part because these objectives are widely pursued, but also because all forms of liberalism and strong voluntarism themselves insist that legal, moral, and other requirements and prohibitions play a necessary part in the formation of self-discipline, a considerable variety of curbs and constraints are and will of certainty remain features of liberal as well as all other politically organized societies.

If self-discipline and hence the reliability as well as the self-reliance of individuals are impossible, however, liberalism—which presupposes all three to a degree distinctive if not unique among *political* ideologies—is hopelessly utopian. If or to the extent that

---

not enough to drive one to the Devil!—But there is no need for that, it has been only a dream! Let us wake up!" (*Daybreak*, bk. 5, sec. 464, p. 194). As Hans Blumenberg argues, however, insofar as they insisted upon the mysteriousness of God's will, its unknowability to humankind, the most radical among them (Blumenberg singles out Nicholas of Autrecourt for this honor) made God into a *deus absconditus* and thereby opened up possibilities closely akin to those that Nietzsche sought. See *Legitimacy of the Modern Age*, pp. 177, 184, 197–200, 346, 387.

(Blumenberg is no doubt correct that for many the combination of the unknowability and the omnipotence of God's will was a source of anxiety rather than self-confidence and that what he calls [in a phrase splendid in its internal dissonances] the "self-assertion of reason" and thinks characteristic of modernity could not develop until "a very decisive renunciation" of the "norm of knowing the Creation from the angle of vision and with the categories of the Creator" had occurred [p. 352]. He argues that this took place between the fourteenth and the seventeenth centuries and presents Hobbes's thought as one of its first full manifestations. As is evident from Chapter 1, I agree with this reading of Hobbes. I am inclined to think, however, that Blumenberg underestimates the self-assurance of figures such as Ockham and Autrecourt and to wonder whether his doing so may reflect the emphasis he gives to reason in his interpretation of modernity. If one were searching for likely sources of self-confidence, wouldn't the best place to look be the notion of omnipotent will—who could be more entitled to be self-confident than an omnipotent deity?—and the next best place notions of human volition that are modeled as closely as possible on images of the divine will?)

liberals succumb to this influential but despairing view, they abandon liberalism. Yet more certainly, if or to the extent that liberals
confuse self-discipline with disciplines of other kinds, or come to
think of the latter as preferable to self-discipline or as desirable in
their own right, they betray liberalism. Indications that these regrettable tendencies are increasingly prominent in professedly liberal theory and practice (they have never been absent from either)
provide the least (but hardly a negligible) reason for applauding and
embracing the correctives supplied by the strong voluntarists.

Are these judgments ahistorical and essentialist? Is liberalism too
amorphous or variable to permit of them except as a (not-likely-to-
be) persuasive definition of "it"? No. Or rather "on the contrary"—
for reasons anticipated in saying that the above are consequential
but minimal advantages gained by turning to the strong voluntarists
to bolster and enhance liberal theory and practice.

Why are diversity and disagreement conspicuous and often cheerfully accepted in liberal theory and practice? We have seen that there
is no single answer to this question, but two distinct yet complementary types of consideration stand out in the reflections of those
protoliberal and liberal political theorists who are closest to strong
voluntarism (for example, Montaigne and Hobbes, Constant, Mill
[as Berlin has construed and appropriated him], and Berlin, Hampshire, and Rawls in the first of the moments of their thinking
discussed earlier). On the one hand, affirming as they do the capacity of individual human beings for reliability and self-reliance, these
thinkers and the liberal practitioners who have influenced and been
influenced by them have fewer reasons to be fearful of variety and
flux in human affairs than do their conservative and radical ideological protagonists. Confident of the capacity of individuals to discipline themselves against the most obviously self- and mutually
destructive forms of conduct, the proponents and members of a
liberal society can disagree with, deviate from, and be indifferent
toward, one another on many matters. (With a delight subtended by
a certain equanimity they can—to use Mill's famous if somewhat
compromised phrase—engage in and welcome a profusion of experiments in living.)

The second type of consideration, resonating as it does with the
most captivating of the themes that have emerged in our explorations, is much the more distinctive and important. As liberals
approach the persuasion of the strong voluntarists, they become

deeply skeptical of more than a minimal and primarily adverbial uniformity or commonality. Their conceptions of and more especially their aspirations for themselves and one another lead them to expect, to cultivate, and to celebrate initiative and independence, singularities and pluralities, dissonances and disagreements, competitions and conflicts. In a willful liberalism, in liberalism at its most engaging, the variability that has been much remarked in liberal theory and practice is due not to lack of resolution or any other form of weakness but to an appreciation for the splendor of these ideas and ideals.

Bibliography of
Works Cited

Ackerman, Bruce. "Constitutional Politics/Constitutional Law." *Yale Law Journal* 99 (December 1989), 453–547.
———. *Social Justice in the Liberal State*. New Haven: Yale University Press, 1980.
Arendt, Hannah. *The Human Condition*. Chicago: University of Chicago Press, 1958.
———. *The Life of the Mind*. 2 vols. New York: Harcourt Brace Jovanovich, 1978.
———. "What Is Existenz Philosophy?" *Partisan Review*, 8 (Winter 1946), 34–56.
Augustine. *Confessions*. Trans. Edward B. Pusey. New York: Modern Library, 1949.
———. *De Libero Arbitrio Voluntatis*. Trans. as *St. Augustine on Free Will* by Carroll Mason Sparrow. Charlottesville: University of Virginia Studies, 1947.
Ayer, A. J. *Language, Truth, and Logic*. New York: Dover, 1946.
Berlin, Isaiah. *Four Essays on Liberty*. London: Oxford University Press, 1960.
Blumenberg, Hans. *The Legitimacy of the Modern Age*. Trans. Robert M. Wallace. Cambridge: Massachusetts Institute of Technology Press, 1983.
The Book of J. Trans. from the Hebrew by David Rosenberg. Interpreted by Harold Bloom. New York: Grove Weidenfeld, 1990.
Cavell, Stanley. *The Claim of Reason*. New York: Oxford University Press, 1979.
———. *In Quest of the Ordinary*. Chicago: University of Chicago Press, 1988.
———. *Must We Mean What We Say?* New York: Scribners, 1969.
Cleveland, Timothy. "Acting, Willing, and Trying," Ph.D. diss., The Johns Hopkins University, 1986.
Dahl, Robert A. *Pluralist Democracy in the United States*. Chicago: Rand McNally, 1967.

———. *A Preface to Democratic Theory*. Chicago: University of Chicago Press, 1956.

Donagan, Alan. *Choice: The Essential Element in Human Action*. London: Routledge & Kegan Paul, 1987.

Dumont, Louis. *Essays on Individualism*. Chicago: University of Chicago Press, 1986.

———. *Homo Hierarchicus*. Chicago: University of Chicago Press, 1980.

Duns Scotus, John. *Philosophical Writings*. Trans. Allan Wolters. Indianapolis: Hackett, 1987.

Figgis, J. N. *The Divine Right of Kings*. London: Cambridge University Press, 1914.

———. *Political Thought from Gerson to Grotius*. New York: Harper, 1960.

Flathman, Richard E. *The Philosophy and Politics of Freedom*. Chicago: University of Chicago Press, 1987.

———. *The Practice of Rights*. New York: Cambridge University Press, 1976.

———. *Toward a Liberalism*. Ithaca: Cornell University Press, 1989.

Fried, Michael. *Absorption and Theatricality*. Berkeley: University of California Press, 1980.

Gierke, Otto von. *Natural Law and the Theory of Society: 1500 to 1800*. Boston: Beacon Press, 1957.

———. *Political Theories of the Middle Ages*. London: Cambridge University Press, 1951.

Hampshire, Stuart. *Innocence and Experience*. Cambridge: Harvard University Press, 1989.

Hobbes, Thomas. *De Homine* and *De Cive or The Citizen*. In *Man and Citizen*, ed. Bernard Gert. Humanities Press, 1972.

———. *A Dialogue between a Philosopher and a Student of the Common Laws of England*. Ed. Joseph Cropsey. Chicago: University of Chicago Press, 1971.

———. *The Elements of Law* and *De Corpore*. In *Body, Man, and Citizen: Selections from Thomas Hobbes*, ed. Richard S. Peters. New York: Collier Books, 1962.

———. *Leviathan*. Ed. Michael Oakeshott. London: Collier Books, 1962.

James, William. *The Will to Believe*. New York: Dover, 1956.

———. *The Writings of William James*. ed. John J. McDermott. New York: Modern Library, 1968.

Levinson, Sanford. *Constitutional Faith*. Princeton: Princeton University Press, 1988.

Lowi, Theodore J. *The End of Liberalism*. New York: W. W. Norton, 1969.

McConnell, Grant. *Private Power and American Democracy*. New York: Alfred Knopf, 1966.

MacIntyre, Alasdair. *Against the Self-Images of the Age*. New York: Schocken Books, 1971.

Moore, G. E. *Philosophical Papers*. London: George Allen and Unwin, 1959.

Nietzsche, Friedrich. *The Anti-Christ*. trans. R. J. Hollingdale. Harmondsworth: Penguin Books, 1968.

——. *Beyond Good and Evil*. Trans. Marianne Cowan. Chicago: Henry Regenry, 1955.

——. *The Birth of Tragedy*. Trans. Francis Golffing. Garden City, N.Y.: Doubleday Anchor, 1956.

——. *The Complete Works of Friedrich Nietzsche*. 18 vols. Ed. Oscar Levy. London: T. N. Foulis, 1911.

——. *Daybreak*. Trans. R. J. Hollingdale. New York: Cambridge University Press, 1982.

——. *The Gay Science*. Trans. Walter Kaufmann. New York: Vintage Books, 1974.

——. *The Genealogy of Morals*. Trans. Francis Golffing. Garden City, N.Y.: Doubleday 1956.

——. *Human, All Too Human*. Trans. R. J. Hollingdale. Cambridge: Cambridge University Press, 1966.

——. *Thus Spoke Zarathustra*. Trans. Marianne Cowan. Chicago: Gateway Editions, 1957.

——. *Thus Spoke Zarathustra*. Trans. Walter Kaufmann. New York: Penguin Books, 1966.

——. *Twilight of the Idols*. Trans. R. J. Hollingdale. Harmondsworth: Penguin Books, 1968.

——. *The Will to Power*. Trans. Walter Kaufmann and R. J. Hollingdale. Ed. Walter Kaufmann. New York: Vintage Books, 1967.

Oakeshott, Michael. *Experience and Its Modes*. London: Cambridge University Press, 1933.

——. *On Human Conduct*. London: Oxford University Press, 1975.

——. *Rationalism and Politics*. London: Methuen, 1962.

Oberman, Heiko A. "*Via Antiqua* and *Via Moderna*: Late Medieval Prolegomena to Early Reformation Thought." In *From Ockham to Wyclif*, ed. Anne Hudson and Michael Wilks. Oxford: Basil Blackwell, 1987.

Ockham, William of. *Predestination, God's Foreknowledge, and Future Contingents*. 2d ed. Trans. Marilyn McCord Adams and Norman Kretzmann. Indianapolis: Hackett, 1983.

Ortega y Gasset, José. *The Revolt of the Masses*. New York: W. W. Norton, 1932.

O'Shaughnessy, Brian. *The Will: A Dual Aspect Theory*. 2 vols. Cambridge: Cambridge University Press, 1980.

Pennock, J. Roland. *Democratic Political Theory*. Princeton: Princeton University Press, 1979.

Perry, Ralph Barton. *The Thought and Character of William James*. 2 vols. Boston: Little, Brown, 1935.

Rawls, John. "The Idea of an Overlapping Consensus." *Oxford Journal of Legal Studies*, 7, no. 1 (1987), 1–25.

——. "Justice as Fairness: Political Not Metaphysical," *Philosophy and Public Affairs*, 14 (Summer 1985), 223–51.

——. "The Priority of Right and Ideas of the Good." *Philosophy and Public Affairs*, 17 (Summer 1988), 251–76.

Bibliography of Works Cited

Raz, Joseph. *The Morality of Freedom*. Oxford: Clarendon Press, 1986.

The Reader's Bible. London: Oxford University Press, 1951.

Rorty, Richard. *Contingency, Irony, and Solidarity*. Cambridge: Cambridge University Press, 1989.

Ryle, Gilbert. *The Concept of Mind*. New York: Barnes & Noble, 1949.

Sartre, Jean-Paul. *Being and Nothingness: An Essay in Phenomenological Ontology*. Trans. Hazel E. Barnes. Secaucus, N.J.: Citadel Press, 1956.

Schopenhauer, Arthur. *The World as Will and Idea*. Translated by R. Haldane and J. Kemp. Garden City, NY: Dolphin Books, Doubleday, 1961.

Taylor, Charles. *Hegel and Modern Society*. London: Cambridge University Press, 1976.

———. *Philosophical Papers*. 2 vols. London: Cambridge University Press, 1986).

Tocqueville, Alexis de. *Democracy in America*. Ed. Phillips Bradley. 2 vols. New York: Vintage Books, 1957.

Todorov, Tzvetan. *The Conquest of America*. New York: Colophon-Harper & Row, 1984.

Truman, David B. *The Governmental Process*. New York: Alfred Knopf, 1957.

Warrander, Howard. *The Political Philosophy of Hobbes: His Theory of Obligation*. Oxford: Clarendon Press, 1957.

Wilson, George. *The Intentionality of Human Action*. Rev. and enl. ed. Stanford: Stanford University Press, 1989.

Winch, Peter. *Trying to Make Sense*. Oxford: Basil Blackwell, 1987.

Wittgenstein, Ludwig. *Culture and Value*. Ed. G. H. Von Wright in collaboration with Heikki Nyman. Trans. Peter Winch. Chicago: University of Chicago Press, 1980.

———. "A Lecture on Ethics." *Philosophical Review*, 74 (January 1965), 3–12.

———. *Lectures and Conversations on Aesthetics, Psychology, and Religious Belief*. Ed. Cyril Barrett. Berkeley: University of California Press, 1967.

———. *On Certainty*. Ed. G. E. M. Anscombe and G. H. von Wright. Trans. Denis Paul and G. E. M. Anscombe. Oxford: Basil Blackwell, 1969.

———. *Philosophical Investigations*. Trans. G. E. M. Anscombe. New York: Macmillan, 1953.

———. *Remarks on Colour*. Ed. G. E. M. Anscombe. Trans. Linda L. McAlister and Margarete Schättle. Berkeley: University of California Press, 1978.

———. *Tractatus Logico-Philosophicus*. London: Routledge & Kegan Paul, 1922.

———. *Zettel*. Eds. G. E. M. Anscombe and G. H. von Wright. Trans. G. E. M. Anscombe. Oxford: Basil Blackwell, 1967.

Index

Index

Index

Library of Congress Cataloging-in-Publication Data

Flathman, Richard E.
  Willful liberalism : voluntarism and individuality in political theory and practice /
Richard E. Flathman.
      p.   cm.
  Includes bibliographical references and index.
  ISBN 0-8014-2661-8 (alk. paper). — ISBN 0-8014-9955-0 (pbk. : alk. paper)
    1. Individualism.   2. Liberty.   3. Liberalism.   4. Voluntarism.   I. Title.
JC571.F523 1992
320.5'12—dc20   91-55559